Chaucer's Gifts

NEW CENTURY CHAUCER

The works of Geoffrey Chaucer are the most-studied literary texts of the Middle Ages, appearing on school and university syllabuses throughout the world. From *The Canterbury Tales* through the dream visions and philosophical works to *Troilus and Criseyde*, the translations and short poems, Chaucer's writing illuminates the fourteenth century and its intellectual traditions. Taken together with the work of his contemporaries and successors in the fifteenth century, the Chaucerian corpus arguably still defines the shape of late-medieval literature.

For twentieth-century scholars and students, the study of Chaucer and the late Middle Ages largely comprised attention to linguistic history, historicism, close reading, biographical empiricism and traditional editorial practice. While all these approaches retain some validity, the new generations of twenty-first-century students and scholars are conversant with the digital humanities and with emerging critical approaches – the 'affective turn', new materialisms, the history of the book, sexuality studies, global literatures, and the 'cognitive turn'. Importantly, today's readers have been trained in new methodologies of knowledge retrieval and exchange. In the age of instant information combined with multiple sites of authority, the meaning of the texts of Chaucer and his age has to be constantly renegotiated.

The series New Century Chaucer is a direct response to new ways of reading and analysing medieval texts in the twenty-first century. Purpose-built editions and translations of individual texts, accompanied by stimulating studies introducing the latest research ideas, are directed towards contemporary scholars and students whose training and research interests have been shaped by new media and a broad-based curriculum. Our aim is to publish editions, with translations, of Chaucerian and related texts alongside focused studies which bring new theories and approaches into view, including comparative studies, manuscript production, Chaucer's post-medieval reception, Chaucer's contemporaries and successors, and the historical context of late-medieval literary production. Where relevant, online support includes images and bibliographies that can be used for teaching and further research.

The further we move into the digital world, the more important the study of medieval literature becomes as an anchor to previous ways of thinking that paved the way for modernity and are still relevant to post-modernity. As the works of Chaucer, his contemporaries and his immediate successors travel into the twenty-first century, New Century Chaucer will provide, we hope, a pathway towards new interpretations and a spur to new readers.

NEW CENTURY CHAUCER

Chaucer's Gifts

Exchange and Value in the *Canterbury Tales*

ROBERT EPSTEIN

UNIVERSITY OF WALES PRESS

CARDIFF

www.uwp.co.uk

British Library Cataloguing-in-Publication Data
A catalogue record for this book is available from the British Library.

ISBN   978-1-78683-168-2 (hardback)
         978-1-78683-169-9 (paperback)
eISBN   978-1-78683-170-5

The right of Robert Epstein to be identified as author of this work has been asserted in accordance with sections 77, 78 and 79 of the Copyright, Designs and Patents Act 1988.

Typeset by Marie Doherty
Printed by CPI Antony Rowe, Melksham.

*For Marcia Cove Epstein
and in memory of Jacob Epstein*

CONTENTS

ACKNOWLEDGEMENTS

A n advantage of working at a relatively small university is that most of one's daily interactions are interdisciplinary. Some years ago (more than I care to acknowledge), I was having lunch at the campus cafeteria with David Crawford, an economic anthropologist. Taking a break from the usual faculty pastime of griping about the administration, David asked me what I was working on. I explained that I had been studying the *Canterbury Tales* through the lens of the social theory of Pierre Bourdieu. David knew Bourdieu's work well; like Bourdieu, he had done field work on North African Berber communities. I went on to tell him that I was frustrated because I was now trying to analyse the *Shipman's Tale*, the Chaucerian tale that I thought should lend itself most readily to Bourdieusian interpretation, but the economics of it – the combination of symbolic and material capital – just didn't seem to be working out. David said, 'You should read Graeber.' That remark led me to David Graeber's *Toward an Anthropological Theory of Value*, which then led me on an odyssey into gift theory.

That initial lunch conversation has never ended. This book has been written largely under the tutelage of David Crawford and of our friend and colleague Dennis Keenan of Fairfield University's Philosophy Department. (David and Dennis team-teach an interdisciplinary course on gift theory.) The experience of tackling this topic has been broadly collegial and interdisciplinary. For some years, I met regularly with an 'economic anthropology reading group', including, in addition to Profs Crawford and Keenan, our colleagues Jay Buss (economics), Eric Mielants (sociology) and Steven Batchelor (history). I have also met monthly with a scholarly writing group, founded by Angela Harkins (religious studies) and including at various times Danke Li and Giovanni Ruffini (history), Elizabeth Petrino and Shannon Kelley (English), and Sarah Diaz (Italian studies); without the insight and support of this group, I can't imagine myself writing a word. I have benefited as well from conversations with colleagues including Marice Rose (art history), Scott Lacy (anthropology), Paul Lakeland, John Thiel, and John Slotemaker (religious studies), Anna Lawrence (history), and Michael Andreychik and Susan Rakowitz (psychology), and with a number of professional anthropologists – Daniel Bass and Hilary Haldane in particular – who have been exceedingly patient with my amateur enthusiasm. I am immeasurably grateful for the generosity of my colleagues in the Fairfield University English Department, especially Peter Bayers, Beth Boquet, Betsy Bowen, Emily Orlando and Nels Pearson.

I sent a large portion of the manuscript of this book to Robert J. Meyer-Lee for his comments. He sent me back the most thorough and extensive reader's report that I have ever received. I have tried to revise the text in accordance with his insights, but Bobby bears no responsibility for its surviving errors or failings. I owe thanks to Helen Fulton and Ruth Evans, who showed interest in an idiosyncratic book proposal and stuck with it. In the later stages of composition I discovered that Roger Ladd had published an article entitled 'Gower's Gifts'; Roger has been generous in offering insights and advice on the topic, and in not objecting to my title. And I am pleased to have an opportunity to thank Derek Pearsall, who attended the panel at Kalamazoo where I first presented the argument on the *Shipman's Tale* that had originated at lunch with David Crawford and that was the germ for this project. Derek's words of support then were a small part of many years of exceptional generosity and wisdom – a gift that I can never repay.

Portions of this book have appeared previously in print. A version of the second chapter was published in *Modern Philology*, 113 (© 2015, University of Chicago Press). The first half of the fifth chapter, under the title 'Sacred Commerce: Chaucer, Friars, and the Spirit of Money', was included in *Sacred and Profane in Chaucer and Late Medieval*

Literature: Essays in Honour of John V. Fleming, edited by William Robins and myself and published in 2010 by the University of Toronto Press. My work on *Chaucer's Gifts* has been supported by research grants from Fairfield University.

Finally, thanks to Miriam, Joseph and Nathaniel, who are the greatest gifts of all (not least for their patience when I talk about gifts).

INTRODUCTION:

Chaucer's Commodities, Chaucer's Gifts

Chaucer's *Canterbury Tales* opens onto a world of commodities. Much of the work describes the contemporary commercial world, where commodities are ubiquitous. The Wife of Bath, a manufacturer of fine commercial cloth, makes a show of wearing her own wares, and other expensive clothes:

> Hir coverchiefs ful fyne weren of ground;
> I dorste swere they weyeden ten pound
> That on a Sonday weren upon hir heed.
> Hir hosen weren of fyne scarlet reed,
> Ful streite yteyd, and shoes ful moyste and newe.   (I.453–57)[1]

Chaucer does not specify what the merchant of the *Shipman's Tale* trades in, but it may well be cloth much like that produced by the Wife of Bath that he 'byeth and creaunceth' (VII.303) when he is in Bruges. There are extensive and explicit references to marketed commodities even in sections of the *Canterbury Tales* that would seem to be removed from the commercial world. In a chivalric romance set in ancient Athens, the narrator pauses in a description of the paintings in the Temple of Diana to remark on the obvious costliness of the paint: 'Wel koude he peynten lifly that it wroghte; / With many a floryn he the hewes boghte' (I.2087–8). Amid a sermon on gluttony, the Pardoner betrays a detailed familiarity with the wide variety of imported wines available to the fourteenth-century English tavern-goer: 'Now kepe yow fro the white and fro the rede, / And namely fro the white wyn of Lepe / That is to selle in Fysshstrete or in Chepe' (VI.562–4).

As with wine, so with people. The Wife of Bath, in her auto-biographical excursus, assesses her passage through a world that has treated her as a purchasable commodity since she was twelve years old and concludes that she should take control of her body as the commodity that it is: 'And therfore every man this tale I telle, / Wynne whoso may, for al is for to selle' (III.413–14).

Chaucer himself was born into a family of wine importers, and later worked as a customs keeper in the bustling commercial port of London. Does he naturally therefore share the Wife of Bath's opinion that everything in this world is for sale, and that only a fool would seek or expect anything other than individual, material advancement? The tales are replete with commodities. Do they contain anything other than commodities?

This line of inquiry reformulates a question often at the heart of Chaucer reception, that of the author's class status and the connections between his social position and the economic perspectives of the *Canterbury Tales*. The Canterbury pilgrims are predominantly middle class; their worlds are most frequently cities and towns; their experiences as well as their language and imagination are informed by the values and practices of the marketplace and commercial transactions. 'Does this mean,' asks Lee Patterson, 'that Chaucer should be understood as a bourgeois writer, or that he understood himself in this way?'[2]

This question gets at such fundamental issues of Chaucerian authorship and interpretation that the various and multitudinous answers could hardly be summarized even in a lengthy discussion. The gamut would include the conservative views of D. W. Robertson and the 'exegetical school' of criticism, for whom Chaucer, as a satirist in an Augustinian moral tradition, is hostile to the worldliness, materialism and cupidity that embodied in bourgeois values. There have been many more critics who have found that social categories and economic conditions were too different in the Middle Ages to be analogous to modern class distinctions and have seen Chaucer's poetic sensibilities as too subtle to be determined or restrained by the simple conditions of his social life, and who therefore, like Derek Brewer, have found in Chaucer 'a certain detachment from *all* class-systems, as well as an acceptance of them'.[3] Others, like Alcuin Blamires, have seen this 'in-between' Chaucer as the wishful product of middle-class readers, and have reacted by casting the poet as a 'reactionary' thoroughly imbricated in 'aristocratic ideology', and the General Prologue as 'the politically astute production of a writer largely enmeshed in the ruling sector of society'.[4]

Yet Aldo Scaglione can just as confidently answer Patterson's question in the affirmative: Boccaccio and Chaucer, he says, are

> not only two of the greatest story-tellers of all time, but also two of the most delightfully 'bourgeois' souls ever to leave records in literature. Indeed their masterworks ... both clearly and eloquently show that their respective authors grew up within the milieu of the contemporary mercantile groups.[5]

Chaucer's bourgeois mentality has seemed just as self-evident to Marxist readers. To David Aers, 'Chaucer's work represents society as a composite of *inevitably* competing groups motivated by individualistic forms of material self-interest, and mediated through access to a market which he saw as encompassing and profoundly affecting most human relationships.'[6] In this, it is the herald of incipient bourgeois social revolution: 'Chaucer's social imagination ... tends to abandon all ideas of fraternity, social justice and the social embodiment of charity, foreshadowing an ideological position that would become commonplace with the triumph of bourgeois individualism in the later seventeenth and eighteenth centuries.'[7]

Patterson's own answer to his question is among the most subtle and sophisticated: that Chaucer's characters evince a sense of autonomous individual identity, independent of class identification and of all economic and historical process – and that this is the most bourgeois thing about them. Chaucer's poetry, to Patterson, thereby helps to normalize commercial and capitalistic mentalities. 'What makes the Wife and the Franklin bourgeois,' Patterson writes,

> is not that they promote specifically bourgeois values, whatever these might be, but that they place their tales in the service of an aristocratic value whose full force can be made available only when it is detached from its social origin … They assume that true values, and their true selves, are not socially determined at all – a claim that we have come to recognize as central to bourgeois ideology.[8]

Yet Patterson does not see Chaucer's treatment of commerce per se as negative or satirical. From tales like those of the Shipman and the Merchant, according to Patterson, 'we can see that Chaucerian poetry does indeed, profoundly and even self-consciously, embrace the ideology of commerce'.[9]

Recent criticism seems to be increasingly willing to accept that Chaucer simply receives as natural the values of the commercial world that he depicts so thoroughly. Helen Fulton points to the 'mercantile ideology' of tales like that of the Shipman, and claims that the

> subject position of the *Canterbury Tales* in general is that of the urban middle classes of the late fourteenth century, both gentry and bourgeoisie. Through the range of pilgrims and their tales, urban life, and in particular the urban economy, are normalized in relation to a land-based feudal economy which is largely located outside tales.[10]

Craig Bertolet has argued that portraits like that of the Cook 'illustrate the association of commerce with civic identity and civic order that was developing in urban life during Chaucer's time'.[11] Lianna Farber has made the case that fourteenth-century writers including Chaucer were approaching a consensus on the legitimacy of trade and commercial economy, based on common notions of value, community and consent.[12]

The degree to which the *Canterbury Tales* is suffused with market exchanges, trade practices and commercial language clearly justifies critical interest in these issues. What is at stake is not merely Chaucer's class standing or his representations of merchants and tradesman but, as it were, the political economy of his poetry – how his fictions represent the real and ideal distribution of resources throughout society, and, even more broadly, how he envisions the natural or just bases for social interactions.[13] To address such profound underlying questions, however, it is necessary to recognize that, as deeply embedded in the commercial world as the *Canterbury Tales* are, some exchanges depicted in them are, at least ostensibly, non-commercial. There are markets and purchases and commerce in the tales, but there are also gifts. Ultimately, the determination of the kind of social and political world envisioned in the *Canterbury Tales* will hinge on a persistent but essential question from the field of economic anthropology: whether the gift is the originary form of commercial exchange, or whether, contrarily, there is a substantive difference between a gift and a commodity.

The field of economics seeks to explain human motivations and decisions in the realm of the market, but the field of economic anthropology has evolved to address the kinds of exchanges that at least seem distinct from market transactions, and to develop theories to explain the relationships among modes of exchange. What kinds of exchange relationships are inherent to human society, and what kinds are historical developments contingent on social and material factors? Above all, are there substantive differences between commercial exchange and gift exchange?

It was Marcel Mauss's 1925 essay *The Gift: The Form and Reason for Exchange in Archaic Societies* that set gift exchange at the centre of the study of culture. Among Mauss's main intentions was to show that there is logic to gift exchanges, just as there is to the money economy, and that gift economies work to redistribute resources, but in a way that makes sense only within a larger symbolic framework.

One of the crucial debates that arose after Mauss was the question of whether the gift is the archaic form of commodity exchange, or if rather there is a substantive difference between commodity and gift. Many answered that there was not, that rather the gift was the archaic form of commodity, for two reasons. One was that the gift, as Mauss described it, seemed fundamentally agonistic, which has been to many interpreters the mark also of competitive commercial exchange. The other reason was that there did not seem to be anything else it could be; that is, there was no clear way to distinguish a gift from a commodity.

This turns out to be a crucial point for this study, because the theories of exchange that have had the greatest influence on contemporary literary criticism – those of Pierre Bourdieu and Jacques Derrida – are both founded on the assumption that there is no fundamental difference between the modes of exchange of gifts and commodities. Bourdieu develops a theory of practice that accounts for exchange in symbolic realms as well as material ones – but that employs the same market-oriented logic, and even the same commercial language, to describe both types of exchange. Derrida, meanwhile, assumes that there can be no 'true gift' if there is any exchange at all. Derrida's redefinition of the 'true gift' precludes any self-interest in the giver, or even any self-awareness, and ultimately any intentionality at all, and it thereby has the effect, apparently intended, of erasing the gift entirely.

To be fair, the project to establish a clear distinction between gift and commodity based on different logics of exchange and different social purposes and functions really began to gain ground only in the 1980s, by which time Bourdieu and Derrida had already formulated much of their theoretical models. A crucial step in the neo-Maussian project came with Christopher Gregory's *Gifts and Commodities*, published in 1982. In his study of Papua New Guinea, Gregory begins with the observation that all societies have both gift exchange and commodity exchange, and he seeks to define the qualitative difference between them. What he finds is that the two types of exchanges stand for two types of relationships. He concludes: 'Commodity exchange relations are objective relations of equality established by the exchange of alienated objects between independent transactors. Gift exchange relations are personal relations of rank, established by the exchange of inalienable objects between transactors who are related.'[14] It is a complex concept, but others have restated it in a more concise form: commodity exchange objectifies people; gift exchange personifies objects.[15]

This is true in the Marxian economic sense. Gregory distinguishes between the production-based value of commodity exchange and the consumption-based value of gift exchange – where 'consumption' should be understood not in the capitalist sense of the consumer of a purchased product but in the sense of a pre-capitalist economy where the consumption necessary to reproduce labour and goods – food, shelter, sex, etc. – is never alienated from the value of the product. But it is also true in a literal sense: commodities are fully alienated from the donor at the moment of transaction. Gifts are never alienated from the donor; on the contrary, they always retain their history. By preserving the memory of the transaction, the obligation for repayment is carried into the future, and the result is the establishment of a social bond between the transactors.

Some anthropologists have been arguing that this alternative view of the gift was actually Mauss's interpretation all along. Many of the leading figures of this revisionist movement were contributors to *La Revue du MAUSS*, founded in the early 1980s by the sociologist Alain Caillé.[16] (The name MAUSS, in addition to evoking the name of the anthropologist from whom the contributors take inspiration, is an acronym standing for 'le Movement Anti-Utilitariste dans les Sciences Sociales'.) Caillé has observed,

> Mauss discovered that the obligation to give – or, rather, the three-fold obligation to 'give, receive and return' – is the basic social rule of at least a certain number of savage or archaic societies and is nothing more than a concrete translation of the principle of reciprocity that supplies the basis for Claude Lévi-Strauss's structural anthropology and which Karl Polanyi contrasts with exchange and redistribution.[17]

The impulse toward reciprocity is the foundation of all social relations, and it is the opposite of the impulse toward individual profit that is the basis of the market economy; only by recognizing this can we see that social exchanges are not always agonistic and intended for domination as the potlatch is, and furthermore – in a political point of primary importance to both Mauss and the neo-Maussians – that the social relations of capitalism and the free market are not the original, natural, exclusive and inevitable organizing principles of society. The motivations for these exchanges are various, but they are always pro-social: the ultimate purpose of gift exchange is not to produce profit for the individual transactor but to establish and maintain relationships between transactors, based on obligations of return. The exchanges cannot always be reduced to the desire for economic profit, nor to the desire for symbolic profit, which mimics the market transaction in seeking individual self-maximization; at the same time, they are not the same as simple generosity or charity.

My goal in this book, therefore, is not just to demonstrate that in a work so replete with commodities as the *Canterbury Tales*, there is anything other than commodities. It is also to show that there *can* be something other than commodities – that gifts are substantively differ-ent from commodities, and that gift exchange operates under its own logic that is distinct from that of commerce and the market. To do so, I will have to directly confront and critique elements of Bourdieu's and Derrida's theories of the gift. I will be drawing on sociological and anthropological theory as it has been developed in the twentieth and twenty-first centuries, by figures such as Gregory and Caillé, as well as Marilyn Strathern, Annette Weiner, Mark Rogin Anspach and David Graeber, to show that there are gifts in the *Canterbury Tales* that are ontologically distinct from commodities, in ways that are as significant for our social world as they are for Chaucer's.

I begin, naturally, with the General Prologue, and with a conspicu-ous and seemingly undeniable example of gift-giving, the extravagant feasts hosted by the Franklin. This feasting can be analogized to the potlatch ceremonies of Northwest American Indians, which have been central to the anthropological study of gift exchange. Like the Franklin's feasts, potlatch is both ostentatiously generous and agonistic, designed to achieve the social and symbolic advancement of the donor at the expense of the recipient. The question for anthropological theory, then, and also for gifting in the General Prologue, is whether this selfish competitiveness is the essential quality of the gift, or the particular quality of certain instantiations of the gift. To answer this, I compare the Franklin to another of Chaucer's pilgrims, the Plowman, whose generosity has not received extensive critical attention. Often dismissed as either a one-dimensional and politically irrelevant allegory for the holy individual, or as a privileged author's fantasy of a politically quiescent peasant, the Plowman in fact lives by a creed that epitomizes the archaic gift economy envisioned by Mauss, and the pre-capitalist, communitarian valuation of land and labour described by the economic historian Karl Polanyi.

Chapter 2 considers the representation of gift exchanges in the tales in the context of contemporary social theory. The *Shipman's Tale* is commonly counted among the most over-determined of the tales for its explicit equation of intimate interpersonal relations – friendship, marriage, sex – with monetary transactions. It would seem therefore to justify those theories of exchange, notably the influential models of practice of Pierre Bourdieu, that portray all human interactions as driven by the desires of individuals for profit in material or symbolic fields. But by applying the approaches of neo-Maussian theorists, I show that, to the contrary, the *Shipman's Tale* dramatizes the persistence of gift-based relations sustained by perpetual obligation, even in a thoroughly monetized and commercialized social context. This revision is intended also to question the sufficiency of Bourdieu's totalizing 'theory of practice' as a putatively universal and transhistorical explanation of the motives for human action.

The third chapter extends the theories introduced in the previous chapter to reconsider the familiar but still little understood principles of reciprocity underlying the actions of Chaucer's comic tales. The genre of fabliau, which frequently balances acts of retribution with almost mechanical efficiency, has often been seen to resemble the operations of the market. But the japes and insults of Chaucer's most representative fabliau, the *Miller's Tale*, more closely resemble the self-perpetuating interactions of gift exchange. Neo-Maussian theorists note that the function of the market is to generate equivalences, and thereby to end relationships; that is, after a commercial exchange, the participants have no further obligation to each other. Gift exchange, on the other hand, creates inequalities and always results in further obligation, thereby extending relationships into the future. Crucially, this is true even when the exchanges are agonistic, or even violent; blood feud can be seen as a kind of gift system. The escalating acts of retribution in the *Miller's Tale* are performed with no expectation of equivalence. In contrast, the two clerks in the *Reeve's Tale* use scholastic reasoning explicitly to justify the pursuit of equivalence – a clear example of scholasticism abetting in the naturalizing of the market. Nonetheless, the tale concludes with a distinct inequality, in that the clerks ride away with the flour, even though their debauches were supposedly justified by its loss. This superfluity can only be explained by a single act of generosity, Malyne's romantic bestowal of the stolen flour on her 'lemman' Aleyn – a naive act, but also a true act of gift-giving amid a series of essentially economic exchanges. A similar dynamic is at work in the *Merchant's Tale*. January's conception of marriage is warped by his selfish and narrow-minded pursuit of personal profit and individual desire. But the intervention of Pluto and Proserpina, divine husband and wife competing with perfectly matched gestures, leads to a state of equivalency that, in the context of marriage, is ultimately pathological.

As the merchant's wife in the *Shipman's Tale* and miller's daughter in the *Reeve's Tale* show, women's roles are crucial to understanding the political economy of the *Canterbury Tales*. Equally important is the fact that women themselves have often been the objects of exchange, and that the status of women has been essential to theories of exchange. In the fourth chapter, I contrast the theories of two of the most influential feminist anthropologists, Annette Weiner and Marilyn Strathern. Since Lévi-Strauss, the idea that the 'exchange of women' was formative to civilization has been both central to anthropological discourse and deeply contentious. Weiner's work, however, posits female agency via the resistance to such exogamous systems through endogamous strategies like incest. I test Weiner's theories against the roles of women in Chaucerian romance, and I analyse virginity in the *Canterbury Tales* as an attempt to establish value outside exchange and to resist the traffic in women. The Wife of Bath, on the other hand, can hardly be said to resist exogamy, and partly due to her persistent, enthusiastic and apparently self-defeating commitment to multiple marriages she is often seen as defeated by or even complicit in a system that commodifies and circulates women's bodies. To explain and, ideally, to recuperate her agency, I apply the very different theories of Strathern, who notes that in gift cultures objects can be personified in exchange – even when the 'objects' are women – and that a woman can be an active participant in a system that allows her to generate multiple personhoods through multiple gift exchanges – even when the gift is her own body. In her tale, I see the Wife of Bath employing a strategy that Sarah Kay, who also adapts Strathern's theories, calls 'the poetics of the gift'. The *Wife of Bath's Tale* exploits ambiguities inherent in gift exchange as a symbolic system to challenge patterns of domination in chivalric romance and in society as a whole.

The satire of the scholastic reasoning of the Cambridge clerks Aleyn and John is part of a broader critique throughout the tales of Church mentalities. The fifth chapter shows Chaucer's extended critique of the accommodation and incorporation of commercial ideology by the Church and its social and intellectual branches. Reading the *Summoner's Tale* alongside the early Franciscan text *Sacrum commercium* and applying the studies of intellectual historian Joel Kaye, I show that Chaucer finds the complex operations of money to be analogous to natural processes, which were then coming to be described scientifically by the 'Oxford calculators' and other university intellectuals. The satirical target of the *Summoner's Tale* is not money itself, nor simple greed, but rather the hypocrisy of friars who claim to abjure the money economy while ignoring their own involvement in its logic and practices. Equally revealing is the honest hypocrisy of the Pardoner, who paradoxically insists on exposing his own intentions – not in order to claim that his intentions are good, but in order to insist that he does not care if his bad intentions result in good. As late medieval scholars were gradually shifting the onus of culpability in ethical exchange from the actual result of just price and profit to the intention of receiving excess profit, Chaucer's Pardoner can be seen as an early advocate of what would become the main ethical justification of capitalism – that it effectively regulates desires to the end of general profit, regardless of the moral status of the individual actors. The portrait of the Pardoner remains a devastating satire, but rather than criticizing the corruption of the salvific mission of the Church by material greed, it reveals that the 'economy of salvation' is, even in its theoretical articulation, truly economic.

Having begun with the Franklin's portrait, I conclude with *Franklin's Tale*, which more than any other tale in Chaucer's collection has been the focus of critical applications of gift theory. Recently, Chaucerians have applied the gift theory of Jacques Derrida to make the case that there is no true generosity in the tale. According to Derrida, true generosity would require an original, unmotivated and therefore impossible act of donation. But this view of the gift is rooted in Derrida's assumption that all exchange must be essentially economic. In his gift theory, Derrida misunderstands Marcel Mauss's original claims, and overlooks the more recent anthropological and sociological work that has uncovered grounds for distinguishing between gifts and commodities. Chapter 6 is therefore dedicated to demonstrating the reality of the gift in the *Franklin's Tale*. I note that the tale first works to set its characters under a number of conflicting constraints, all of which are justified in the terms of contract. The cascading acts of generosity at the climax of the tale constitute wilful rejections of contractual language and legalistic restraints, in favour of older modes of association based on donation and obligation. I relate this to David Graeber's influential recent historical analysis, which traces the use of state power and law to convert obligations into debt. 'A debt,' Graeber says, 'is just the perversion of a promise.'[18] In Graeber's terms, the *Franklin's Tale* can be seen as an allegory of nascent globalization – but it is a process that Chaucer, while anticipating, can also imagine resisting.

I am seeking here to respond to interpretations that claim to show that all exchanges are inherently profit-driven and thus essentially commercial, or that even those objects of exchange in the *Canterbury Tales* that seem to be gifts are in fact archaic commodities, because all exchange is inevitably commercial. Such analyses are often rooted in a presumed critique of commercial or capitalist social relations, but they have the effect of naturalizing market relations by making all other forms of social relations impossible. Above all, therefore, this book intends to show that in different modes of exchange Chaucer dramatizes the potential for different types of socially generated value than those presumed by market transactions. If we can learn to recognize them, then we can see that there are alternatives to commercialized social relations, in Chaucer's world, and more importantly (since they are more doubted now than ever, and more threatened) in ours.

1

THE FRANKLIN'S POTLATCH AND THE PLOWMAN'S CREED:

The Gift in the General Prologue

Among the first things that a reader of the General Prologue to the *Canterbury Tales* is likely to observe is that it depicts a cross-section of fourteenth-century English society. This is the spirit of the most famous observation on the poem, John Dryden's praise of its diversity and verisimilitude: "Tis sufficient to say, according to the proverb, that here is God's plenty. We have our forefathers and great-grand-dames all before us, as they were in Chaucer's days.'[1]

Most readers will soon make the additional observation, however, that it is not a representative cross-section. It may comprehend, as Dryden maintains, all of immutable human character, and it may as well portray the variety and range of social stations, but the distribution of class and caste positions among the pilgrims is hardly proportional to their contemporary numbers. Only two of the pilgrims introduced in the General Prologue – the Knight and his Squire – can properly be said to belong to the First Estate; they travel with the Knight's Yeoman 'and servantz namo' (I.101). And yet two out of twenty-eight is more than 7 per cent – a statistical over-representation for fourteenth-century England. The Second Estate, meanwhile, is represented by the Prioress, Second Nun, Monk, Friar, Clerk and Parson, and perhaps the Pardoner and the Summoner – a much greater over-representation.

All the remaining pilgrims can be said to belong to the Commons, but in relation to the Third Estate's percentage of the populace it is nonetheless under-represented on this pilgrimage. Yet only one of the Canterbury pilgrims, the Plowman, is described as engaging regularly in the kind of agricultural labour that would have been the lot for the vast majority of the population. (The Reeve has a trade – carpentry – and has risen to become an estate manager and an overseer of peasant labourers.) Most over-represented of all are a minority of the Third Estate – artisans, tradespeople, property owners, professionals and managers, mostly from cities and towns: the Merchant and the Shipman, the Man of Law and the Physician, the Five Guildsmen and their Cook, the Franklin, the Wife of Bath (a successful cloth-manufacturer), the Miller, the Reeve, and the Manciple. Most of these portraits focus on the pilgrims' professional activities. Add to this the very worldly activities of most of the clerical figures and you have what Patricia Eberle has called 'a lively interest in the world of getting and spending, the world of commerce'.[2] Eberle questions a conventional assumption about Chaucer's poetry as intended primarily for a 'courtly' audience; she concludes instead that in the General Prologue 'Chaucer creates a new kind of implied audience, by implying that his audience will bring a commercial outlook to bear on his text, for the first time in any of his works, and perhaps also for the first time in any work of English literature.'[3]

The General Prologue is set in a tavern, and the tale-telling project that defines the *Canterbury Tales* is introduced by its ostler. The thoroughgoing commercialism of Harry Bailey and the narrative world over which he presides make all the more significant the examples of non-commercial exchange that are rarer but undeniably present. For all the commodities in the General Prologue, there are also gifts. If the General Prologue, which sets the stage for the tale-telling that follows and introduces the social world of the work as a whole, is so profoundly commercial, then the instances of gift-giving must either be another form of market exchange – commodities in disguise – or they must be evidence, however exceptional, of an alternative logic of exchange.

I. The Franklin's potlatch

It snows food in the Franklin's house:

> An housholdere, and that a greet, was he;
> Seint Julian he was in his contree.
> His breed, his ale, was alweys after oon;
> A bettre envyned man was nowher noon.
> Withoute bake mete was nevere his hous,
> Of fissh and flessh, and that so plentevous
> It snewed in his hous of mete and drynke;
> Of alle deyntees that men koude thynke,
> After the sondry sesons of the yeer,
> So chaunged he his mete and his soper.
> Ful many a fat partrich hadde he in muwe,
> And many a breem and many a luce in stuwe.
> Wo was his cook but if his sauce were
> Poynaunt and sharp, and redy al his geere.
> His table dormant in his halle alway
> Stood redy covered al the longe day.   (I.339–54)

His home is stocked at all times with the finest wine, ale, bread. The ovens are constantly baking fresh pies of fish and meat. The wide selection of delicacies available changes constantly with the seasons. He has pens full of partridges and ponds stocked with fish. He expects his chef to serve these foods with finely spiced sauces, and to make sure he keeps the kitchen supplied with luxury cooking utensils. The side tables in his halls stand ready at all times to be lined with newly baked dishes. The home is in a state of perpetual feast.

What are we to make of this ostentatious feasting? Whatever its motivations, they would seem to lie outside the usual vectors of market exchange. In his country, the Franklin is considered the embodiment of Julian, patron saint of hospitality, and he is called the very son of Epicurus. The feasting is therefore associated with generosity and pleasure, neither of which precisely aligns with the profit-motive of commercial transaction. Indeed, for Craig Bertolet, the differences between descriptions of the Cook (a hired servant of the Five Guildsmen) and the financially and socially independent Franklin 'illustrate the difference between the pleasure and the business of food. The Franklin enjoys both the preparation and the presentation of food while the sore-ridden Cook regards food merely as a commodity.'[4]

But because of the public nature of the Franklin's feasting, many have always seen it as performing 'social work' beyond the satisfaction of individual pleasure or even simple generosity. There have always been readers who have found the Franklin to be nouveau riche, shallow, materialistic and even vulgar. (R. K. Root compared him to a 'Toledo oil-magnate'.[5]) His ostentatious generosity has been seen as his effort to compensate for insecurities about his status as a free but untitled landholder. He has been taken as an object of satire of the Third Estate, but not all critics have seen the portrait as satirical: Jill Mann notes that the description of the Franklin's feast shares many of the details of conventional satires of gluttony, but none of their condemnatory tone.[6]

For D. W. Robertson, who saw the Franklin as embodying 'the entirely superficial nobility of a wealthy man of the middle class who is … blind to anything beneath surface appearances',[7] the Franklin's feast is conspicuous for being a bourgeois duplication of an aristocratic indulgence. The extravagance of the late medieval feast is rather notorious: it is one of the social phenomena that Johan Huizinga is most interested in exploring in *The Autumn of the Middle Ages*.[8] A number of modern observers, noting the records of remarkable consumption at such feasts, have drawn analogies to one of the traditional customs most studied and debated in the field of anthropology. Stephen Mennell, for instance, has claimed that the grand aristocratic banquets that dot the historical records as well as smaller-scale events of households of many sizes 'were a means of asserting social rank and power': 'In this respect, there are possibly parallels in social function between the late medieval banquets and the famous institution of potlatching among the Kwakiutl Indians of British Columbia.'[9]

'Potlatch' refers to elaborate rituals of feasting and gift-giving practised by the native tribes of the northern Pacific coast of North America.

These feasts are generally occasioned by significant events – births, deaths, weddings, coming-of-ages observances, sometimes to save face in the aftermath of an embarrassing incident. They were and are practised by a wide variety of peoples in this region, but potlatch became most elaborate, and garnered the greatest interest of anthropologists, as it was practised among the Kwakiutl people of the northern portion of Vancouver Island, especially during the 'Fort Rupert Period' of 1849 to 1925.[10]

The medieval banquet is parallel to the potlatch, Mennell suggests, in that 'it is probable that sheer volume and indeed waste of food was inherent in and necessary to the social function of such events'.[11] Volume and waste do seem central to the Franklin's feasting. Despite the references to Epicurus and St Julian, Chaucer's description says little about the Franklin's subjective enjoyment of the food, and no mention is made of who benefited from the Franklin's hospitality. Instead, the overflowing details of the passage give an overall impression of daunting superfluity.

This is hardly to claim that the Franklin's feasts, or medieval banquets generally, were socially identical to the practice of potlatch.[12] But potlatch has always been central to the anthropological theory of the gift, and the different ways in which the practice has been received and analysed reveal competing models for understanding the social power and meaning of the Franklin's generosity and other acts of giving in the *Canterbury Tales*.[13]

Foundational anthropologists like Franz Boas and Bronislaw Malinowski were drawn to the study of potlatch because the practice seemed to offer a clear example of a social practice that could not be explained by conventional economic models. Boas and Malinowski saw particular significance in potlatch practices because they seemed to be driven by a symbolic logic that was fundamentally non-economic: whatever inspired the waste and self-destructiveness commonly observed in potlatch, it could not be the individual material profit assumed as the basis for classical economics, because the participants seemed to pursue actions that were clearly against their own material self-interest.[14] Potlatches could be extraordinarily extravagant.

They could go on for days, serving tremendous amounts of food, and offering many expensive gifts. The ethnological museums of North America brim with astonishingly accomplished potlatch artefacts: the sculptures and totems used as welcoming signals; the enormous bowls and spoons used to serve the copious food; the elaborately crafted gifts; the intricately carved chests in which gifts were stored or presented. Potlatch was, furthermore, as Mauss emphasized, part of an economic system based on redistribution of wealth. This gift-giving was part of a system of exchange that made sense only within a symbolic matrix, in which symbols and status were inextricably linked with, and as important as, material goods. Most of all, Kwakiutl potlatch was intensely competitive. The host of the potlatch would seek to make symbolic gains in the act of giving gifts, by demonstrating his wealth and his status, and by translating material wealth into symbolic authority. Hosts of potlatches were often competing to lay claim to titles, or to control narratives or the right to tell them, and thereby to control the authority that the narratives could bestow. The gift-giving was also agonistic in that it imposed an obligation of repayment on the recipient. Giving a gift too rich to be returned would be an act of extreme humiliation to the recipient; he would be permanently in the debt of the donor, and therefore subordinated. Potlatch hosts strove for such acts of domination, while also demonstrating their power through their capacity to donate, to consume, to expend, even to destroy tremendous amounts of wealth, sometimes wilfully bankrupting themselves in the process. At the height of the Fort Rupert Period, Kwakiutl families were observed burning valuable items, blankets for instance, both as demonstration of the family's resources and in order to remove the items from the gift exchange economy, so that competing families or leaders would not have access to them.[15] This is the Kwakiutl equivalent of lighting a cigar with a hundred dollar bill. It is more than just the ultimate display of conspicuous consumption: it is gift-giving that preserves the symbolic profit of the donor while eliminating the material profit of the recipient.

In his essay on the gift, Mauss focused on three main instances of gift economies: that of the New Zealand Maori; that of Melanesia;

and the Kwakiutl potlatch. Mauss noted that the first two of these are relatively benign forms of exchange. They are based on constant give-and-take, on gifts and obligatory compensations, but they are less, or less obviously, agonistic. For Mauss, it is the agonistic element of potlatch that is its defining feature, and that is the hallmark of its significance to the theory of the gift. All gift exchange is rooted in a culture-wide network of obligation that Mauss terms 'prestations totales', usually translated as 'total services'.[16] But potlatch takes this to extremes:

> [W]hat is noteworthy about these tribes is the principle of rivalry and hostility that prevails in all these practices. They go as far as to fight and kill chiefs and nobles. Moreover, they even go as far as the purely sumptuary destruction of wealth that has been accumulated in order to outdo the rival chief as well as his associate (normally a grandfather, father-in-law, or son-in-law). There is total service in the sense that it is indeed the whole clan that contracts on behalf of all, for all that it possesses and for all that it does, through the person of its chief. But this act of 'service' on the part of the chief takes on an extremely marked agonistic character. It is essentially usurious and sumptuary. It is a struggle between nobles to establish a hierarchy amongst themselves from which their clan will benefit at a later date.[17]

Mauss therefore grants a special title to the kind of 'institution' embodied in potlatch: '*total services of an agonistic type*'.[18]

The interpretation of Mauss's essay has itself been intensely contested over the decades. Much depends on how Mauss understands potlatch in relation to the elementary gift economies, and on what he means when he calls it an 'exaggerated' form of exchange. To some, it has come to mean that potlatch manifests the gift economy *in extremis*, and therefore that its idiosyncrasies, including its extremely agonistic qualities, represent the essential and definitive elements of exchange. This would mean that potlatch is the fullest, most essential and most natural instantiation of exchange – the gift laid bare.[19]

This interpretive tendency was augmented by postmodern approaches to gift theory, which sought to deconstruct some of Mauss's more benign views of gift exchange. Derrida, in 'The Gift of Time', critiques Mauss's claims about the voluntarism of donation in Maori or Melanesian culture, arguing that there is no original gift, every gift being in fact an obligatory repayment of an earlier gift: 'These conditions of possibility of the gift (that some "one" gives some "thing" to some "one other") designate simultaneously the conditions of the impossibility of the gift.'[20] For Derrida, the word 'gift' has no meaning if it is connected in any way to expectations of exchange or reciprocity. (As I will argue in chapter 6, this betrays a fundamental misunderstanding on Derrida's part of how Mauss and neo-Maussian anthropologists conceive of the meaning and function of the gift.) Derrida is therefore especially critical of Mauss's analysis of potlatch. Mauss, he remarks, 'speaks of it [pot-latch] blithely as "gifts exchanged." But he never asks the question as to whether gifts can remain gifts once they are exchanged.'[21] Derrida notes that Mauss at one point characterizes the competitive practices of potlatch as 'madly extravagant'.[22] Derrida in turn characterizes this portion of Mauss's text as a 'passage of madness'.[23] Its rationality is torn asunder, he claims, as Mauss persists in trying to treat potlatch as a species of gift while simultaneously acknowledging that it is part of a system of exchange.

Pierre Bourdieu argues that potlatch is not exceptional at all, since every gift in every culture is an act of symbolic violence, a transaction in which the donor seeks to dominate and subordinate the recipient:

> Generous conduct, of which the potlatch (a curio for anthro-pologists) is simply the extreme case, might seem to suspend the universal law of interest and 'fair exchange', whereby nothing is ever given for nothing, and to set up instead relationships which are their own end ... But in reality such denials of interest are never more than *practical disclaimers*.[24]

Elsewhere Bourdieu adds, 'From ordinary acts to extraordinary acts of exchange, of which the potlatch is the extreme example (as an act of giving beyond the possibilities of return, which puts the receiver in an obliged and dominated state), the difference is only of degree.'[25] In all exchanges, that is to say, the motivation of the giver is to gain symbolic profit for himself and, through symbolic violence, to dominate and subjugate the recipient by burdening him with an obligation to return that the recipient may struggle to fulfil. Potlatchers, by extending their gift-giving so as to make return nearly impossible, simply do it to a greater extreme, and therefore more successfully, than others do. What is more, the logic of profit and domination in gift exchange is analogous to the profit and domination of commercial exchange.

Under the influence of sociologists like Bourdieu, scholars in many fields, including history and literature, have come to see potlatch not as abnormal but as normative, and agonistic exchange as the elemental, essential, even original form of social interaction. Martha C. Howell, for instance, has studied the social nature of commerce in the late medieval and early modern periods. Whereas historians have commonly characterized the late medieval period as a transitional time when traditional gift-based cultures and relationships were supplanted by the commercial culture of nascent capitalism, Howell shows that the bourgeois of England, France and the Low Countries 'exchanged gifts even more exuberantly, in greater volume, and in more social arenas at the end of the Middle Ages than ever before'.[26] The question, then, is the ontological status of the gift, in the conception of men of the time, place and status of men like Chaucer's Franklin and his ilk. Howell acknowledges that the gift 'did different work' in this period than it had previously, and that among the most conspicuous changes was that the gift became thoroughly monetized.[27] But she insists that the monetized gift is still a gift, largely because she adopts Bourdieu's view that gift-giving is fundamentally a symbolically violent act motivated by self-interest and individual profit. Howell quotes Bourdieu's remark that gifts possess a 'structural ambivalence which predisposes them to fulfill a political function of domination'.[28]

Many elements of Howell's view of late medieval gift-giving, and of Bourdieu's theory of the logic of the gift, can be seen in Chaucer's portrait of the Franklin. The essential elements of potlatch, in anthropological terms, can be found in his home: not just the ostentatious feasting, but also the agonistic self-interest, and the symbolic violence of donation. That the Franklin is St Julian 'in his contree' (I.340) indicates that the effect of his generosity is to enhance his reputation. This is complicated by the fact that we don't know who, if anyone, eats the food: Chaucer describes at length the preparation and service of the food, but he says nothing about who attends the feasts. The passage gives the odd impression of an ornate feast in an empty house. The Franklin nonetheless performs generosity, and the performance attains its meaning through its generalized sense of the power of the donor, and the intimation of unreturnable obligation on implied recipients. After the image of the permanent 'table dormant' ever ready to be laden with food, Chaucer transitions immediately into descriptions of the possessions and positions that define the Franklin's social status:

> At sessiouns ther was he lord and sire;
> Ful ofte tyme he was knyght of the shire.
> An anlaas and a gipser al of silk
> Heeng at his girdel, whit as morne milk.
> A shirreve hadde he been, and a contour.
> Was nowher swich a worthy vavasour.   (I.355–60)

The Franklin presides at court sessions, he has been sheriff and auditor of the county, and, Chaucer concludes, 'Was nowher swich a worthy vavasour' (I.360). The last word conveys both his standing and his striving, suggesting both a landholder and a vassal, elevated yet nonnoble; he possesses, as Susan Crane says, an 'insecure social rank'.[29] Amid these subtle points of legal and social standing, a pair of very telling physical details appear: an 'anlaas' and a silk 'gipser' hanging at the Franklin's belt. The luxurious accoutrements that complete the Franklin's display of wealth and power are a decorative dagger and a silk purse – materializations of symbolic violence and wealth as signifier.

It is appropriate that the Franklin's portrait is followed immediately by that of the Five Guildsmen:

An Haberdasshere and a Carpenter,
A Webbe, a Dyere, and a Tapycer –
And they were clothed alle in o lyveree
Of a solempne and a greet fraternitee.
Ful fressh and newe hir geere apiked was;
Hir knyves were chaped noght with bras
But al with silver, wroght ful clene and weel,
Hire girdles and hir pouches everydeel.
Wel semed ech of hem a fair burgeys
To sitten in a yeldehalle on a deys.
Everich, for the wisdom that he kan,
Was shaply for to been an alderman.
For catel hadde they ynogh and rente,
And eek hir wyves wolde it wel assente;
And elles certeyn were they to blame.
It is ful fair to been ycleped 'madame,'
And goon to vigilies al bifore,
And have a mantel roialliche ybore.   (I.361–78)

Like the Franklin, the Guildsmen are attempting to gain social advancement through public displays of their wealth and success. But their resources are nothing like the Franklin's. Their greatest ambition is to make alderman – a joke in part because their dream, like their livery, is uniform among the five of them, and in part because this seems truly to be their wives' ambition more than theirs. What's more, some critics have noted that guildsmen of these trades – haberdashers and carpenters and the like – had little hope of becoming aldermen of any considerable town.[30] In comparison to the Franklin, their symbolic aspirations are as modest as their material means – because, in the totalizing system of exchange, the two arenas are inseparable.

These middle-class men at the heart of the General Prologue seem, then, to personify a world in which gifts, whatever they might have symbolized in previous social orders, have been incorporated into a money economy and now serve to reinforce monetized social relations.

As Howell maintains, this society is not necessarily truly capitalist in the modern sense, as the rituals of non-economic exchange are still expected, but the goal of all exchanges, the purely economic as well as the ostensibly non-economic, is individual profit and advancement. The value of donation is in its display of social resources and the potential to deploy those resources to gain social and symbolic profit from acts of generosity that cannot be matched or returned. As Bourdieu would have it, all gifts are potlatch, in that they are essentially and inevitably agonistic, competitive, individualistic and symbolically violent, designed primarily for domination.

Contemporary theorists, however, have been revising the perception of Mauss's intentions. David Graeber argues that when Mauss called potlatch 'exaggerated' he meant that it was a 'particular agonistic variation' of the gift economy, 'even, in some ways, a slightly pathological one'.[31] If so, then Mauss saw potlatch, which he called 'total services of the agonistic type',[32] as one direction in which gift economy could evolve, but not an original or normative or even representative one. Mauss also refers to potlatch as 'the monster child of the gift system'.[33] Potlatch does indeed contain many elements that would eventually be found in the commercial economy, but as a gift system potlatch, to Mauss, is revealing but non-normative. After all, one of Mauss's main purposes in writing *The Gift* was to formulate an anthropological critique of commercial and capitalistic values. In fact, in Graeber's political re-reading, Mauss's vision was truly communistic: Mauss was trying to show the earliest societies to be based not on competition among individuals for dominance, but instead on agreements among all individuals *not* to compete with each other, for the benefit of the society as a whole. At the conclusion of *The Gift*, Mauss writes,

> Thus we can and must return to archaic society and to elements in it. We shall find in this reasons for life and action that are still prevalent in certain societies and numerous social classes: the joy of public giving; the pleasure in generous expenditure on the arts, in hospitality, and in the public and private festival.[34]

This does not sound very much like Mauss's own description of potlatch, nor does it really seem to capture the essence of the Franklin's feast. Despite the allusion to Epicurus, the verses on the Franklin's feast do not evoke much pleasure, as there does not seem to be anyone there to enjoy it; it is a catalogue of presentation without any accompanying consumption. But the point, from a neo-Maussian perspective, would be that the competitive, agonistic and self-interested nature of the Franklin's feast make it exceptional rather than normative. The normal view of exchange, according to Mauss, is one based on collective welfare, and on the pleasure of donation, independent of profit to the donor. Most important, Mauss conceives this mentality as opposite to capitalism and market values. According to Graeber, Mauss understood potlatch as a deviant form of gift economy, and therefore analogous to the market economy and to capitalist economic formations.

This is not to say that potlatch does not constitute true gift-giving. Though it is competitive in the extreme, to neo-Maussians (or 'anti-utilitarianists', as they sometimes figure themselves) the fundamental nature of the gift is seen in the potlatch not because it is competitive but because it is primarily motivated by the desire to form and extend social relations. In the case of potlatch, and other archaic practices of exchange, the social bonds that are formed are agonistic and tend toward domination. But if this is all they were and all that they could be, then such primitive exchanges could be seen as the original and natural form of the market and the ancestor of capitalism. There are, that is, a multiplicity of ways in which the social relations formed in exchange can be constructed.

The point is not that gifts like those provided by Chaucer's Franklin are not true gifts; rather, the point is that the Franklin's feasts, like potlatch, are, in Mauss's terms, gifts 'of an agonistic type'. In deploying an action that is ostensibly generous in order to achieve domination and gain social profit, the Franklin's feasting is a perfect example of what Pierre Bourdieu terms 'symbolic violence'. Like potlatch, therefore, the Franklin's feast is an example of gift exchange, but not necessarily a normative form of it. They are gifts not because they are agonistic, but because their purpose is to generate social relations and to perpetuate obligations. The crucial question to ask in order to address the values of the General Prologue, therefore, is whether any of the other pilgrims also engage in gift-giving, but in a less agonistic form. Are there examples among the pilgrim portraits of donations based on principles of reciprocity but also motivated by intentions for mutual benefit rather than material or symbolic profit and domination? Readers of the *Canterbury Tales* are likely to have an immediate answer – though they may not consider it a satisfactory one.

II. The Plowman's creed

Like the Franklin, the Plowman also lives by an ethic of generosity, though of another sort:

> With hym ther was a Plowman, was his brother,
> That hadde ylad of dong ful many a fother;
> A trewe swynkere and a good was he,
> Lyvynge in pees and parfit charitee.
> God loved he best with al his hoole herte
> At alle tymes, thogh him gamed or smerte,
> And thanne his neighebor right as hymselve.
> He wolde thresshe, and therto dyke and delve,
> For Cristes sake, for every povre wight,
> Withouten hire, if it lay in his myght.
> His tithes payde he ful faire and wel,
> Both of his propre swynk and his catel.
> In a tabard he rood upon a mere.   (I.529–41)

The 'pees and parfit charitee' of the Plowman is clearly distinct from the Epicureanism and hospitality of the Franklin's house, and readers have almost invariably recognized the Plowman as one of the 'ideal' figures of the General Prologue, along with his brother the Parson and the Knight (and sometimes the Clerk, depending on the reader's sympathies). These pilgrims stand in contrast to the satirical portraits making up the bulk of the prologue.

Yet the Plowman's portrait is seldom seen as a legitimate social critique of other figures in the General Prologue. Critical objections to the Plowman tend to take two main forms. The first is that the figure of the Plowman in general as well as the particular features of this Plowman render him an embodiment of abstract ideals of holiness, or of ethical values so pure that they are equally abstract.[35] In either case, he is seen as admirable but cut off from the world of real, lived experience and complex humanity depicted so vividly in the other pilgrim portraits. Jill Mann, who is among those who believe Chaucer's Plowman may have been influenced by Langland's, remarks,

> The Parson and the Ploughman indeed correspond to the ideal of the estates writer, but Chaucer seems to be showing us that this ideal is inadequate to account for the workings of society ... They exist in a separate sphere which is as exclusive and specialised as those inhabited by the other pilgrims.[36]

The second common objection is that the realistic qualities of the portrait commend the Plowman for his obedience and complacency. Critics of many different periods and political perspectives have seen Chaucer, in the wake of the Great Rebellion, as representing the ideal peasant labourer as politically quiescent and self-abnegating. Thus, Gardiner Stillwell, writing in 1939, says that the Plowman is 'a colorless figure for a good reason, namely that the real ploughman of the time was revolting against everything that Chaucer stood for'.[37] Stephen Knight, writing in 1986, agrees that the Plowman is a reaction to the politically rebellious peasant, noting that 'not visualized at all, he is presented in terms of his busy and honest actions as he lived up to high standards in "pees and parfit charitee" – in every way he is the dutiful senior peasant'.[38] And Alcuin Blamires, writing in 2000, finds the political perspective of the General Prologue as a whole 'reactionary' and sees the clearest evidence for this in the Plowman's portrait:

> It has always been hard to find much to say about this earnest, boringly conscientious, compliant man ... He lives in 'pees and

parfit charitee' instead of breaking the king's peace. His neighbour-
liness knows no bounds, for 'thogh hym smerte' (whatever the
cost to himself) he nurtures no smouldering resentments. So far is
he from graspingness that he will even work for free, 'withouten
hire'. And 'His tithes payde he ful faire and wel' both in labour
and in produce, so he is a most obedient subject in his payment
of taxes.[39]

Generally, then, the Plowman is seen as a religious ideal or a
spiritual allegory, an embodiment of transcendent values that in their
abstract perfection are completely alien to the realities of this world,
in which case he is deemed a politically toothless critique of dominant
social values; or, he is seen as a historical and political ideal of peasant quietude and passivity, and therefore as the reactionary fantasy
of a fundamentally conservative author. I would like to suggest that
in both cases the opposite is closer to the truth. If the Plowman is an
allegorical embodiment of religious values, they are values that are
philosophically nearly indistinguishable from the values of the marketplace that dominate the rest of the General Prologue. But if he is
seen as a historical embodiment of the ethics of a medieval, agrarian
political economy, then the creed articulated in the Plowman's portrait
is not only a profound critique of the commercial values illustrated so
thoroughly in the rest of the text, but in fact it resembles the kind of
critiques voiced by anthropologists like Marcel Mauss and economic
historians like Karl Polanyi.

In the religious sense, the 'pees and parfit charitee' that guides the
Plowman's life is an ethic of sacrifice. He donates his labour, 'thogh
him gamed or smerte', and willingly donates his property in the form of
tithes to the Church, and he does all 'For Cristes sake'. From one perspective, this is the essence of generosity – gifts that cost the giver dearly
but are purely disinterested in motivation, inspired only by abstract
notions of goodness without hope of return. But if, as a Christian figure,
the Plowman hopes for salvation, then there certainly are expectations
of return. In fact, it had been assumed since ancient times that religious
sacrifice operated by the same principles of *do ut des* that undergirded

commercial exchange in secular law. Since the beginnings of sociology, theorists have distinguished the goals of religious sacrifice from pure material exchange, but they have also noted that they operate by an analogous underlying logic. Max Weber described this as 'the economy of salvation': 'Almost always ... some kind of theodicy of suffering has originated from the hope for salvation.'[40] For Bourdieu, this becomes 'the *economy of sacrifice*, in which exchange is transfigured into self-sacrifice to a sort of transcendental entity'.[41] Many Chaucer critics are inclined to see traditional Christian principles as the only possible bulwark against the rising tide of bourgeois ideology and hegemony, but to see Chaucer as depicting all figures of religious authority as hopelessly corrupt and implicit in market relations.[42] But from a Bourdieusian perspective, the more important point is not that the clergy has allowed itself to be seduced from its ideals, but rather that the clerical ideal itself operates under the same principles of exchange as the commercial economy, and therefore cannot constitute a true refutation or critique of them. The Plowman performs his righteous deeds 'For Cristes sake', but the terms of exchange are still fundamentally contractarian, giving in order to receive, just as one would find in market exchanges, though the contract is with God. In Bourdieu's terms, religious sacrifice is not a critique of commercial values, but an extension of them. It is assiduously disguised and euphemized in a host of ways, but it is ultimately a duplication of the other material exchanges in the General Prologue, including the ultimately self-interested generosity of the Franklin's feast.

If, on the other hand, one reads the Plowman politically, then his portrait can be seen as a profound critique of commercial mentalities. Of his Plowman Chaucer says, 'God loved he best with al his hoole herte / At alle tymes, thogh him gamed or smerte, / And thanne his neighebor right as hymselve' (I.533–5). This formulation of the 'Golden Rule' is so familiar to us that we are likely to glide over it as an empty commonplace of personal morality. But Jill Mann notes, 'There is little association of the typical peasant with love of his neighbour, although a large number of complaints about his avarice may indicate that charity was a feature in the ideal of this estate.'[43] Chaucer seems deliberately to be rooting the Plowman's morality in his generalized feeling of commitment to community. This is even clearer in lines that, I think, are often misinterpreted: 'He wolde thresshe, and therto dyke and delve, / For Cristes sake, for every povre wight, / Withouten hire, if it lay in his myght' (I.536–8). Those reading the Plowman as an allegorical figure or a religious symbol are inclined to take these lines to mean that the Plowman offers his labour as a sacrifice to Christ. Those reading it more politically and historically instead tend to claim that he is offering his labour for free to his lord or to landowners in general, so little does he value his own work and so abjectly does he perform servile obedience to landed authority. But it is clear from the lines that the Plowman's foremost devotion is not to the Lord or to his lord but rather to 'every povre wight' – the general needs of common people'.[44]

The critical inclination to view the Plowman as a servile vassal may miss a more significant historical and social tension at the heart of this brief portrait. Christopher Dyer has observed that Chaucer's Plowman 'is not, as is sometimes alleged, an employed servant plowman, but rather an independent peasant with his own draught animals and equipment'.[45] That is, he is not a servant on a manorial estate, ploughing with the lord's team for an annual salary, but a relatively wealthy peasant who works for daily payment with the oxen, plough and gear that are among his own 'catel'. In post-plague England, as has been noted often, the interests of such independent ploughmen would have conflicted with those of lords and landowners trying to keep the cost of labour down; this was the basis of the Statute of Labourers, which sought to prevent workers from freely marketing their labour. But Dyer explains that tensions also arose between wealthier and poorer peasants:

> There had always been a peasant elite – both customary and free tenants – who had large enough holdings to prosper in the growing market in the thirteenth century. After the Black Death as land became cheaper they could hope to increase the size of their holdings, and some were able to do this … They had problems in making very large profits, especially from conventional arable farming, because of the dearness of labour and the long-term decline in the price of corn. Traditionally they had employed the

cottagers and smallholders of the village, and taken young people into their houses as servants, but all types of workers were in short supply after the Black Death. They had suffered heavy losses in the plagues, and some survivors had taken the opportunities to acquire land and therefore were no longer seeking employment.[46]

It is conventional to view the Plowman as the ideal employee, from the perspective of landowning employers of the second half of the fourteenth century – docile, selfless and devoted to his lord. But in fact there is no mention anywhere in the passage of a lord, or any employer of the Plowman. It might be more accurate to see the Plowman as the ideal employer, viewed not from above but from below.

Langland's Piers is of a similar status to Chaucer's Plowman, and Piers complains at some length about the malingerers, beggars and unsatisfied workers whom he sees as inhibiting his own productivity. In one of that poem's most chilling passages, he summons Hunger to coerce reluctant labourers into agricultural work. 'Piers Plowman's encounter with the wasters and beggars,' Dyer remarks, 'implies that a deep gulf had opened between the more substantial peasants and the cottagers and laborers.'[47] Yet these are precisely the people to whom Chaucer's Plowman donates his labour. Piers demands that those who would eat help him to plough his half-acre, and he tries to distinguish between the lazy and greedy and the deserving poor. Chaucer's Plowman 'wolde thresshe, and therto dyke and delve, / For Cristes sake, for every povre wight, / Withouten hire, if it lay in his myght' (I.536–8).

Why would the Plowman do this? If we answer simply that it is 'charitee' offered '[f]or Cristes sake', we may be accepting, as I noted above, a certain kind of calculation on the Plowman's part, one in which secular sacrifice is proffered in exchange for eternal reward. But we may also be revealing our assumption that the Plowman's sense of collective and communal obligation can have no temporal reason – no political-economic logic. This is the kind of reasoning that Marcel Mauss sought to explain in his essay on the gift, and particularly in his concept of '*système des prestations totales*'.[48] 'Prestations totales' is the term Mauss introduces in *The Gift* to describe the system of inviolable obligations that runs throughout a society. It is among the most disputed terms in Mauss's much disputed book. 'Prestation' is translated in a variety of ways, including 'services', but it is not a common word in French. It is most often used in modern French in the context of public administration, to mean benefits owed in particular circumstances, similar to the American use of the word 'entitlement'.[49] Or, contrarily, as Chris Hann and Keith Hart explain, it can refer to 'a service performed out of obligation, something akin to "community service" as an alternative to imprisonment'. But Hann and Hart also note that it 'cannot be translated into English and is something of a feudal relic in French', and Mauss may have selected it deliberately for its archaism.[50] In its feudal context, it means the fees or obligations owed by a vassal to a lord.[51]

By the phrase 'prestations totales', Mauss seems to be suggesting the obligations like those of a peasant to a lord, but generalized throughout society. Its definition is implicit in Graeber's explanation of Mauss's theory of why social welfare seems just:

> His answer, quite different from Marx's, was that a relation of wage labor was a miserable and impoverished form of contract. Because … the elementary form of social contract is, for Mauss, precisely, communism: that is, an open-ended agreement in which each party commits itself to maintaining the life of the other.[52]

This seems to me the clearest and most reasonable way of understanding the Plowman's donation of his labour. He is a peasant with an inherent sense of the social obligation to work the land, but the primary obligation that he feels is not to his lord (Chaucer mentions no feudal overlord) nor to the Lord (though he dutifully pays his tithes to the Church) but rather to 'every povre wight', the rural community of common people like himself. This impetus resembles what Marshall Sahlins has termed 'generalized reciprocity', defined by David Graeber as 'the kind of open-ended responsibility that prevails among close kin, all of whom will do whatever they can to help the other, not because they expect repayment, but simply because they know that in a similar crisis, the other *would* do the same'.[53] These are the stated values of the Plowman's creed.

If we do not tend to recognize these as the Plowman's values, it may be because we are forgetting what economic historians have identified as peasant values. I am thinking particularly of Karl Polanyi, who famously wrote about the 'Great Transformation', the economic revolution that converted land into a marketable commodity, and that was therefore central to the creation of the modern capitalist economy and the ideology that underpins it.[54] What made this process so significant was that it not only changed the value of the land but also it changed the way the value of land was conceived. After, the land's value is calculated in terms of the labour and capital required to work it and the commodities that it can produce. Before, land is never really a commodity – alienable from owner – and is understood to produce both material value and symbolic value, that is, the social relations formed through the working of land. Polanyi was trying to address a central issue of economic history, that even in the industrial age peasants seemed to calculate the value of land and labour differently than landowners did. Polanyi sees this transformation as culminating in the Industrial Revolution but originating in Chaucer's England:

> Commercialization of the soil was only another name for the liquidation of feudalism which started in Western urban centers as well as in England in the fourteenth century and was concluded some five hundred years later in the course of the European revolutions, when the remnants of villeinage were abolished. To detach man from the soil meant the dissolution of the body economic into its elements so that each element could fit into that part of the system where it was most useful.[55]

The divide demarcated by Polanyi's 'Great Transformation' runs through the General Prologue. Consider, for instance, the 'commodity fiction' that represents Nature and work as 'land' and 'labour':

The crucial point is this: labor, land, and money are essential elements of industry; they also must be organized in markets; in fact, these markets form an absolutely vital part of the economic system. But labor, land, and money are obviously *not* commodities; the postulate that anything that is bought and sold must have been produced for sale is emphatically untrue in regard to them ... Labor is only another name for a human activity which goes with life itself, which in turn is not produced for sale but for entirely different reasons, nor can that activity be detached from the rest of life, be stored or mobilized; land is only another name for nature, which is not produced by man; actual money, finally, is merely a token of purchasing power which, as a rule, it not produced at all ... The commodity description of labor, land, and money is entirely fictitious.[56]

The General Prologue to the *Canterbury Tales* begins with a famous description of nature in springtime: the sweet showers of April, the gentle west wind, the path of the sun rising upward through the heavens. Entirely embedded within this vision of the natural world is agriculture – the 'tendre croppes' (I.7) that, like the flowers in the heath, are inspired to grow by personified water, air and light.

Chaucer's pilgrims themselves, however, live in a commercial world of 'fictitious commodities', in which land, like labour and social relations, has been artificially abstracted as elements in a money economy. This is perhaps most conspicuously true of the Man of Law, the heart of whose professional practice is in land transactions: 'So greet a purchasour was nowher noon: / Al was fee symple to hym in effect; / His purchasyng myghte nat been infect' (I.318–20). 'Purchasyng' and 'fee symple' are legal terms from the buying and selling of landed property. The Man of Law is a specialist in this particular 'fictitious commodity'. Neither the fragrant showers of April nor the sweet breath of Zephirus inspire his relationship to land, which he transacts as commodified property.

But virtually all Chaucer's pilgrims inhabit the novel side of Polanyi's transformation, where nature (land), work (labour) and human relations (money) are treated as marketable commodities. This is true of our Franklin, whose generosity is linked to social advancement and facilitated by a cornucopia of commodities extracted from property that he owns but does not work, unseen land tended by unseen labourers. It is also true of the Monk, who, riding away from the lands of the monastic estate, uses an ideology of economistic utility to remove himself from a direct relationship to the land through physical labour – 'What sholde he studie and make hymselven wood, / Upon a book in cloystre alwey to poure, / Or swynken with his handes, and laboure, / As Austyn bit? How shal the world be served?' (I.184–7) – and to justify individual pleasures derived from products taken from the land – 'A fat swan loved he best of any roost' (I.206). It is true also of the Friar, whose relations with his fellow men are purely commercial, whether he is receiving – 'He was an esy man to yeve penaunce, / Ther as he wiste to have a good pitaunce' (I.223–4) – or giving – 'His typet was ay farsed ful of knyves / And pynnes, for to yeven faire wyves' (I.233–4). It is true, naturally, of the bourgeois pilgrims as a whole, whose mentalities are shaped by what Polanyi calls the 'One Big Market',[57] from the Merchant – 'His resons he spak ful solempnely, / Sownynge alwey th'encrees of his wynnyng' (I.274–5) – to the Physician – 'For gold in phisik is a cordial, / Therefore he loved gold in special' (I.443–4). It is particularly true of the Wife of Bath, whose wealth and social status derive from the commodification of land value through the international woollen cloth industry – 'Of clooth-makyng she hadde swich an haunt / She passed hem of Ypres and of Gaunt' (I.446–7) – which would soon, through the acceleration of the process of rural enclosure, become a prime example of the transformation of nature into the 'fictitious commodity' of land.[58] It is true as well of the Reeve and the Manciple, not because they are greedy scoundrels (though they are), but rather because, like Uriah Heep, they have learned to outdo their social superiors at the commodification of land value and the commercialization of relationships. The Reeve's young lord knows the land only as a source of commodities, and the Reeve controls the accounts of the expenditures and the yields, and understands them better than the lord does:

Wel koude he kepe a gerner and a bynne;
Ther was noon auditour koude on him wynne.
Wel wiste he by the droghte and by the reyn
The yeldynge of his seed and of his greyn.
His lordes sheep, his neet, his dayerye,
His swyn, his hors, his stoor, and his pultrye
Was hoolly in this Reves governynge,
And by his covenant yaf the rekenynge,
Syn that his lord was twenty yeer of age.   (I.594–601)

The complex administrative and commercial analysis required to run an agricultural estate allow the Reeve to take advantage of his young and inexperienced lord. But as Dyer observes, a reeve was more likely to face daily conflicts with the peasants under his charge: 'Some reeves made a profit, but not everyone relished this office, because it inevitably involved a conflict of interest between the lord, for whose revenues the reeve was responsible, and the peasants from whom he was expected to collect rents and enforce labor services.'[59] The peasant's perspective is familiar from the first speech of the 'Second Shepherds' Play':

Ther shall com a swane
As prowde as a po;
He must borow my wane,
My ploghe also;
Then I am full fane
To graunt or he go.
Thus lyf we in payne,
Anger, and wo,
By nyght and day.
He must haue if he langyd,
If I shuld forgang it;
I were better be hangyd
Then oones say hym nay.[60]

This is the kind of antagonistic relationship that Chaucer's Plowman eschews, choosing instead to donate his labour and forge bonds of communal interdependence.

The Plowman, therefore, stands across Polanyi's great divide from most of the other pilgrims. Alongside him would seem to stand 'his brother' the Parson. But it would be wrong to see them purely as idealized embodiments of otherworldly charity and sacrifice.[61] Both portraits contain elements of calculation according to the values of the money economy. The Parson's virtue is defined largely negatively:

> He sette nat his benefice to hyre
> And leet his sheep encombred in the myre
> And ran to Londoun unto Seinte Poules
> To seken hym a chaunterie for soules,
> Or with a bretherhed to been withholde;
> But dwelte at hoom, and kepte wel his folde,
> So that the wolf ne made it nat myscarie;
> He was a shepherde and noght a mercenarie.   (I.507–14)

The Parson does not pay a less qualified clerk to mind his parish; he does not leave his flock and go to London; he does not seek a higher-paying position as a chantry priest or a chaplain for a guild. This is all admirable; he is, as the guiding metaphor of the entire portrait shows, a good shepherd to his flock. But this also shows that the Parson is to a large extent measuring his sacrifice by how much more he could be making if he were to sell his services. He is doing this for a transcendental ideal of service to God, but his estimation of value is predicated on the existence of a market in which he is choosing not to participate.

On the other hand, the Parson also supports his parishioners in other ways:

> Ful looth were hym to cursen for his tithes,
> But rather wolde he yeven, out of doute,
> Unto his povre parisshens aboute

Of his offryng and eek of his substaunce.
He koude in litel thyng have suffisaunce.   (I.486–90)

Rather than threatening excommunication for the insufficient payment
of tithes, the Parson is more likely to return to the poor of his parish
a portion of their donations. There is in this gesture a sense of chari-
table sacrifice for a transcendental ideal – the Parson sometimes gives
part of his personal income to the poor, while making do on very
little himself. But the income that accrues to him in the form of tithes
comes from the very people he is giving money back to. The Parson
is facilitating a kind of communal redistribution of wealth. In explain-
ing that the economy is instituted, Polanyi identifies three modes of
economic process: reciprocity, which he sees as predominating within
kinship groups; redistribution, which he finds to occur more broadly
within all societies; and exchange, which can be instituted only with
the introduction of money and markets.[62] Following anthropologists,
particularly Malinowski, Polanyi identifies redistribution as the prime
organizing principle of primitive societies, but he insists that it is present in some form in all societies, even those in which free-market
or centralized demand models have been instituted. In this process,
a large portion of the goods or wealth produced are delivered to a
centralized authority, which can store it and redistribute it in order to
guarantee the survival of all the members of the society.[63] Chaucer's
Parson sees part of his office as overseeing the return of the peasants'
own wealth to the neediest among them. It is a simple redistribution
of wealth, based on a communitarian sense of fairness and collective
responsibility.[64]

His brother the Plowman, meanwhile, also measures value, in part,
according to the commercial and market standards of labour and property. He has to, for, like his brother's parishioners, he owes tithes and
taxes on them: 'His tithes payde he ful faire and wel, / Both of his
propre swynk and his catel' (I.539–40). But Polanyi insists that in primitive and archaic societies economy was 'embedded in the labyrinth of
social relations'.[65] Chaucer's Plowman works the land but measures the
value of the land both in the material that it produces and in the social

relations that it produces. He uses his work of the land to forge and foster social bonds and to reinforce community and kinship.

Lee Patterson, in another representative assessment of the Plowman, calls him 'psychologically opaque and socially quiescent' and says that his portrait 'assiduously effaces the very real economic struggles of Chaucer's contemporary world'.[66] There is truth in this: the Plowman would better satisfy a certain kind of historicism if he were brandishing a pitchfork and burning down the Savoy Palace. But from the perspectives of anthropology and broader economic history, Chaucer's Plowman is not only historically and psychologically 'realistic' but also a singular reproach to the market-oriented political economy that dominates the rest of the General Prologue.

Ultimately, though, the reservation that many readers harbour regarding the Plowman is that he and the Parson seem ideal rather than real: they seem to lack the specificity and therefore the vivacity of the other pilgrims, and so whatever ideal values they represent do not seem relevant to true, lived experience. For Jill Mann, for instance, these brothers figure the idealized representatives of the Second and Third Estates from estates satire, but have little of the spark of creative energy that Chaucer generated by mixing the satirical portraits from that tradition with precise observation and detail from true life:

> I do not think that Chaucer's aim in these two portraits can have been solely to endorse the idea that society coheres through the mutual benefits arising from the interchange of services ... This is the basis on which society *should* be organized; but the isolation of these two figures in the *Prologue* shows us that the actuality is something different.[67]

There is certainly some truth to such criticisms. But underlying them is an assumption that competitive self-interest is the only real motivation for exchange, and that any other possible reasons are ideal and not part of true, lived experience. It is important to understand, therefore, that the significance of the Plowman's creed does not lie in his selfless charity. The Plowman's generosity does not prove that true exchange is benevolent, any more than the Franklin's feasting proves that all gifts are selfishly self-motivated. Nor is it particularly significant that some people, like the Plowman and Parson, are more virtuous than other people, like just about everyone else. What the Plowman's portrait does demonstrate is that there are other ways of measuring value and other motivations for exchange than those of the marketplace, and these alternatives are fully real, and actually exist, and always have.

I am also sympathetic to those who, like Mann, have reservations about the Parson's and Plowman's portraits on aesthetic grounds. There is something to the critical commonplace that the depiction of the ideal is less interesting than the satirization of the flawed particular. It does occur to me, however, that though many readers consider the Clerk to be an ideal scholar, few claim that his scholarly ideals are not *real* – no doubt because most of those who advance interpretations of the pilgrim portraits are scholars. There might be greater recognition of the validity of the Plowman's ideals if more of his interpreters were medieval peasants.

The General Prologue portraits of both the Franklin and the Plowman illustrate gift exchange. The Franklin's gifting imitates in its motivations the self-interested and competitive logic of the marketplace, but this is not because market values are natural, eternal and inevitable; rather, it is because the mentalities of gift exchange was changing in the increasingly market-oriented context of the late medieval haute bourgeoisie. The market as an instituted process is evident in the portrait of the Plowman, which shows that gift-giving could be, and was, rooted in motivations materially and symbolically different from those of commercial exchange. Such non-commercial intentions are just as real, just as logical and just as viable as the profit motive of the marketplace, and also just as elemental to the social reality that informs and is dramatized by the *Canterbury Tales*. If we neglect them, or misread them simply as rudimentary reflections of commerce, then we will arrive at a warped understanding of Chaucer's world, and our own.

THE LACK OF INTEREST IN
THE *SHIPMAN'S TALE*:

Chaucer and the Social Theory of the Gift

Is there any interest in Chaucer's *Shipman's Tale?*
I mean this question in several senses, but not primarily the
most obvious one. In terms of critical attention, the *Shipman's Tale*
has been accruing compound interest. None of the other *Canterbury
Tales* has such a reputation for being over-determined as the *Shipman's
Tale* does, but this has often been seen as its point, and indeed as
its virtue, as it seems to construct precise parallels between complex
monetary transactions and subtle human relations. E. T. Donaldson
remarks that the 'reduction of all human values to commercial ones
is accomplished with almost mathematical precision ... Sensitivity to
other values besides cash has been submitted to appraisal and, having
been found nonconvertible, has been thrown away.'[1] Helen Fulton has
observed that 'the plot of the *Shipman's Tale* rests on a commercialism
which is so over-determined that it becomes humorous'.[2] As interest in
economics in literature has increased in recent years, so has attention
to the *Shipman's Tale*, and as William E. Rogers and Paul Dower suggest there has been a trend away from seeing the tale as a critique of
mercantile values to seeing it as an embodiment of those values.[3] Lee
Patterson finds that the tale 'threatens to coopt its readers to its own
sardonic world of self-interest'.[4] And Lianna Farber finds scholastic

philosophy establishing the naturalness of exchange value, and she therefore asserts that the *Shipman's Tale* 'works to blur the distinction between a "natural" world and a "commodified" one, suggesting that the two work in much the same manner already'.[5]

If Chaucer studies has been adopting a vision of a purely mercantile society comprised of atomized agents motivated by individual profit, it is perhaps because contemporary social theory has been moving in this direction as well. In particular, this view of the *Shipman's Tale*, of individuals in inevitable competition for resources both material and immaterial, resembles, and may reflect the influence of, the theories of Pierre Bourdieu. Bourdieu begins his essay 'Is a Disinterested Act Possible?' by asking, 'Why is the word interest to a certain point interesting? Why is it important to ask about the interest that agents may have in doing what they do?'[6] His answer is that without specific interests, the actions of individuals would be unintelligible. Interest is interesting because self-interest is the only interest. Bourdieu devised his totalizing 'theory of practice' in order to provide a consistent model for human social action in multiple contexts, both economic and non-economic, and central to this theory is the view that all human choices are rooted in self-interest.

As Bourdieu's theory borrows economic terminology to describe individual human calculations and strategies in both economic and non-economic fields, and as it analogizes the self-interest inherent in economic transactions to all human interactions, it would seem particularly suited to elucidating the *Shipman's Tale*.[7] The tale begins, 'A marchant whilom dwelled at Seint-Denys, / That riche was, for which men helde him wys' (VII.1–2), and it is throughout concerned with such interconnections of economic and symbolic capital.

The claim of this chapter is that the *Shipman's Tale* is not as deterministic as it has been taken to be, and that instead its characters repeatedly evince motivations not accountable by a purely economic model of human action, nor by theories of symbolic action founded on utilitarian principles. These discrepancies reveal insufficiencies in the currently dominant models of value theory, particularly Bourdieu's, and justify the project under way by anthropological and sociological theorists to reinterpret Marcel Mauss's foundational essay *The Gift* in order to redefine interest, self-interest and disinterestedness in human interaction. Bourdieu provided a theory of practice, based on a logic of action in symbolic as well as material fields, that could be applied transhistorically and transculturally, making it influential in areas like medieval studies. But neo-Maussians, notably David Graeber and Alain Caillé, criticize Bourdieu's social theory for its generalization of all human motivation as based on individual, competitive self-interest. They offer instead a view of motivation and interest based on mutual indebtedness, communal value and shared pleasures. These critiques enlighten previously neglected parts of the *Shipman's Tale* and promise to reshape our understanding of the characters' motivations and the tale's meaning; just as important, the evidence of the *Shipman's Tale* helps to expose the insufficiency of a purely Bourdieusian model of cultural logic and to reveal the value of the newer approaches.

I. Interest-free loans

What I am primarily asking in my initial question, therefore, is whether there is any interest charged on the loans that run through the *Shipman's Tale*. The presence or absence of interest beyond principal is the key factor in distinguishing between a loan and gift. And gift theory, historically and in its recent developments, is at the heart of the greater issue: whether self-interest is the only interest.[8]

The monetary exchanges in the *Shipman's Tale* begin at the merchant's home in St. Denis. While the merchant is in his counting-house, his wife and the monk perform their elaborate *pas de deux* in the garden, wherein she ultimately informs him that she is in debt by 100 francs, and he agrees to give her the money, for the promise of a sexual assignation. Afterward, the merchant informs the wife that he must travel to Bruges to purchase merchandise. The monk then asks the merchant for a loan of 100 francs – for a week or two, he says, to purchase 'certein beestes' (VII.272). The merchant agrees and gives the monk the 100 francs, telling him to 'Paye it agayn when it lith in youre ese' (VII.291). Daun John returns to his abbey in Paris, and the merchant goes to Bruges, where he 'byeth and creaunceth' (VII.303) – that is, he purchases goods for both cash and credit. Meanwhile, Daun John rides back to St. Denis, gives the wife the 100 francs he had borrowed from her husband, spends the night with her, and returns to Paris. When the merchant returns home, he explains to his wife that to pay for the merchandise in Bruges he had to take a loan of 20,000 shields, and that he now must go to Paris 'To borwe of certeine freendes that he hadde / A certeyn frankes' (VII.333–4) so that he can repay the debt. When he arrives in Paris, he visits the monk and tells him about his business dealings. Daun John, taking a hint, or pretending to, informs the merchant that he has already repaid the loan of 100 francs to the merchant's wife. The merchant, after repaying his Bruges debt to 'certeyn Lumbardes' (VII.367), returns again to St. Denis. He admonishes his wife for not telling him about the monk's repayment of the 100 francs. She admits having received it and already having spent it on her 'array' (VII.418) and asserts, famously, that she will pay him back in bed.

The unavoidable impression from this synopsis is that the tale consists of a series of borrowings and repayments. In fact, it is an open series, persisting beyond the end of the tale: the wife is still to pay her debt '[f]ro day to day' (VII.415) in bed, and the merchant presumably must still pay back the parties in Paris from whom he borrowed money to pay off the debt from Bruges.

There are no explicit references to interest in the tale, and this in itself is not surprising. Lending at interest was still illegal in the late Middle Ages under usury laws. But since the arrival of Italian banking houses in Flanders in the thirteenth century, Bruges had developed into one of the commercial and financial centres of Europe, with a wide variety of sophisticated financial instruments available to those seeking commercial or consumer credit.[9] Not all the credit that Chaucer's merchant takes is necessarily in the form of loans. Since he is a regular purchaser at the Bruges market, he could simply buy on a line of credit extended to him by a cloth-seller; this has always been common practice among vendors on occasion, to facilitate sales. But the debt of 20,000 shields is explicitly a monetary, commercial loan from an Italian bank. Lending at interest did exist, and in places like Bruges it was not only common but often licensed. Raymond de Roover explains that 'an attitude of leniency prevailed in the Low Countries during the fourteenth and fifteenth centuries, and it became customary to grant dispensation to usurers licensed by the secular authorities'.[10] Italian bankers, like Jewish money-lenders, could, for a price, secure the (always tenuous) protection of local lords or princes. Alternatively, there were a variety of ways to obscure a bank's profit on the lending of money. Interest could be euphemized as a 'fee' on a transaction, or the bank could take its profit as a percentage of the revenue from the venture.[11] The most common form of loan devised to circumvent the usury ban was the 'bill of exchange', which involved borrowing in one currency and repaying in another currency.[12] This is what Chaucer's merchant seems to employ, borrowing from an Italian banking house in Bruges in shields, the basic unit of account in Flanders, and paying back another branch of the same firm in Paris in francs. Helen Fulton thinks that the merchant 'makes a one-thousand-franc profit on the currency conversion'.[13] This is not entirely certain. It would be unusual, though not impossible, for the borrower to make a profit on a currency exchange: the bill of exchange was devised, after all, to make money for the bank, not the borrower, and currency was almost always worth less abroad than at home.[14] And the merchant seems pleased at the end of the Paris transaction not because he has made a profit but because he anticipates making one, perhaps from the retailing of the merchandise: 'And hoom he gooth, murie as a papejay, / For wel he knew he stood in swich array / That nedes moste he wynne in that viage / A thousand frankes aboven al his costage' (VII.369–72). But even if the merchant is the arbitrageur that Fulton believes him to be, it is clear that the bank making the loan expects to gain a profit through interest disguised as an exchange rate.

But the merchant repays the Lombards both with cash from his own stores in St. Denis and with money that he borrows in Paris. Why would the merchant take out a second loan to pay back the first? And why in the end does he consider himself 'cleerly out of dette' (VII.376)? (It should be noted that when the merchant refers to his 'freendes' in Paris from whom he hopes to borrow, he is almost certainly not thinking of Daun John. The monk's personal debt to the merchant is too small to be of significant use to the merchant in these large-scale business transactions. Though, obviously, exchange rates fluctuated, 100 francs was in Chaucer's time the equivalent of only about 150 shields.[15]) It may be that the merchant's Paris associates are themselves chapmen, rather than bankers, in which case they may be purchasing a share in the merchandise for a portion of the profits. Or it could be that the merchant of St. Denis has a good name among them and is trusted to repay the loan, just as they might need to borrow money from him in a similar situation. As merchants, our protagonist himself notes, 'hir moneie is hir plogh' (VII.288): they cannot do business without occasionally laying out large amounts of cash on the expectation of future sales, and it might be in their interest to lend to each other, rather than to borrow money at interest from bankers.

In this thoroughly monetized and mercantile environment, the loans may entail explicit or euphemized payments of interest, but even in the absence of interest obligations all the parties to all the loans engage in the transactions with some expectations of gain, in the form of future business, a share of profits, a potential source of future revenue or the value of having a good name as a debtor. What is less clear is whether this is also true regarding the personal loans among the characters of the tale. In their colloquy in the garden, the wife initially propositions the monk with a request for a loan, with the promise of sexual favours offered apparently as interest: 'Daun John, I seye, lene me thise hundred frankes, … / For at a certeyn day I wol yow paye, / And doon to yow what plesance and service / That I may doon, right as yow list devise' (VII.187, 190–2). Eventually, however, they agree that the transaction is not a loan but a payment for services: 'This faire wyf acorded with daun John / That for thise hundred frankes he sholde al nyght / Have hire in his armes bolt upright' (VII.314–16).

The 100 francs the merchant gives to the monk, on the other hand, is explicitly a loan, ostensibly to fund another transaction. But while the monk proposes to pay the merchant back in 'a wyke or tweye'

(VII.271), the merchant sets no time limit on the loan and expects no repayment beyond the initial amount: 'Paye it agayn whan it lith in youre ese' (VII.291). The monk later tells the merchant that he has settled the account with the merchant's wife by giving her 'the same gold ageyn' (VII.357), and the merchant repeats to the wife that the monk 'hadde an hundred frankes payed / By redy token' (VII.389–90).

In the literary, historical and theoretical contexts of the tale, interest in some form was conceivable and feasible.[16] Even the earliest scholastic writers on economics granted that payment beyond principal could be allowed in certain situations, such as a penalty when lateness has caused specific loss to the lender. Scholars consistently distinguished between a commercial purchase or a loan, and a 'free gift', which, being given without expectation of restitution or profit, must be morally blameless.[17] Some analysts added that payment to a creditor beyond the principal of a loan could be allowable if it is not contractually obligated, but a voluntary gift.[18] The notion of a debtor voluntarily making superfluous payment to one of his creditors is an ethicist's fantasy, of course. It is not surprising that such distinctions would eventually allow some payments of interest to be euphemized as gifts.[19] Even most schoolmen seem to have understood that in the context of business and commerce no one does anything without a profit motive. And yet Chaucer's merchant grants the monk a loan and unilaterally asserts that he will charge no interest and set no date for repayment. What is his motivation – his *interest* – in doing so?

Then, as now, one would grant such a loan only to a friend or relative. That is, it is a kind of gift – the species of exchange that stands apart from commercial transaction. Which is not to say that it is motiveless, or even necessarily 'free'. Marcel Mauss defined the gift as 'the present generously given even when, in the gesture accompanying the transaction, there is only a polite fiction, formalism, and social deceit, and when really there is obligation and self-interestedness'.[20] Mauss's objective in his seminal study was to explain why people are motivated to give and exchange gifts, and most contributions to gift theory over the last century have been essentially glosses on Mauss's *The Gift*.[21] One of the most influential of these has been Bourdieu's.

Bourdieu explains that one of the signal features of his contribution to gift theory is that 'it relates gift exchange to a quite specific logic, that of the economy of symbolic goods and the specific belief (*illusio*) that underlies it'.[22] Among Bourdieu's chief concerns is that in comparison to the fully elaborated system of self-interest and motivation offered by economic analysis, the actions of individuals within a system not governed by the material exchange systems of capitalism could seem illogical and even unintelligible. Much of his work, therefore, focuses on what he calls 'anti-economic sub-universes' which seem to reverse or reject the economic field: the Berber village; the Roman Catholic Church; the nineteenth-century Parisian avant-garde; twentieth-century academia; and so on. These realms are governed by economies of symbolic goods, just as regular and predictable as the economies of material goods in any market culture. Bourdieu emends and extends Mauss's definition of the gift to claim that all gifts and in fact all human actions are self-interested and strategic efforts to gain advantage in one or another of infinite possible fields of competition.

This hallmark feature of Bourdieu's philosophy of the gift, in which all exchanges, transculturally and transhistorically, are fundamentally agonistic and motivated by individual profit, has come under critique by a number of theorists. In particular, the economic anthropologist David Graeber has criticized Bourdieu's 'theory of practice' as an example of 'formalism' – that branch of social theory that seeks to explain human values and motivations in economic terms.[23]

Bourdieu would vehemently deny this charge, and in fact did so, for instance in *The Logic of Practice*: 'Economism recognizes no other form of interest than that which capitalism has produced ... It can therefore find no place in its analyses, still less in its calculations, for any form of "non-economic" interest.'[24] Bourdieu's concept of multiple 'fields' is specifically intended to expand the explanation of human agency beyond the purely commercial and economic. He insists, furthermore, on the autonomy of individual fields, and he claims that this puts his theories 'light years beyond economism, which consists of applying to all universes the *nomos* characteristic of the economic field'.[25]

Nonetheless, Bourdieu uses the language of economics to describe non-economic fields. His terminology borrows directly and intentionally from economics – symbolic capital; symbolic profit; symbolic interest – and he insists that non-economic fields operate according to an 'economy of symbolic goods'.[26] Bourdieu is not unaware of this paradox, and in some instances he justifies this decision by noting that economics is the one social science most advanced in its descriptions of human motivation. But that, for Graeber, is precisely the problem. Despite Bourdieu's insistence that the economic field is only one among an infinite number of overlapping but autonomous fields, within any one of these fields, as Graeber points out, 'it is a matter of self-interested calculation, making rational decisions about the allocation of scarce resources with the aim of getting as much as possible for oneself'.[27] In the 'theory of practice', Graeber sees only the war of all against all – and that is why Graeber characterizes Bourdieu not merely as a formalist but also as a 'neo-liberal', a proponent of free-market principles and global capitalism.

Such a charge directed at so prominent a Marxist as Pierre Bourdieu is, to say the least, surprising. But Graeber's point is that, while Bourdieu attacks the social relations inherent to capitalism, he insists that the calculations of individual profit and competition associated with capitalism and market society are the exclusive governing principles of all human practice. Bourdieu is extending to pre-, non- or anti-economic contexts the rational intentionality that economists identify in the marketplace. The commodities being sought and contested are symbolic rather than material, but the mentality is always competitive and individualistic – the self-maximization that economists invariably assume as the motivation of individual agents within a market system. Any other motivations, as perceived by an observer or by the agents themselves, are the *illusio*, the false criteria that mask the true.

The world of the *Shipman's Tale* is a commercial culture, but it is also a gift culture.[28] With its detailed attention to competitive self-interest and individual profit as motives for human interaction, the *Shipman's Tale* would seem to dramatize just the kind of confluence of gift and commodity practices and mentalities that Martha Howell catalogues and describes in Bourdieusian terms, one in which gifts possess a 'structural ambivalence which predisposes them to fulfill a political function of domination'.[29] Yet in light of Graeber's critique, we can see that many of the most important actions in the *Shipman's Tale* resist and even refute the ostensible motivations ascribed to them by Bourdieu's model of interpretation.

The merchant has no economic interest in lending the 100 francs to the monk. In fact, he is at pains to point out to Daun John that parting with ready money can put him in economic jeopardy. He is overstating the peril: the size of the loan the monk is requesting, as I have noted, is pocket change in comparison to the amounts of his usual business dealings. The merchant is undeniably reluctant to cough up the money. It would be natural to assume, then, that the merchant visits the monk when he is in Paris in order to collect the 100 francs, or, in the case that the monk would be unable to repay him, to 'capitalize' on the debt – to benefit from his own symbolic profit. He would not demand repayment directly, though; rather, he would pretend that the visit was social and had nothing to do with collecting a debt, and this would be a perfect example of the 'euphemization' of a monetary transaction.

In fact, when the merchant arrives, the monk acts as if he knows that the merchant is really there to collect the money. He does this only because he is actually seeking an opportunity to tell the merchant that he paid his wife, but in rushing his friend out the door he successfully makes the merchant think that he, the merchant, is responsible for exposing the euphemism and threatening the friendship. Indeed, when the merchant later admonishes his wife, it is not because she failed to give him the money, but rather because in not telling him about the repayment it made it seem as if he had gone to see his friend in order to get repaid – an unacceptable violation of the rules of the game:

> Ye sholde han warned me, er I had gon,
> That he yow hadde an hundred frankes payed
> By redy token; and heeld hym yvele apayed,
> For that I to hym spak of chevyssaunce;
> Me semed so, as by his contenaunce.   (VII.388–92)

For all these reasons, one sometimes finds even the closest readers of this tale asserting that the merchant really does go to the monk to collect the debt.[30] But Chaucer goes out of his way to tell us that he does not:

> And whan that he was come into the toun,
> For greet chiertee and greet affeccioun,
> Unto daun John he first gooth hym to pleye;
> Nat for to axe or borwe of hym moneye,
> But for to wite and seen of his welfare,
> And for to tellen hym of his chaffare,
> As freendes doon whan they been met yfeere.   (VII.337–41)

The point is reiterated at the end of the tale, when the merchant explains to his wife that he faced embarrassment when he visited the monk and brought up the topic of business. Daun John, the merchant says,

> heeld hym yvele apayed,
> For that I to hym spak of chevyssaunce;
> Me semed so, as by his contenaunce.
> But nathelees, by God, oure hevene kyng,
> I thoughte nat to axen hym no thyng.   (VII.390–4)

Chaucer is as explicit as he can be about the merchant's motivations: he visits his friend to see how he is doing, to enjoy his company and to tell him of his business affairs – because that is what friends do. This motivation can be dismissed as insufficient only if we proceed from an a priori assumption that human motivation is explicable only by competitive, individual self-maximization.

True, Bourdieu is always at pains to emphasize that *conscious* motivation is irrelevant. If people are generous or kind or altruistic, it is because they have been conditioned to be so, or because they unconsciously recognize, through what he typically calls their 'sense of the game', that there is a profit to be gained through being so. To

Bourdieu, then, friendship would in this transaction be the *illusio* that masks the true intentions. But there is a kind of inescapable circularity to this reasoning. As Graeber remarks,

> On some level, what Bourdieu is saying is undeniably true. There is no area of human life, anywhere, where one cannot find self-interested calculation. But neither is there anywhere one cannot find kindness or adherence to idealistic principles: the point is why one, and not the other, is posed as 'objective' reality.[31]

The merchant lives in a world where interest, if never explicit, is always expected, and money is a tool for competitive transactions and individual advancement. And yet he extends to the monk an open-ended, no-interest loan, and would never even consider asking him to pay it back. One could say that he does all this to gain a symbolic profit in the field of friendship. Or one could say, as Chaucer explicitly does, that he does it because they are friends. The former formulation is more reasonable only if one assumes that individual profit is the purpose of friendship.

In contradistinction to such interpretations of the gift as essentially agonistic, competitive and individualistic, Graeber offers Mauss's concept of 'total prestations'. To Graeber, this means those exchanges that 'created permanent relationships between individuals and groups, relations that were permanent precisely because there was no way to cancel them out by repayment. The demands one side could make on the other were open ended because they were permanent.'[32] Whereas Bourdieu assumes that the purpose of any social transaction is to generate a material or symbolic profit for one participant over the other, anthropologists like Graeber maintain that gifts are exchanged in order to establish and maintain alliances that extend beyond the transaction and that are, in their elementary form, essentially non-competitive, because the participants recognize such relationships to be, in the greater scheme, in their collective interest.

Economic anthropologists like Graeber emphasize the meaningful distinctions between gift exchange and market transactions. In a market context, the relationship between the participants ends with the completion of the transaction. The relationship is based on the debt, and is cancelled when the debt is paid. That is why accounts need to be kept. In contrast, Graeber says of gift-based relationships, 'No accounts need to be kept because the relationship is not treated as if it will ever end.'[33]

In a number of ways, the merchant of the *Shipman's Tale* seems to act in greater accord with Bourdieu's model than with Graeber's. He is a great keeper of accounts. It is clear, even when he lends a relatively small amount to a friend, that he is not likely to forget the expense, and he makes Daun John acutely aware of it as well; there may, in fact, be an element of agonistic exchange in the way the loan places an onus of obligation on the monk. Nonetheless, there is a real distinction between the types of relationships the merchant maintains. When the merchant pays off his Bruges debt in Paris, his relationship with those Lombard bankers is concluded: he has no further obligation to them, nor they to him, and unless he chooses, for business purposes, to transact with them again in the future, he need never have anything to do with them again. They are not friends or kinsmen, after all; they are merely business associates. But the merchant's relationship with the monk is not a market exchange or a professional contract. He would only extend an open-ended, interest-free loan – a gift – to a friend. In Bourdieu's social model, 'friendship' is the *illusio* that facilitates the exchange, the purpose of which is to generate profit. From Graeber's neo-Maussian perspective, this gets it precisely backwards: the exchanges, and the obligations they entail, exist to perpetuate the relationship. The granting of the loan has the effect of sustaining the friendship and extending it, due to its open-ended nature, indefinitely into the future. The merchant does not ask Daun John for the money when he visits him in Paris. In part, this may be because he does not want to expose the euphemism at the heart of their transaction, or because the continuation of the obligation of the repayment grants him ongoing symbolic profit. But it also may be that he requires no interest and sets no time limit because the loan's purpose is not profit but the continuation of the relationship. Such a motivation is no less logical or natural than seeking individual profit. As Graeber says of such relationships based on 'total prestations', 'Most of us treat our closest friends this way.'[34]

II. Gratuitous sex

The most over-determined element of the *Shipman's Tale* is its monetization of married sex. This entails, unavoidably, a commodification of the wife's body. Feminist readings of the tale, however, have sought to demonstrate that the wife engages actively and deliberately in the tale's economy. Thus Cathy Hume argues that though the wife's power is 'severely restricted' outside the home, at home with her husband she is 'allowed to get away with paying him back in bed' though she is 'pushing at the limits of her social boundaries, to secure even this'.[35] And Holly Crocker finds that 'the wife herself becomes an active player' and 'a trader in the economy of this tale'.[36]

Certainly, the wife is a player in the game, and to some extent the tale and her role in it exemplify Bourdieusian principles. The source of the wife's notoriety, the thing that makes her scandalous even to this day, is her brazen violation of what Bourdieu calls 'the taboo of calculation':

> Housewives, who have no material utility or price (the taboo of calculation and credit), are excluded from market circulation (exclusivity) and are objects and subjects of feeling; in contrast, so-called venal women (prostitutes) have an explicit market price, based on money and calculation, are neither object nor subject of feeling and sell their body as an object ... The logic of the prevailing economic universe introduces, within the family, the rot of calculation, which undermines sentiments.[37]

The gimlet-eyed *Shipman's Tale* exposes sentiment as the *illusio* of marriage and reveals the calculation of both material and cultural profit that underlies the bourgeois household.

But while an individualistic and competitive model of social exchange can afford the wife agency, it also, as with her husband, simultaneously limits her agency by severely restricting the range of motivations for social action. And like the merchant, the wife actually demonstrates a variety of drives and intentions that are not entirely subsumable to Bourdieu's theory of practice. For while the wife plays to win, she also plays for fun, and as critics like Graeber point out, pleasure does not calculate the way profit does, nor the way that Bourdieu maintains it does.[38]

The *Shipman's Tale* is a fabliau, even if in its understated wit and its precise attention to codes of behaviour in social situations it is closer to a comedy of manners, and we should not be surprised that appetite and carnality animate it. Male sexual desire is at the heart of the *Shipman's Tale*, and its female counterpart is primarily depicted as women's desire for fine 'array', which the wife as well as the narrator justify as an extension of men's property and status. As far as we know, the wife does not want to have sex with the Daun John; she wants to clear her debts. Daun John, who is hardly a brazen and experienced lothario like Nicholas in the *Miller's Tale*, may not want sex with the wife as much as he wants to score some sort of social point by sleeping with the merchant's wife.[39] The merchant and his wife, meanwhile, quite unlike the typical married couple of fabliau, have an active sex life, but critics have been reluctant to allow them this free expression of conjugal desire; some suggest, for instance, that their sex is an expression of the merchant's fetishizing of profit: he is sexually aroused when he is out of debt.[40]

But the relationship between the merchant and his wife, like the relationship between the merchant and the monk, seems to contain, in addition to elements of economics and exploitation and competition, an irreducible element of attraction, and in fact affection, that neither is fully converted into monetary value nor parallels economic competition in a separate but analogous field of symbolic competition.[41]

When, during their conversation in the garden, the monk makes a gently bawdy allusion to the dalliances of married people, the wife replies, 'In al the reawme of France is ther no wyf / That lasse lust hath to that sory pleye' (VII.116–17). She goes on to declare, 'Myn housbonde is to me the worste man / That evere was sith that the world bigan' (VII.161–2), and finally confessing that she has spent 100 francs '[f]or his honour, myself for to arraye' (VII.179), she claims, 'And if myn housbonde eek it myghte espye, / I nere but lost; and therfore I yow preye, / Lene me this somme, or ellis moot I deye' (VII.184–6). In all this, the wife paints her marriage as loveless and sexless and her husband as avaricious and cruel – the stereotypical *senex amans* of fabliau tradition.

But there is little indication elsewhere in the text that any of these insinuations are true. The merchant takes pleasure in a great many things, including feasting his friends and dealing in business as well as sex with his wife. He can hardly be accused of watching his wife too jealously, and he does not deny her money, but only, as she admits, keeps her on an allowance that he insists is sufficient. In her characterization of her husband, the wife is playing on the expectations of the monk – and of the reader – and on the conventional, jaundiced view of marriage as an arena of material and emotional competition. It is this – the merchant holds the purse strings and condescends to his wife's needs and desires, while she uses sex and guile to try to gain equal control – but it is not exclusively this. Chaucer could easily have made the merchant the kind of ogre that the wife claims him to be, someone combining the worst characteristics of his other fabliau husbands – John of the *Miller's Tale*, Symkyn of the *Reeve's Tale*, January of the *Merchant's Tale*. Instead, Chaucer gives us multiple occasions to see the couple share what seem to be true affection and physical pleasure. When the merchant returns from Bruges, for instance, 'with his wyf he maketh feeste and cheere' (VII.327).

Even more notable are their relations in the final scene. When the merchant arrives home from Paris, he and his wife retire to the bedroom, 'And al that nyght in myrthe they bisette' (VII.375). In the morning, the merchant wakes up and once again approaches his wife amorously:

> Whan it was day, this marchant gan embrace
> His wyf al newe, and kiste hire on hir face,
> And up he gooth and maketh it ful tough.
> 'Namoore,' quod she, 'by God, ye have ynough!'   (VII.377–80)

The wife here employs the language of sufficiency that her husband had used against her in denying her more spending money. She claims now to have paid her debt, and in a few lines she will explain precisely the mercantile arrangement that ostensibly determines their relations.

But in the next line Chaucer writes, 'And wantownly agayn with hym she pleyde' (VII.381). The word 'agayn' in Middle English usually means 'in return' or 'in response', and that is how this instance is glossed by the Riverside editors. (Chaucer uses it in this sense in the *Shipman's Tale* at VII.37, 134 and 357.) But it could also mean, as in modern usage, 'one more time'. (The *MED* cites a line from Chaucer's *Astrolabe* as an early instance of its use in this sense.) '[W]antownly', meanwhile, clearly means 'lasciviously', and 'pleye' can mean many things, including to amuse yourself or others, or to joke or jest, or to use playful language, but also it can mean to have sex. The wife has already referred to sex as 'that sory pley' (VII.117), and in the *Merchant's Tale* January says to May, 'It is no fors how longe that we pleye ... / For we han leve to pleye us by the lawe' (IV.1835, 41).

So what action is indicated by the line, 'And wantownly agayn with hym she pleyde'? I think that the wife has sex with her husband again, having just said that she was not obligated to. It is also possible that she engages in foreplay, or merely teases him in a flirtatious manner, or some permutation of the three. But whatever kind of playfulness or amatory pleasure it is, the wife is not marking it in her accounts of her sexual obligations to her husband.

Bourdieu's answer to the question 'Is a Disinterested Act Possible?' is, emphatically, no. By way of explanation, he introduces the term he understands as the opposite of 'interested':

> The word 'gratuitous' refers, on the one hand, to the idea of unmotivated, arbitrary: a gratuitous act is one which cannot be explained ... a foolish, absurd act – it matters little – about which social science has nothing to say and in the face of which it can only resign. This first sense conceals another, more common meaning: that which is gratuitous is that which is for nothing, is not profitable, costs nothing, is not lucrative. Telescoping these two meanings,

the search for the *raison d'être* of a behavior is identified with the explanation of that behavior as the pursuit of economic ends.[42]

That which is gratuitous is both free and pointless; it is without interest, and therefore it is meaningless and unintelligible.

But in this final scene of the *Shipman's Tale*, the wife, having evoked the over-determined analogy of sex to money, immediately undermines it by having sex that provides her with no economic advantage – monetary or symbolic. The sex is, in Bourdieu's own terms, 'gratuitous'.

What has Bourdieu done, really, but exclude from consideration any motivations other than competitive, individual self-interest? There is in fact an intelligible way of reading the wife's actions: she likes her husband and she likes having sex with him, and despite her claims that their marriage is a business-like arrangement of sex for money they have a personal connection that is sometimes expressed sexually.

Bourdieu freely admits the validity of libido as an explanation of action. In fact, he suggests that desire is the core of human motivation, which he figures, using an appropriately monastic image, as fundamentally competitive:

> *Libido* would also be entirely pertinent for saying what I have called *illusio*, or investment … If I had to summarize in an image all that I have just said about the notion of the field, and about *illusio* which is at the same time the condition and the product of the field's functioning, I would recall a sculpture found at the Auch cathedral, in the Gers, which represents two monks struggling over the prior's staff. In a world which, like the religious universe, and above all the monastic universe, is the site par excellence of *Ausserweltlich*, of the extraworldly of disinterestedness in the naive sense of the term, one finds people who struggle over a staff, whose value exists only for those who are in the game, caught up in the game.[43]

This image of two ostensibly pious men struggling to control a symbol of power and authority says much about Bourdieu's conception of desire, but one must ask how well this image represents libido in the carnal sense. If these two monks were seeking physical gratification, would not their struggle be of a very different nature? (When, in the *Merchant's Tale*, May claims to 'strugle with a man upon a tree' (IV.2374), we know what kind of struggle she means.) Only one of the monks can get the staff; is this true of sexual pleasure?

Elsewhere, Bourdieu calls on social science

> to extend economic calculation to *all* goods, material and symbolic, without distinction, that present themselves as *rare* and worthy of being sought after in a particular social formation – which may be 'fair words' or smiles, handshakes or shrugs, compliments or attention, gossip or scientific information, distinction or distinctions, etc.[44]

One can see that individuals in a given social formation might be motivated to seek smiles or handshakes, but does it really make sense to imagine a 'profit of smiles'? Similarly, we are familiar with a fabliau world in which individuals compete for advantage in everything, including sexual gratification. But can even such 'nakedly' self-interested motivations be translated into economic terms? We could say that the wife in the *Shipman's Tale* seeks to maximize her own pleasure. But when she 'plays' with her husband, she sets her own physical pleasure in opposition to the economic metaphor that she playfully invokes.

The fact is that neither smiles nor shrugs, nor foreplay nor orgasms, are apportioned through society in the same way that economic resources are. They can, of course, be found in abundance where material wealth is not, but more important, they are not zero-sum and do not follow the laws of economics that pertain to money or material resources. I can give someone a smile without suffering a commensurate loss of smile of my own – and I invite the reader to extend this analogy to the sexual interactions hitherto delineated. Pleasure can be gained when it is given. So what reason is there to describe it in economic terms at all?

III. The gift that keeps on giving

As his invocation of the image of the monks and the staff suggests, Bourdieu admits libido as an operative term for core motivations precisely because he sees all desire as individualistic and competitive. This would not seem to allow the possibility that pleasures could be increased when they are shared or social. It is a conception of pleasure, therefore, that conforms to a market model of desire and negotiation. This is the root of Graeber's objection to contemporary value theory:

> When market theorists think about a pleasurable, rewarding experience, the root image they have in mind seems to be eating food ('consumption') – and not in the context of a public or private feast, either, but apparently, food eaten by oneself ... [O]ne need only imagine how different the theory might look like if it set off from almost any other kind of enjoyable experience: say, from making love, or from being at a concert, or even from playing a game.[45]

When Chaucer's merchant emerges from his counting house, he takes pleasure in dining with friends: 'And richely this monk the chapman fedde' (VII.254). A comprehensive theory of value must account for this kind of pleasure.

To address such limitations built into purely utilitarian models of social action, some social theorists have been seeking to develop alternative theories of value. This project has been the particular focus of the scholars associated with *La Revue du MAUSS*, founded by Alain Caillé. Caillé and Jacques Godbout have taken up Bourdieu's interest in the words 'interest' and 'gratuitous'. They note that in addition to meaning 'free' and 'meaningless', 'gratuitous' (*gratuit*) 'still harbors a hint of grace, of what is gracious, of what makes it possible for something unexpected to appear out of nowhere, something generous, associated with birth, with begetting'.[46] Significantly, the value of the gift is for Caillé and Godbout tied to pleasure: 'The deeper meaning of the word disinterested (*gratuit* in French) has been misunderstood by mercantile logic. There is an equivalence in the gift precisely because of its disinterestedness: a disinterested gift *gratifies* the one who gives it as much as the one who receives it.'[47] Caillé and Godbout find room for pleasure in their model of exchange because they limit the meaning of the transaction neither to the object exchanged nor to the moment of transaction. Rather, they locate value also in the relationship formed by the transaction when, as in a gift exchange, a sense of obligation results and persists. Whereas economic models recognize only 'exchange value' and 'use value', Caillé and Godbout propose a third mode of evaluation: 'bonding-value': 'what an object, a service, a particular act, is worth in the world of ties and their reinforcement'.[48] Thus it is the ineradicable obligation, and not any elusive 'disinterestedness', that defines the gift: 'The gift involves the partners in a state of indebtedness that characterizes any intense social bond.'[49] A state of indebtedness, in which the accounts can never be settled, is what delineates the gift relationship from the market relationship, which moves ever toward equivalence: 'This assertion of long-term equality reflects something bizarre and "gratuitous". For how does the observer know that in the long term gifts and counter-gifts will balance out? At what theoretical moment does everything become even?'[50]

Just such a state of perpetually indebted disequilibrium is dramatized at the conclusion of the *Shipman's Tale*, which in light of Caillé and Godbout's theories takes on an entirely different cast from its conventional interpretation. The merchant brings up his concerns about the monk to his wife only reluctantly:

> 'By God ... I am a litel wrooth
> With yow, my wyf, although it be me looth.
> And woot ye why? By God, as that I gesse
> That ye han maad a manere straungenesse
> Bitwixen me and my cosyn daun John.
> Ye sholde han warned me, er I had gon,
> That he yow hadde an hundred frankes payed
> By redy token; and heeld hym yvele apayed,
> For that I to hym spak of chevyssaunce;

But nathelees, by God, oure hevene kyng,
I thoughte nat to axen hym no thyng.
I prey thee, wyf, ne do namoore so;
Telle me alwey, er that I fro thee go,
If any dettour hath in myn absence
Ypayed thee, lest thurgh thy necligence
I myghte hym axe a thing that he hath payed.'   (VII.383–99)

The merchant is not thinking about their marriage bed in mercantile terms, and he is not demanding that his wife give him the money that his friend says he paid back. Nor is he particularly angry that she did not tell him about the money. He simply admits, amid the pleasure of their sexual reunion, that he is 'a litel wrooth' because her 'necligence' had put him in the position of seeming to ask for repayment from a friend. He therefore only asks that, in the future, she tell him if she has received payments from his debtors, in order to avoid such potentially embarrassing situations.

The wife responds with her notorious commodification of the wife's body:

'Ye han mo slakkere dettours than am I!
For I wol paye yow wel and redily
Fro day to day, and if so be I faille,
I am youre wyf; score it upon my taille,
And I shal paye as soone as ever I may.'   (VII.413–17)

But when that is – the due date for repayment of this marital debt – is not specified. Instead, after noting that she spent the money for his 'honour' (VII.421), she says,

'As be nat wrooth, but let us laughe and pleye,
Ye shal my joly body have to wedde;
By God, I wol nat paye yow but abedde!
Forgyve it me, myn owene spouse deere;
Turne hiderward, and maketh bettre cheere.'   (VII.422–6)

The merchant, seeing that there is 'no remedie' (VII.427), forgives her, and asks only that in the future she be not so 'large' and '[k]eep bet thy good' (VII.432–3).

This is comical, of course. The wife has cheated on the merchant, and she has avoided being caught in that particular indiscretion. But all the same, the tale ends with laughter, amicability, and sex – with 'pleye'. It does *not* end with a precise equivalency of sex and money. Neither party is actually calculating the franc-value of marital sex, nor are they setting real terms on when the debt shall be repaid. That the wife says in jest, and the merchant, with a sigh, gives up and takes what's offered. This concluding scene is almost always taken as the quintessential commodification of sex and subordination of marriage to the calculation of the marketplace. But their relationship here reflects not the conclusive equivalence of the market transaction, but rather the perpetual 'dynamic of indebtedness' that Caillé and Godbout see in gift exchange. Money and sex will always be exchanged in this relationship, but there is no expectation of ever settling accounts, and each shall always be in debt to the other. In Caillé and Godbout's terms, marital sex in the *Shipman's Tale* is not a commodity at all. It is the gift that keeps on giving.

The problem with using the language of the market economy to describe all human relations is that, in addition to being superfluous, it has the effect of naturalizing commercial relationships, of making the economic transaction the elementary form of exchange. Just as Graeber sees this as a problem of contemporary value theory, it also seems to have been a feature of recent literary criticism. Perhaps the (presumably unconscious) effect of market theorists is responsible for the trend, observed by Rogers and Dower, of contemporary critics seeing the *Shipman's Tale* not as a critique of market values but as an illustration of the naturalness and inevitability of those values. 'Put bluntly,' Lee Patterson writes, 'the *Shipman's Tale* argues that the correspondence between business and marriage, however dismaying, is an inevitable part of being human.'[51] But this is precisely what the *Shipman's Tale* does *not* do. On the contrary, the tale shows that whatever the effects of capitalism and the money economy on society and human relations, they are absolutely not inevitable, original or natural to the human condition.

As Graeber acknowledges, there is no area of human interaction where one cannot find individual self-interest at work, and I know of no sociological model more effective than Bourdieu's in describing its operation. It is also true that the world of the *Shipman's Tale* is one of pervasive commercial mentality, which clearly influences the personal relationships; I would hardly wish to sentimentalize the kinds of friends and spouses we encounter in this story. And yet, in this most thoroughly economic and monetary tale, the characters themselves still have access to other measures of social worth and other modes of human interaction. To reduce all motivations in the tale to economic-minded competition is to obscure Chaucer's achievement and as well as his intentions, and also to place philosophically unnecessary and politically undesirable limitations on the range of human motivations and interactions. There is something ultimately irreducible in the human connections in this tale – in the affection and attraction between merchant and wife, in the fondness of the merchant for friendship and the pleasure he takes from companionship and generosity. These are rare enough in fabliau – to say nothing of the real world – that we should not seek to erase them when they actually present themselves. This may make the characters and the tale harder to fit into an overarching theory of practice, but it also makes them more interesting.

GIVING EVIL:

Excess and Equivalence in the Fabliau

It is the drunkenly obstreperous Miller who, interrupting the orderly plans of the Host after the *Knight's Tale*, introduces both the concept of 'quiting' and the genre of fabliau into the *Canterbury Tales* scheme:

> 'By armes, and by blood and bones,
> I kan a noble tale for the nones,
> With which I wol now quite the Knightes tale.'   (I.3125–6)

Almost immediately, 'quiting', or the declared intention to do so, begins to duplicate itself. Even before the Miller has completed his own prologue, the Reeve is vowing to pay back the Miller for perceived slights. 'Quiting' quickly evolves into one of the organizing principles of the poem.

The term and concept of 'quiting' is so frequently and conspicuously used throughout the collection of tales that it would not seem to require definition. It means 'to pay', often in the monetary sense, but it also means more broadly 'to pay back' and more specifically 'to take revenge on'.[1] Because all these senses seem to be rooted in commerce, self-interest and aggression, 'quiting' has come to be seen as arising from mentalities of the marketplace, and such market mentalities have been seen as the underlying logic of the *Canterbury Tales*. To R. A. Shoaf, 'quiting' is the clearest expression of the commercial imaginations of Chaucer's characters as well as the principles of exchange underlying the work as a whole:

> In fact, every pilgrim 'quites' someone or something with the tale he or she tells (even the Knight, who 'quites' his version of disorder in the world). Every pilgrim is an unredeemed, unself-conscious narcissist. Selfhood depends on taking a position, but if one's position is only in opposition to ... then one's opponent radically circumscribes one's self. Not in opposition, then, but in relationship, in mutual and just exchange, is freedom of the self posited. The Canterbury pilgrims repeatedly fail in such relation-ship, fail in community, because they are forever opposing or 'quiting' someone or something; even though we occasionally hear some such formula as 'God save al this faire compaignye'... we are never allowed to forget at the same time that, for example, the Friar and the Summoner cannot stand each other ... And since the sphere of economics, the marketplace, is the space where community, mutual and just exchange, is most visible and strenu-ously tested, Chaucer posits economics, 'quiting,' as the structure of relations in *The Canterbury Tales*.[2]

Similar interpretations, for similar reasons, have accrued to Chaucer's fabliaux. The outdated argument, originating with Joseph Bédier, that fabliau was to the bourgeoisie as romance was to the First Estate, was largely refuted by Charles Muscatine and others, and most critics today would say that fabliaux were not more middle class than romance in either their origins or their audience.[3] Nonetheless, there persist perceptions of the genre as fundamentally commercial and market-oriented in its imagination. Even while refuting the claim that the bourgeoisie constituted the genre's original audience, Muscatine concludes that fabliaux are informed by a drive for material profit: 'No matter what social biases they variously exhibit, they celebrate uniformly one set of values: the ethic of cleverness, of profit, and of elementary pleasure. In historical perspective this unabashed material-ism and hedonism has not become respectable until very recently.'[4]

Gabrielle Lyons links the rise of fabliau to the advent of the money economy in the thirteenth century; Simon Gaunt adds that the French fabliaux 'continually undermine discourses which posit stable social hierarchies, parodying other genres which sustain such discourses … poking fun at conventional morality, and overturning received views of social order'.[5]

But the association of the fabliau with the market economy may simply be due to the fact that the stories are peopled by characters that, as Patricia Eberle says, 'are usually very closely involved in the world of getting and spending'.[6] Or the connection may be rooted in the mechanistic inevitability with which the fabliau plot so often seems to work out. Though Muscatine would later refute the middle-class origins of the fabliau, in *Chaucer and the French Tradition* he presents the genre as quintessentially bourgeois, and it may not be coincidental in doing so he refers to the 'economical' plotting of the tales: 'The fabliau is the most protean genre of the bourgeois tradition, and will supply us with virtually all of its stylistic traits. Perhaps the commonest (some fabliaux have little else) is a blunt economy of plan and procedure.'[7] Such observations of the 'economy' of narration are a commonplace of fabliau criticism. Thomas D. Cooke's observation is representative: '"The Shipman's Tale" is very similar to the French fabliaux in its economy and symmetry.'[8] The choice of words might seem like a mere semantic coincidence, but this understanding of the economic operation of the fabliau is linked to the much more widely accepted conception of one of its essential qualities, known to criticism as 'fabliau justice'. One of the original expositors of this term was Paul A. Olson, who explained that the *Reeve's Tale* consists of a series of actions and reactions, each calculated to be precisely commensurate with its precedent. It is a pattern, Olson concludes, that shapes the competitive nature of the work as a whole: 'The Reeve is only one of a series of pilgrims who expose their fellows mercilessly; the Summoner, the Friar, the Manciple, all do the same thing. Each provisionally brings himself under the retributive economy which the Reeve so ably dramatizes.'[9]

Conventionally, then, criticism sees 'quiting' as of a piece with fabliau. In both cases, actions and motivations are viewed as selfish, competitive and aggressive, and are perceived to work out with mechanistic commensurability. The actions and motivations are often immoral, but the attitudes of the tales themselves seem to be amoral, non-judgmental, as the plots play out to sometimes surprising but inevitable conclusions. For all these reasons, the genre of fabliau, and its extension in the 'quiting' structure of the Canterbury frame narrative, are associated with the commercial economy, and analogized to the motivations and processes of the marketplace.

I believe, however, that Chaucer's handful of fabliaux does not conform so readily to a market model of exchange. Rather, they drama-tize a number of different kinds of exchange, some resembling the market and some resembling the gift. The most emblematic of them, the *Miller's Tale*, is driven by markedly incommensurate retribution. Ultimately, though seemingly paradoxically, it is the most aggressive and violent elements of the fabliaux that most bespeak the logic of gift exchange. Some of the fabliaux do indeed evince the logical operation of the money economy. The difference between the two modes is not between hate and love, nor between violence and pacifism; rather, it is the difference between superfluity and equivalence.

I. The *Miller's Tale* and the logic of the feud

Among the juxtapositions that the *Miller's Tale* mines for comedic effect are the contrasts between the clerks Nicholas and Absolon. John the carpenter is defined first and foremost by his jealousy, but he finds Absolon so innocuous that he is largely indifferent even when the par-ish clerk sings love songs to Alison outside their window while they are in bed together.

Nicholas, though in the end he is not as clever as he thinks he is, is confident that he can devise a plan to spend the night with Alison. Absolon, on the other hand, has no plan whatsoever when he approaches Alison a second time, other than a vague hope for a kiss. This shows that Absolon is not by nature competitive or aggressive (this is in fact a large part of what he is mocked for) and also that strategic planning is not his strong suit.

Absolon enters into the competitive and retributive scheme of the tale with a vengeance, as it were, when he realizes that he has been tricked and humiliated by Alison:

> This Absolon gan wype his mouth ful drie.
> Derk was the nyght as pich, or as the cole,
> And at the wyndow out she putte hir hole,
> And Absolon, hym fil no bet ne wers,
> But with his mouth he kiste hir naked ers
> Ful savourly, er he were war of this.
> Abak he stirte, and thoughte it was amys,
> For wel he wiste a womman hath no berd.
> He felte a thyng al rough and long yherd,
> And seyde, 'Fy! allas! what have I do?'
> 'Tehee!' quod she, and clapte the wyndow to,
> And Absolon gooth forth a sory pas.
> 'A berd! A berd!' quod hende Nicholas,
> 'By Goddes corpus, this goth faire and weel.'
> This sely Absolon herde every deel,
> And on his lippe he gan for anger byte,
> And to hymself he seyde, 'I shal thee quyte.' (I.3730–46)

As Absolon awakens to a world of insult and retribution, what does he mean by the phrase, 'I shal thee quyte'? That is, does he understand his own impulse and commitment to 'quyte' those who have abused him as a payment of price? It might be more accurate to interpret it not as payment but as payback, and the best context in which to understand such an impulse is the Maussian model of gift and counter-gift.

That violent retribution could be a part of the realm of the gift would come as no surprise to those familiar with the canonical debates of economic anthropology. In the conclusion of *The Gift*, Mauss focuses on the parallelism and proximity of fighting and gifting:

> In all the societies that have immediately preceded our own, and still exist around us, and even in numerous customs extant in our

popular morality, there is no middle way: one trusts completely, or one mistrusts completely … Two groups of men who meet can only either draw apart, and, if they show mistrust towards one another or issue a challenge, fight – or they can negotiate.[10]

Mauss, as the greater context of the argument makes clear, is not opposing fight to gifting, but rather demonstrating the analogies between them. Unless men manage to have nothing to do with each other, then they must either exchange blows or exchange gifts. There is, he says, no middle way.

Much of Mauss's preceding argument also shows that there can be violence inherent in gifts. It is on this note that some critics have made the connection between gift exchange and the social relations represented by fabliau. Christian Sheridan, like many others, locates the impetus for the invention of French fabliau in the 'commercial revolution of the long thirteenth century'.[11] But rather than figuring the genre as a narrative embodiment of commercial ideals, Sheridan points to 'the different models of economic and social organization that crisscross the fabliaux'.[12] The tales are constantly negotiating between the logic of gift exchange and the logic of monetary exchange. This is a crucial observation, and potentially valuable to the understanding of Chaucer's fabliaux as well, but in order to distinguish between gift exchange and market exchange, Sheridan relies on the gift theory of Bourdieu. The defining characteristics of the gift, Sheridan says, are, first, the time between the gift and the counter-gift, and secondly, the essentially agonistic nature of the gift. The lapse of time between the two parts of the transaction 'allows the parties to "misrecognize" the obligations gifts entail'.[13] The agonistic nature is an expression of the true impetus for the gift, in a drive for symbolic profit and domination, for in gift economies the goal is always 'to vanquish one's trading partner so that he or she is no longer able to exchange'.[14]

Lapse of time would not seem entirely applicable to violent reciprocity of a fabliau like the *Miller's Tale*. At the moment that Absolon understands what has been done to him, he is permanently disabused of his romantic fantasies – 'For fro that tyme that he hadde kist hir ers, / Of paramours he sette nat a kers, / For he was heeled of his maladie' (I.3755–7) – and set entirely upon revenge. He immediately goes across the street and asks Gerveys the smith if he may borrow the 'hoote kultour' (I.3776) in the fire. Paying no heed to Gerveys's banter, and refusing even to tell him what he needs it for – 'I shal wel telle it thee to-morwe day' (I.3784) – Absolon seizes the coulter and returns to John's house to use it.

The lapse of time is central to Bourdieu's gift-exchange model because it would seem to distinguish between gift exchange and monetary transactions, while still allowing Bourdieu to define the gift as essentially agonistic, a tool for domination. As Carl von Clausewitz said that 'War is the continuation of politics by other means', so Bourdieu sees gifts as the continuation of war by other means.[15] In contrast, Claude Lévi-Strauss, following Mauss, writes, 'There is a link, a continuity, between hostile relations and the provision of reciprocal prestations. Exchanges are peacefully resolved wars, and wars are the result of unsuccessful transactions.'[16] Thus, gift exchange and war are not the same thing: they are at opposite poles of a continuum.

Mauss recognized the passage of time is an important element of gift exchange, but not necessarily for the same reasons put forward by others, including Derrida as well as Bourdieu. Rather than obscuring obligation and allowing for the euphemization of the gift, as per Bourdieu, or because the participants need to attempt a radical (and impossible) forgetting of the donation, as per Derrida, some modern interpreters of Mauss would say that time is necessary because the point of the gift is the obligation that lives in the intermediate period between gift and return. As I emphasized in the previous chapter, Mauss in his essay on the gift meant to show that the gift could be agonistic but that it was not essentially or inevitably so. What is needed is a conceptual framework incorporating reciprocal violence into the logic of gift exchange, without reducing the gift itself to violence and domination. Marc Rogin Anspach, another social theorist associated with the MAUSS collective, seems to provide a way forward.[17]

Like other neo-Maussians, Anspach contrasts gift to purchase in terms of inequality and equivalence. The market serves to establish equivalences between objects or actions; the parties to an exchange settle upon a price that allows for a perception on both sides of equal exchange. Therefore, no obligations result from the transaction, and no relation is formed between the parties. But since the purpose of gift exchange is to produce social relations, all exchanges of gifts are unequal by design; there will always be an obligation on one party to reciprocate, and the relationship cannot be cancelled out. This is just as true when the exchange arises from animosity, when the resulting relationship is antagonistic, and when the reciprocal action will be an escalation of violence. Thus, the logic of the feud is a gift-logic.

To Anspach, the difference between the motivation to provide a gift and the motivation to mete violence lies in the perspective of the agent. Anspach figures this as 'a difference of temporal orientation'.[18] When a gift is donated,

> the giver may not want the return gift to match his initial gift – he may hope his own generosity will outshine the other's – but, even in the case of such competitive giving, he is apt to be insulted if the other makes no attempt at all to reciprocate. The giver does want the receiver to recognize his positive gesture; he *looks forward* to the return. In this sense, gift-giving involves an orientation toward the future.[19]

On the other hand, when a cycle of 'negative reciprocity' is under way,

> it will tend to continue indefinitely into the *future precisely because* the same kind of future orientation is lacking. For example, someone may insult someone else on the spur of the moment, without any thought of the consequences. The other may react to what has happened by killing him. He will do so as reparation for the past offense, and not because he looks forward to being killed in turn ... In the same way, each new murder may call for reprisal, without equilibrium's ever being reached ... The avengers seek to wipe out a past event and end up provoking its repetition.[20]

Thus, for Anspach, 'positive reciprocity is really negative reciprocity in reverse'.[21]

This explains why the unending cycles of violence in blood feuds – Montagues and Capulets; Hatfields and McCoys; Bloods and Crips; Swedes and Geats – can look so illogical to outsiders. It is not just that both sides in a feud continue to meet violence with violence – anyone can understand the feeling of injured honour and the desire for vengeance that it inspires. More perplexing is that the feuding party does not seem to recognize that his own reciprocal act of violence can, must and will result in a counter-act of even greater violence. That is because, Anspach says, he is looking backward, not forward.

Anspach's theories provide a reason to see Absolon's 'quiting' as payback rather than payment. To be sure, 'quiting' is often evoked within an idiom of commercial exchange. Chaucer's Summoner, forestalling the Host's attempts to get the Friar to temper his slanders, says, '"Nay … lat hym seye to me / What so hym list; whan it comth to my lot, / By God, I shal hym quiten every grot"' (III.1290–2). For the Summoner, to 'quite' is to pay back vituperation in monetary equivalence – to the penny, as it were. And yet neither the Summoner nor the Friar truly expect to achieve a market-like balance that would allow their interaction to be completed and their relationship to be suspended without further dependence or obligation. It is clear, from the sudden eruption of their argument at the end of the *Wife of Bath's Prologue*, that they have been quarrelling since before the pilgrimage began, and when Fragment Three ends with the Summoner declaring, 'My tale is doon; we been almoost at towne' (III.2294), few readers would expect that the animosity between the two has been settled by the exchange of tales.

On other occasions, 'quiting' is more explicitly like vengeance and unlike purchase, in that it does not create equivalences, and is not intended to. The term is used in this sense in a text whose comic sensibility closely resembles that of the fabliau, the 'Noah' play from the Towneley Cycle:

> *Noe.* We! hold thi tong, ram-skyt
> Or I shall the still.

Vxor. By my thryft, if thou smyte,
I shal turne the vntill.

Noe. We shall assay as tyte.
Haue at the, Gill!
Apon the bone shal it byte.

Vxor. A, so! Mary, thou smytys ill!
Bot I suppose
I shall not in thi det
Flyt of this flett:
Take the ther a langett
To tye vp thi hose!

Noe. A! wilt thou so?
Mary, that is myne!

Vxor. Thou shal thre for two,
I swere bi Godys pyne!

Noe. And I shall qwyte the tho,
In fayth, or syne.[22]

Though Noah and his wife 'qwyte' each other with blows, they have no expectation of equivalence. Instead, they meet each offence with a vow of increased retribution – the wife promises to give Noah 'thre for two' – despite the obvious result that the reactions will be increasingly severe. Inevitably, the conflict escalates, and it never resolves into equilibrium. When the feuding couple stop fighting, it is only because they are exhausted, and in that exhaustion they find the opportunity to look forward together to God's peace.

When in the *Miller's Tale* Absolon makes the inward vow, 'I shal thee quyte', he is dwelling on the injury he has suffered. He continues to dwell on it as he approaches Gerveys's smithy:

Who rubbeth now, who froteth now his lippes
With dust, with sond, with straw, with clooth, with chippes,
But Absolon, that seith ful ofte, 'Allas!'
'My soule bitake I unto Sathanas,
But me were levere than al this toun,' quod he,

> 'Of this despit awroken for to be.
> Allas,' quod he, 'allas, I ne hadde ybleynt!'   (I.3747–53)

He is, as Anspach says, looking backward, and therefore when he plans his revenge he does not think of the counter-payment that must inevitably lie on the other side. Rather, he requites the insult with a drastic increase in the offence and injury. It is rather odd, really, that the exchanges in the *Miller's Tale* would be perceived as mechanistically equivalent in the manner of the market economy when one considers the offence Absolon receives alongside the one he delivers in return. Absolon calls to Alison, appropriately, with a promise of a lover's gift:

> 'I am thyn Absolon, my deerelyng.
> Of gold,' quod he, 'I have thee broght a ryng.
> My mooder yaf it me, so God me save;
> Ful fyn it is, and therto wel ygrave.
> This wol I yeve thee, if thou me kisse.'   (I.3793–7)

In fact it is a gift that he delivers, though one of extreme violence. The comic quality of this climactic action of the *Miller's Tale* is the very epitome of what is often called 'cartoon violence', but Chaucer pointedly describes the injury to Nicholas's flesh in alarmingly precise physical detail:[23]

> This Nicholas anon leet fle a fart
> As greet as it had been a thonder-dent,
> That with the strook he was almoost yblent;
> And he was redy with his iren hoot,
> And Nicholas amydde the ers he smoot.
> Of gooth the skyn an hande-brede aboute,
> The hoote kultour brende so his toute,
> And for the smert he wende for to dye.   (I.3806–13)

This fabliau does not consist of a series of exchanges calibrated for commensurability. On the contrary, the events are antic, threatening always to spin into anarchic chaos. The acts and counter-acts snowball, becoming increasingly intense, violent and destructive, right up to the climax. The list of violations with which the tale concludes –

> Thus swyved was this carpenteris wyf,
> For al his kepyng and his jalousye,
> And Absolon hath kist hir nether ye,
> And Nicholas is scalded in the towte.
> This tale is doon, and God save al the rowte!   (I.3850–4)

– represents not an equation, but rather a catalogue of violent offenses. The story stops here for us; it could go on, accumulating in intensity, indefinitely.

It is counterintuitive that acts of violent retribution should operate in the manner of gift exchange. But gift economy is not defined by generosity, altruism or 'charite'. It is, rather, defined by a logic that sees the goal of exchange as the generation of social relations and the maintenance of obligations that ensure their continuation. This is what makes gift exchange distinct from market exchange, in which the goal of each party is only personal profit, by way of an agreement on equivalent exchange, resulting in no further obligations and no social bonds. If all exchanges, malevolent or benign, were directed toward equivalence, with the goal of optimizing utilitarian profit for both transactors, then economic models would pertain in all situations; the market would be naturalized, and the gift would be erased. Only by recognizing the social dimension of exchange – by locating its purpose in the production of social relations rather than in the utility of the object of exchange – can we distinguish gift exchange from market exchange. And this means accepting that the social relations that result from exchange can be agonistic as well as benevolent. As Alain Caillé says, 'It is not just positive goods or acts of kindness that circulate; so too do insults, acts of vengeance, curses and wrongdoing, and they circulate in precisely the same way. If we cannot give evil, how can we give good?'[24]

II. 'The flour of il endyng': scholasticism and equivalence in the *Reeve's Tale*

The gift, then, is not defined by violence, symbolic or otherwise. Nor is violence the opposite of the gift. In Caillé and Godbout's terms, the opposite of the gift is equilibrium:

> [A] gift's debt is never 'paid off'; instead it is reduced or reversed (inverted) by a gift greater than the debt. If nature abhors a vacuum, the gift abhors equilibrium, though it cannot distance itself from it beyond a certain threshold, without risking the disruption of a relationship or a chain of giving. This abhorrence of equilibrium is not generally taken into consideration in theories dealing with typologies of the gift. They are almost all founded, at least implicitly, on the postulate of the quest for equivalence. But equivalence represents the death of the gift. It is a way to 'put to an end' the chain of the gift, to strip it of that tension which is its dynamic. By the same token, the absence of equilibrium spells the end of a mercantile relationship.[25]

The opposite of the gift is equivalence. And that is why the opposite of the *Miller's Tale* is the *Reeve's Tale*.

In his prologue, the Reeve insists that laws of equivalence allow and require that he respond to the *Miller's Tale*: 'For leveful is with force force of-showve' (I.3912). 'It is lawful to repel force with force.' The Reeve is citing a legal doctrine, as his clerical characters will, to justify an act of retribution.[26] But the doctrine that he invokes is as much mechanical as it is legal: he is vowing to meet the Miller's action with an equal and opposite reaction. This is the kind of mechanistic equilibrium and legalistic commensurability that Olson, among others, sees as fundamental to the *Reeve's Tale* and to 'fabliau justice' more generally. But it is less a defining feature of the genre of fabliau than it is a particularity of the *Reeve's Tale*, one that sets it off from the fabliau that precedes it.

Although the Reeve introduces the two clerks of his tale as a pair of revellers, when they petition their warden to allow them to take the college's grain to be ground by Symkyn, who has been 'a theef outrageously' (I.3998) since their manciple became ill, they are planning neither lustful play nor revenge. Rather, they intend to re-establish equitable fair and legal commercial relations with the miller:

> Testif they were, and lusty for to pleye,
> And, oonly for hire myrthe and revelrye,
> Upon the wardeyn bisily they crye
> To yeve hem leve, but a litel stounde,
> To goon to mille and seen hir corn ygrounde;
> And hardily they dorste leye hir nekke
> The millere sholde not stele hem half a pekke
> Of corn by sleighte, ne by force hem reve;
> And at the laste the wardeyn yaf hem leve. (I.4004–12)

John and Aleyn are not vowing to pay the miller back for his thievery. They are confident that they can assure that the miller will deliver them all the flour that their grain provides, and that he will take no more than he is paid for. Symkyn has been a 'market-betere' (I.3936) in more sense than one, and John and Aleyn intend to restore market equilibrium.

When the clerks arrive at Symkyn's mill, they express fascination with the technology of corn milling, announcing that they will observe the process:

> 'By God, right by the hopur wil I stande,'
> Quod John, 'and se howgates the corn gas in.
> Yet saugh I nevere, by my fader kyn,
> How that the hopur wagges til and fra.'
> Aleyn answerde, 'John, and wiltow swa?
> Thanne wil I be bynethe, by my croun,
> And se how that the mele falles doun
> Into the trough; that sal be my disport.' (I.4036–43)

They are doing this, of course, to try to prevent Symkyn from siphoning off a portion of their flour, but their interest may not be entirely feigned.

The mill is a complex contraption designed to maintain equivalence through transformation. In this regard it is like the operation of the commercial economy, and like the *Reeve's Tale* itself.

The tension in the tale is between the clerks, who seek to enforce the impersonal equilibrium of the commercial transaction – they intend 'To grynde oure corn and carie it ham agayn' (I.4032) – and the miller, who is motivated not just by a drive for unmerited profit, but also by an animus for the clerks and their ilk, by a spite that compels him to seek the clerks' humiliation and to increase his power over them. When John and Aleyn pretend interest in the operation of the mill in order to monitor its proper output, Symkyn sees only the arrogance of clerks imagining they can outwit a miller:

> This millere smyled of hir nycetee,
> And thoghte, 'Al this nys doon but for a wyle.
> They wene that no man may hem bigyle,
> But by my thrift, yet shal I blere hir ye,
> For al the sleighte in hir philosophye.
> The moore queynte crekes that they make,
> The moore wol I stele whan I take.
> In stide of flour yet wol I yeve hem bren.
> "The gretteste clerkes been noght wisest men,"
> As whilom to the wolf thus spak the mare.
> Of al hir art counte I noght a tare.'   (I.4046–56)

Symkyn vows to increase his theft in proportion to the clerks' affectations of cleverness, and to corrupt the commercial arrangement with the false substitution of bran for flour. His inward sneer reveals that he is not motivated purely by greed. He is particularly resentful of 'the sleighte in hir philosophye' (I.4050). He seems to suspect that there is something in their scholastic methods that contrives to subdue his own interests and to check his drive for control and profit. In this regard, his dismissal of the clerks' training resembles the confident, though short-lived, affirmation by John the carpenter in the *Miller's Tale* of the superiority of the common man's simple belief to the pointy-headed abstractions of Nicholas's university education:

> This man is falle, with his astromye
> In some woodnesse or in som agonye.
> I thoghte ay wel how that it sholde be!
> Men sholde nat knowe of Goddes pryvetee.
> Ye, blessed be alwey a lewed man
> That noght but oonly his bileve kan! (I.3451–6)

But Symkyn's resentment of scholastic reasoning seems particularly misplaced. John and Aleyn have made no claim to greater sophistication or understanding; on the contrary, they are pretending to be interested in the function of the mill because it is an unfamiliar technology: 'For John,' says Aleyn, 'y-faith, I may been of youre sort; / I is as ille a millere as ar ye' (I.4044–5).

Symkyn sets John and Aleyn's horse loose, proving 'Yet kan a millere make a clerkes berd' (I.4096), and forcing the clerks to petition him for lodging for the night. But again, Symkyn mocks the clerks for their abstruse philosophical reasoning:

> Myn hous is streit, but ye han lerned art;
> Ye konne by argumentes make a place
> A myle brood of twenty foot of space.
> Lat se now if this place may suffise,
> Or make it rowm with speche, as is youre gise. (I.4122–6)

This mockery and resentment may seem misguided, or even paranoid. The Miller seems to see some connection between the clerks' philosophical methods and the economic arrangement they are seeking to enforce. Symkyn is lampooning the kind of scholastic reasoning that is proverbially called 'angels on pinheads' – picayune, empty and irrelevant disputation. But in Symkyn's jab, it is more like angels *for* pinheads – the substitution of substances to give a false impression of equivalence, all justified by scholastic argumentation. Symkyn seems to be implying that scholastic disputation is ultimately intended to justify certain forms of exchange.

In fact, John and Aleyn do consistently try to enforce commercial forms of exchange. It is they, not the miller, who insist that they will pay for their food and lodging. First, 'for the love of God they hym bisoght / Of herberwe and of ese, as for hir peny' (I.4118–19), and then John adds, 'Get us som mete and drynke, and make us cheere, / And we wil payen trewely atte fulle' (I.4132–3). Symkyn seizes this opportunity to provide as sumptuous a meal as he is able, sending Malyne into town for bread and ale and roasting a goose, presumably so that he can charge the clerks for it all. But his suspicions of a connection between scholastic thought and logic of trade in fact prove justified. Unable to sleep because of the snoring of the miller and his family, and stewing on the miller's trickery and theft, Aleyn says to John,

> Som esement has lawe yshapen us,
> For, John, ther is a lawe that says thus:
> That gif a man in a point be agreved,
> That in another he sal be releved.
> Oure corn is stoln, sothly, it is na nay,
> And we han had an il fit al this day;
> And syn I sal have neen amendement
> Agayn my los, I will have esement.   (I.4179–86)

As a number of commentators have pointed out, Aleyn is invoking a common principle of medieval civil law. In fact, in two fifteenth-century manuscripts of the tale, including Hengwrt (MS Peniarth 392D), scribal marginalia identify the principle: *Qui in uno gravatur in alio debet relevari*, a gloss from the *Corpus Iuris Civilis*. Mary Braswell further explains that 'esement' is the specific legal term for the right of one individual to make use of another's property, some sense of which persists in contemporary legal usage.[27]

It is often asserted that characters in fabliau are motivated by appetite, or at least by a generalized spirit of individual competition, and therefore that the 'fabliau justice' that seems to operate in the tales works itself out through a natural, almost Newtonian series of causes and effects. Robert Frank observes, '[t]he clerk, especially the student, had a reputation as an inveterate and successful sexual adventurer' in late medieval tradition, and adds that in the *Reeve's Tale* 'the clerks swive because they are clerks'.[28] This would seem to be true of Nicholas in the *Miller's Tale*, but not Absolon. That may be the point of the satire of Absolon, who is after all not a student and also is relatively deficient in the intellectual astuteness ascribed to Nicholas (or that Nicholas claims for himself).[29] The clerks of the *Reeve's Tale* may be somewhere in between: the joke perhaps is that Aleyn is the kind of intellectual who feels compelled to cite a legal doctrine to justify his own fornicating.

The legal principle that Aleyn cites may be unnecessary to the narrative context, but like the one the Reeve himself quotes in his prologue to the tale, it articulates a fundamentally economic sense of justice. Aleyn emphasizes that the resolution of their story depends on substitutions, and in particular on the generation of equivalencies among unlike but competing sets of values: if a man is 'agreved' in one field, he is to be 'releved' in another, and the law functions to contrive the appropriate substitution in the other field. One might be due monetary payment in compensation for physical injury, or one might, as Aleyn posits, receive restitution for lost grain in illicit sex. In this conception, the organization of the tale truly reflects the world of economic competition and marketplace values in which fabliaux are invariably set.

Nicholas's sexual advance on Alison in the *Miller's Tale* initiates a series of offences and injuries that accumulate and compound throughout the tale. At this point in the *Reeve's Tale*, in contrast, the clerks have only tried to re-establish commercial relations with the miller, but have suffered abuse and humiliation. Here, at the hinge of the tale, Aleyn invokes a doctrine of equivalent compensation, and the tale swings back in the clerks' favour: Aleyn sleeps with the miller's daughter; John takes advantage of his wife; in the subsequent struggle, Symkyn is beaten, through the detailed contrivance of fabliau plotting; the clerks return to Cambridge, their grain restored.

This seemingly mechanical determinism of plotting is crucial to the aesthetic effect and the reception of fabliau. The genre is notorious for its immorality, but also for its amorality, and the negotiation of competing interests through the substitution of unexpected but appropriate rewards and punishments is the fabliau's dramatization of the workings of the marketplace. The goodness or badness of individual motivations become irrelevant in a system that subordinates all claims of value to a competitive formula of equivalence generation. The contrasts between Chaucer's first two fabliaux, however, reveal that this calculation of equivalence is not general to the genre, but is distinctive to the *Reeve's Tale*. Furthermore, Chaucer, like Symkyn, seems to associate this drive toward equivalence, at once legalistic and economic, with scholasticism.

J. A. W. Bennett has noted that King's College, Cambridge – assumed to be the original for Chaucer's 'Soler Halle' – was particularly well endowed with books on law, and he takes the clerks to be law students.[30] Regardless, university clerks at Cambridge, though more so at Oxford and Paris, drove the increasingly complex debates on economic analysis, ethics and justice so important to late medieval thought as well as to late medieval commercial practices. There can be an assumption in discussing this philosophical history that economic philosophy was received from Aristotle, and that in glossing the Aristotelian tradition the medieval scholastics – themselves not only cloistered scholars but mostly mendicants devoted to ideals of voluntary poverty – gradually if grudgingly conformed to the realities of a swiftly burgeoning economic world beyond the university walls. In fact, scholastic economic thought was original, innovative and intentional. Odd Langholm, in his extensive historical analysis of scholastic economics, emphasizes that 'Latin Aristotelian economics was a medieval invention. It was inspired by attempts to explain Aristotle, but is essentially a projection of medieval ideas into the ancient texts.'[31] Lester Little, in his influential study *Religious Poverty and the Profit Economy in Medieval Europe*, explains that the mendicants who dominated scholastic thought were products of the urban, commercial centres of late medieval Europe – like St Francis, son of a wealthy cloth merchant of Assisi. The theology of spiritual poverty that they embraced could only have been conceived in a context of wealth and money, and they brought to their intellectual debates an innate understanding of and, to some extent, sympathy for the mentalities underlying commerce and mercantilism. The institutions in which they found intellectual homes – the universities –were established as alternatives to the traditional centres of learning in Benedictine monasteries, and were distinguished by their fundamental worldliness – they prepared students for a wide variety of careers, including secular ones, and they developed pedagogies and critical approaches rooted in disputation to prepare students for the world outside their walls.[32] These university scholars inherited a patristic tradition of negative attitudes toward property and wealth and suspicion of professional trade, money and profit. Scholasticism from the beginning was determined to establish philosophical and ethical justifications for the money economy and commercial practices – from the private property, to profit in trade, to the justness of market prices, and eventually, after centuries of struggle with the problem of usury, for lending at interest – and where necessary they would also contribute to the invention of legal fictions to legitimize specific commercial practices.

Joel Kaye has recently argued that by the fourteenth century a 'new model of equilibrium' informed scholastic understanding of economics, politics and natural science.[33] The upshot of this scholastic tradition is what R. Howard Bloch calls a 'scholasticism of exchange':

> The application of logic to business served to oil the rusty ideological machinery of a relatively inert economy … It created, according to a dynamic dialectical model, the conditions under which concepts and techniques essential to effective exchange were naturalized. To dwell upon the logicization of profit, price, or interest is also to recognize that money is an always already modalized form of property whose purpose is to catalyze substitution – a kind of metalanguage akin to logic itself.[34]

The university students of Chaucer's *Reeve's Tale* intentionally and explicitly apply this kind of 'scholasticism of exchange' to their relations with the miller, and this logic informs the structure of the tale. Symkyn points to the economic nature of philosophical argumentation when he suggests that the clerks use their scholastic reasoning to make a narrow room equivalent to a space a mile wide, goading them to 'make it rowm with speche, as is youre gise' (I.4126). As Bloch observes, 'The sale and the syllogism are coequal operations; one oriented toward the reduction of asking price and bid to selling price, and the other toward the reduction of thesis and antithesis to synthesis or sentence.'[35] Aleyn's legalism makes it more explicit, using a point from his Cambridge schoolwork to justify the exchange of sex for lost property, and of vitiated lineage for injured pride, and the second half of the tale realizes the principle.

I would suggest, in fact, that this is the core of the tale's satire. The miller's name is Symkyn, diminutive of 'Symond', or Simon. Symkyn's association with the sin of simony is most obviously manifested in his two major preoccupations – the property he acquires through the dowry of the daughter of the parish priest, and the legitimizing of this property through the virginity and marriageability of his own daughter Malyne – which embody the secular acquisition of ecclesiastical property and the bourgeois appropriation of ecclesiastical authority. But the symbolic simony in the tale runs deeper than this. It is revealed in the clerks' reasoning, which points to the complicity of the scholastic philosophers in the rising tide of market values and the commercial economy, for which they provide ethical justification and legal cover. Chaucer seems to be characterizing the scholastic project of liberalizing economic philosophy, which was conspicuously gaining momentum and sophistication in his lifetime, as simony on a grand scale. It represents not merely the sale of clerical offices or the expropriation of Church wealth, but a more comprehensive embodiment of the sin with which Simon Magus approached the Apostles – the commercialization of ecclesiastical authority and prerogative. 'Pecunia tua tecum sit in perditionem: quoniam donum Dei existimasti pecunia possideri,' says St Peter, the rock on which the Church is founded, to the magician. 'Keep thy money to thyself, to perish with thee, for thou has thought that the gift of God may be purchased with money.'[36] Simony consists in the commercialization of gifts. Chaucer's clerks, in a manner that even the miller Symkyn recognizes as representative of contemporary scholastic philosophy, justify, promulgate and enforce the mentalities and social relations of the commercial economy.

The greater irony is that, while the clerks are working to maintain a commercial equilibrium among the characters in the tale, gift exchange, with its intentional disequilibrium and obligations, persists. To some extent, the *Reeve's Tale* may seem to accept the logic and inevitability of these commercial mentalities. As Bloch notes, the overall effect of the scholastic project is to 'naturalize' the market through logic. It is significant, therefore, that the value equations that the Cambridge clerks are so assiduous to enforce in the tale do not work out as precisely as they at first appear. Elizabeth Edwards has noted that the precise exchanges and equivalencies of the *Reeve's Tale* are apparently unable to subsume female sexual pleasure. The women in this tale, as in other fabliau, are 'represented as escaping with enjoyment',[37] Edwards says, because women represent both 'exchange value' and 'use value' in the Aristotelian and Thomistic economic scheme, and ultimately, 'The profit of female pleasure is incalculable.'[38]

Edwards's analysis is persuasive and important, but as I noted in the previous chapter, it is not only female pleasure that proves to resist calculation in Chaucer's fabliaux.[39] Whenever critics analyse these tales economically, they invariably stumble upon some troubling and seemingly inexplicable superfluity, some calculation error in the texts' equations. This has often been observed in the *Shipman's Tale*, despite the fact that no fabliau is more explicitly concerned with market calculations and precise monetary transactions. Lee Patterson, for example, argues:

> The Shipman's Tale describes the process by which the circulation of a hundred franks among three people generates, as if by magic, a profit for all of them. The wife repays her creditors, the monk enjoys the wife and the merchant gets in the place of a reluctant sexual partner one eager to do his bidding.[40]

There is a critical fallacy at work here. Chaucer's fabliaux are assumed to be the products of a commercial mentality and to perfectly figure the calculations of the marketplace; when the calculations do not seem to work out as predicted, it is then taken as evidence of the mysterious powers of capitalism to generate excess profit.

The resistance to calculation in Chaucer's fabliau is not due to any putative 'magic'. And though, as I argued in the previous chapter, economic models of exchange do not readily account for sexual pleasure, nor really for any shared, pro-social forms of motivation, the ultimately unequal distribution of reward in a tale like the Reeve's is also not due to the special economic status of female sexuality. Rather, even the most commercial of Chaucer's fabliau include alternative models of exchange and value persisting alongside the terms of the marketplace.

Consider the cake of flour. Aleyn frames his citation of the doctrine of 'esement' by vowing,

> Ye, they sal have the flour of il endyng.
> This lange nyght ther tydes me na reste;
> But yet, na fors, al sal be for the beste.
> For, John ... als evere moot I thryve,
> If that I may, yon wenche wil I swyve ...
> Oure corn is stoln, sothly, it is na nay,
> And we han had an il fit al this day;
> And syn I sal have neen amendement
> Agayn my los, I will have esement.   (I.4174–8, 4183–6)

They have had their grain stolen, and they have been harried and humiliated at the miller's home. In compensation, he declares that he will have the 'esement' of sex with the miller's daughter. When Aleyn declares that Symkyn and his family 'sal have the flour of il endyng', the pun on 'flour' emphasizes that he contrives his sex with Malyne not simply as a retributive injury to the miller, but as precise compensation for the loss of their corn. And yet at the conclusion of the tale the clerks ride back toward Cambridge having 'swyved' the miller's wife and daughter, and also having recovered their half bushel of stolen flour. If their property is restored, then what justifies the 'esement' of illicit sex? And if the sex is compensation for the theft, then why do they also recover the property?

The reason the flour does not in the end compute in the tale's economic equations is because it has in the course of the narrative ceased to be a commodity and become instead a gift. In the mock-aubade with which Aleyn and Malyne part at dawn, he takes his leave with the language of courtly love:

> Fare weel, Malyne, sweete wight!
> The day is come; I may no lenger byde;
> But everemo, wher so I go or ryde,
> I is thyn awen clerk, swa have I seel! (I.4236–9)

His patently insincere promise to remain ever true to her is made especially comic by his self-identification as a loyal clerk, where in romance he would be a true knight. But it inspires Malyne to reveal, in the same language of *fin'amor*, the location of their stolen meal:

> 'Now, deere lemman,' quod she, 'go, far weel!
> But er thow go, o thyng I wol thee telle:
> Whan that thou wendest homward by the melle,
> Right at the entree of the dore byhinde
> Thou shalt a cake of a half a busshel fynde
> That was ymaked of thyn owene mele,
> Which that I heelp my sire for to stele.
> And, goode lemman, God thee save and kepe!'
> And with that word almoost she gan to wepe. (I.4240–8)

Malyne may be pathetic to believe him and to return his avowals of love, but that does not diminish her motivations. She gives her 'deere lemman' the flour partly out of guilt, and partly because giving gifts at parting is what lovers do. And the reason that lovers give gifts is precisely what makes gifts distinct from commodities – because it generates obligation and disequilibrium that extends relationships into the future. To Caillé and Godbout, 'an essential quality of the gift' is 'the spontaneous movement of one soul towards another'.[41] Malyne does not give the flour as payment, and does not give it because it is merited due to expenditure or injury. It is a spontaneous act, moral and personal. The reader may well find her pitiable in her delusion, but this is the only moment of agency she is allowed in the tale, and it stands apart from and in contrast to the amoral competition of market forces. That is why it is not fully integrated into the market calculations of the rest of the tale. As Christopher Gregory explains, market exchange subsumes human relationships to the value of commodities; gift exchange uses objects to generate and maintain human relationships.

To the Reeve, the tale is all about equivalence. It shows, he concludes, that the clerks are fully compensated for their injuries, that the beguiler will always be beguiled, and that the Reeve himself has 'quited' the Miller for his tale. But the Reeve is not Chaucer; the tale in many ways shows the opposite of what the Reeve maintains, namely that human relations are not reducible to profit, competition and equivalence, and that the philosophies that seek to justify and naturalize such marketplace mentalities, then and now, are overly limiting of the range of human motivation for exchange.

III. 'A wyf is Goddes yifte': utility, balance and marriage in the *Merchant's Tale*

When Caillé and Godbout seek to explain the perpetual indebtedness of the gift relationship, and the anti-sociality of a relationship based on precise equilibrium, they look to marriage for an illustration. Ideally, a marriage is

> a gift relationship ... one where *each* considers that she or he benefits from something special and can never give in return everything received from the other, so that both feel they owe more than they reap. Inequality becomes part and parcel of the relationship and drives it forward. A couple that 'functions' well lives in a state of constant reciprocal indebtedness that it considers normal and inexhaustible and where there is no sense of

egalitarian accounting ... A couple that seeks equality, that seeks to balance the books in its exchanges, is a couple whose dynamic leads to permanent rivalry, towards the establishment of a mercantile relationship, and towards rupture.[42]

In their depiction of a dysfunctional marriage, Caillé and Godbout could be describing the *Merchant's Tale*.

January is a man who has 'folwed ay his bodily delyt / On wommen, ther as was his appetyt' (IV.1249–50) for his entire life, until in old age he determines to marry, declaring, 'Noon oother lyf ... is worth a bene, / For wedlok is so esy and so clene, / That in this world it is a paradys' (IV.1263–5). The satire here is broader than is typical in Chaucer's comic tales. January is a foolish figure, a *senex amans* like John the carpenter, but he is not just a character in that comic type. He so embodies the type that the tale verges on burlesque. He is ridiculed, obviously, for taking a young wife when he is old and imagining it to be an ideal condition. And as criticism has often noted, he is satirized for the profane hedonism of his sensual delectation; he praises marriage as 'a full greet sacrement' (IV.1319) while understanding it only as a sanctioned way to indulge in his accustomed lechery, and he turns the Song of Songs into 'olde lewed wordes' (IV.2149) by using the poetry as a literalistic invitation to conjugal dalliance. But also part of this satirical portrait is January's purely instrumental conception of marriage, taking an institution that necessarily shared and communal, as well as sacramental, purely as a means for individual pleasure. Though he is old, he fantasizes about the physical pleasures that await him without ever extending to his prospective partner the same kind of subjective experience. When he expresses this to his counsellors, he figures his sexual appetites in terms of the consumption of food:

> 'But o thyng warne I yow, my freendes deere,
> I wol noon oold wyf han in no manere.
> She shal nat passe twenty yeer, certayn;
> Oold fissh and yong flessh wolde I have fayn.
> Bet is,' quod he, 'a pyk than a pykerel,

> And bet than old boef is the tendre veel.
> I wol no womman thritty yeer of age;
> It is but bene-straw and greet forage.'   (IV.1415–22)

January's analogy of women to food is revealing. His hedonism is rooted in a fundamentally consumerist view of pleasure. Such a perspective accords with David Graeber's characterization of market-oriented models of pleasure:

> When market theorists think about a pleasurable, rewarding experience, the root image they have in mind seems to be eating food ('consumption') … The idea seems to be of an almost furtive appropriation, in which objects [t]hat had been parts of the outside world are completely incorporated into the consumer's self.[43]

January therefore takes a mental inventory of the qualities he most desires in a wife, and he constructs a composite ideal, focusing primarily on a catalogue of physical attributes: 'He purtreyed in his herte and in his thoght / Hir fresshe beautee and hir age tendre, / Hir myddel smal, hire armes longe and sklendre' (IV.1600–2). And then, from the buffet of women available to him as a rich knight of Pavia, he selects the one he finds most appealing:

> He seyde ther was a mayden in the toun,
> Which that of beautee hadde greet renoun,
> Al were it so she were of smal degree;
> Suffiseth hym hir yowthe and hir beautee …   (IV.1623–6)

January figures his consumerist and utilitarian understanding of marriage to be perfectly natural. 'A wyf,' he says, 'is Goddes yifte verraily' (IV.1311).

Even more than Chaucer's other fabliaux, the *Merchant's Tale* hinges on the suppression and then revelation and enactment of female desire. Essentially absent for the first half of the tale, May is depicted only as the object of January's sensual aspirations. Then, at the precise centre of the tale, on the wedding night, the narration suddenly shifts to her perspective. In the middle of a line, May goes from being object of January's sexual fantasies to the subject experiencing the undesired and uninvited ministrations of the aged lover:

> And Januarie hath faste in armes take
> His fresshe May, his paradys, his make.
> He lulleth hire; he kisseth hire ful ofte;
> With thikke brustles of his berd unsofte,
> Lyk to the skyn of houndfyssh, sharp as brere –
> For he was shave al newe in his manere –
> He rubbeth hire aboute hir tendre face.   (IV.1821–7)

The sudden and radical shift to May's perspective recasts the scene in terms of her rejection of his body and his desires – 'She preyseth nat his pleyyng worth a bene' (IV.1854) – and initiates the trajectory of the second half of the tale.

When Damyan's love letter brings the opportunity of a sensual indulgence of her own, May does not seem to be motivated primarily by revenge. 'Certeyn,' she thinks, 'whom that this thyng displese / I rekke noght' (IV.1982–3). Rather, given what she must experience for January's sexual pleasure, she is simply seeking satisfaction of her own appetites, even as the poem satirically depicts her agreement to tryst with Damyan as the noble mercy of the lady for the amatory plaints of the courtly lover: 'Lo, pitee renneth soone in gentil herte!' (IV.1986)

Yet the tale is structured to emphasize the perfect balance between the goose and the gander. In addition to January's utilitarianism, the tale's most distinctive feature is its equilibrium. In its details and its structure, the *Merchant's Tale* thematises balance. It is present in the name of the main character. January is winter to May's springtime, but his name also evokes Janus, the double-faced god of portals. It is present, too, in the blatantly named counsellors, Placebo and Justinus, who provide him with equal measures of fatuous flattery and prudent sagacity, leaving only January's callow selfishness to lead him to the obviously wrong choice. And it is present in the carefully calculated introduction of the wife's consciousness and desire as counterpoise to masculine presumption.

The motif of marriage perfectly balanced in its competitiveness, self-interest and recrimination extends to the odd and unexpected appearance of the divine machinery. Pluto and Proserpina, duplicating and expanding on the human action, engage in a debate on the relative worthiness of January and May, as well as an analogous disagreement as to the wisdom or folly of Solomon. The god and goddess vow to intervene for the husband and the wife, respectively, leading to the obscenely comic climax of the tale. January's utilitarian, self-serving and fundamentally economic engagement in marriage has left May no choice but to meet it on the same terms and to pursue equivalent satisfaction for herself.

It is tempting to ascribe the rigorous equitability of exchange in the *Merchant's Tale* to the mercantile perspective of its teller. But this is, ultimately, an unnecessary invocation of the 'dramatic principle'. It is enough simply to recognize the variety of modes of exchange that are contained within Chaucer's fabliaux. The *Miller's Tale* is animated by the disequilibrium of feud and violence. The *Reeve's Tale*, through the contrivances of the clerks' ideology, seeks a commercial balance, but is ultimately unbalanced again by the impulsive gifting of Malyne. But the *Merchant's Tale* dramatizes a marriage maintained in perfect equilibrium. That is the clearest expression of its pathology. As Caillé and Godbout predict, this marriage is a mercantile relationship, and therefore locked in 'permanent rivalry' that is equivalent to 'rupture'.

This is not to say, of course, that May is unjustified in her determination, as the Wife of Bath would have it, to fry January 'in his owene grece' (III.487). It would be no more true to claim that the Reeve's greedy, thieving, violent miller is superior to his mild clerks; or that the aggressive, competitive and anarchic impulses of the *Miller's Tale* are preferable to the *Reeve's Tale*'s drive toward legalistic commensurability. The greater point is that fabliaux do not strictly express or enforce a commercial sense of justice. The genre, in Chaucer's hands, should not be taken to naturalize the market relations or to embody a bourgeois conception of social relations. Markets and commercial exchange can be manifested in fabliaux, but these are not the only kinds of relations the form can imagine. In fact, monetized relations can seem in fabliau to be a novel form. January, discovering late in life the prospect of purchasing sanctified pleasure through marriage, seems to be awakening to a brave new world of profit through exchange. Symkyn is suspicious of the novelty of Aleyn and John's reasoning, as the clerks seem to be ushering in a new world order in which human relations will be objectified and utilitarian, and all qualities will be measured by a single set of relative valuations. The fact that they are clerks, and that their sense of economic justice derives from their clerical education, is the core irony of the *Reeve's Tale*. But the negative, though pro-social, exchange of the *Miller's Tale* shows that non-commercial motivations, and the relations generated by them, can be just as elemental to fabliau. Malyne's transformation of the ontological status of the flour demonstrates the persistence of the possibility of the gift even in a pervasively commercial context. And the bitterly cynical equilibrium of the *Merchant's Tale* shows that a mercantile balance in marriage relations is no more natural than it is desirable.

4

THE EXCHANGE OF WOMEN AND
THE GENDER OF THE GIFT

Chaucerian romance depends on the exchange of women. Even the women in Chaucer's romances recognize this. In a prayer to Diana in the *Knight's Tale*, Emily declares, 'Noght wol I knowe compaignye of man' (I.2311) and asks that the goddess cause Palamon and Arcite to love each other,

> And fro me turne awey hir hertes so
> That al hire hoote love and hir desir,
> And al hir bisy torment, and hir fir
> Be queynt, or turned in another place.   (I.2318–21)

But without waiting for any response from the gods, Emily continues,

> And if so be thou wolt nat do me grace,
> Or if my destynee be shapen so
> That I shal nedes have oon of hem two,
> As sende me hym that moost desireth me.   (I.2322–5)

Emily seems to intuit that in chivalric romance it is impossible that a woman might not be the object of competitive male desire, even in the realm of prayer.

Most modern critics have concluded that Emily is right. Roberta Krueger has argued that 'romance mystifies the exchange of women'.

By way of the classic example of Chrétien's *Yvain*, Krueger shows that the customary chivalric role of defending the woman 'assures not the protection of a maiden's autonomy, but her value as a possession or prize for those knights between whom she is the object of dispute. Within the chivalric honor system, the woman becomes an object of exchange.'[1]

Of course, this condition is not restricted to romance, or to literature, or to the Middle Ages. Virtually from its inception, anthropological theory has held that meaning and value are generated through exchange, particularly the exchange of gifts between kinship groups based on mutual expectations of reciprocity. Most notably, Claude Lévi-Strauss theorized that the pressures toward exogamy engendered by the incest taboo led family groups of early humans to exchange women in marriage, leading them into necessary, lasting alliances and laying the foundation for civilization itself: 'The total relationship of exchange which constitutes marriage is not established between a man and a woman, where each owes and receives something, but between two groups of men, and the woman figures only as one of the objects in the exchange, not as one of the partners between whom the exchanges take place.'[2]

There has also been a strong tradition of resistance to Lévi-Strauss's model. Gayle Rubin, in a foundational feminist re-interpretation, both affirms and critiques Lévi-Strauss's concept. 'The "exchange of women",' Rubin writes,

> is a seductive and powerful concept. It is attractive in that it places the oppression of women within social systems, rather than in biology. Moreover, it suggests that we look for the ultimate locus of women's oppression within the traffic in women, rather than within the traffic in merchandise.[3]

But Rubin continues,

> The 'exchange of women' is also a problematic concept. Since Lévi-Strauss argues that the incest taboo and the results of its

application constitute the origin of culture, it can be deduced that the world historical defeat of women occurred with the origin of culture, and is a prerequisite of culture.[4]

Negotiating between the explicatory power of the concept and the seemingly totalizing inevitability and inescapability of women's oppression in Lévi-Strauss's formulation, Rubin reconsiders the Freudian basis of Lévi-Strauss's use of the invocation of the incest taboo, and argues that the subjection of women to exchange between men is neither biologically nor historically inevitable, but rather socially constructed and contingent. There remains, however, a tension in her analysis between the clear centrality of the exchange of women in much of culture, and the way in which this paradigm seems to relegate women to the passive, inert and depersonalized status of objects. Nearly all subsequent treatments of this topic have drawn on Rubin's essay, and nearly all seem to share its ambivalence in response to this perceived dichotomy. Thus Karen Newman rejects the model of women in exchange for its totalizing reduction of women to passive objects, and asserts that 'we have exhausted the usefulness of "the traffic in women" paradigm as it is currently used in feminist analysis'.[5]

On the other hand, some feminist theorists, notably Luce Irigaray, have embraced an anthropological model of the exchange of women on account of its power to explain the objectification of women:

The society we know, our own culture, is based upon the exchange of women ... The law that orders our society is the exclusive valorization of men's needs/desires, of exchanges among men. What the anthropologist calls the passage from nature to culture thus amounts to the institution of the reign of hom(m)o-sexuality. Not in an 'immediate' practice, but in its 'social' mediation ... and heterosexuality has been up to now just an alibi for the smooth workings of a man's relations with himself, of relations among men. Whose 'socio-cultural endogamy' excludes the participation of that other, so foreign to the social order: woman ... The economy – in both the narrow and the broad sense ... requires that women lend themselves to alienation in consumption, and to exchanges in which they do not participate, and that men be exempt from being used and circulated like commodities.[6]

When Irigaray says 'the anthropologist' she means (and cites) Lévi-Strauss, and when she refers to 'the society that we know' she means late capitalism. Lévi-Strauss's model of the exchange of women is useful to her because her critique of the treatment of women in Western capitalism makes no distinction between commodities and gifts, and it assumes continuity between the exchange of women in archaic gift economies and the commodified status of women in contemporary commercial society.

As feminist anthropologists and philosophers have struggled to respond to and to reform Lévi-Strauss's theoretical formulation, critics of medieval romance have striven to account for the position of women in the conventions of the genre. Chaucer addresses these issues of subjectivity and objectivity, of agency and exchange, in his romances in the *Canterbury Tales*, and his own most agential female character, the Wife of Bath, seeks to represent her own subjection to the 'traffic in women' and to respond to it and potentially to 'break' it. In all these efforts, the results have been mixed.

This chapter considers the problem of women and the gift in Chaucer in light of the strikingly divergent theories of two of the most prominent feminist anthropologists. Both Annette Weiner and Marilyn Strathern represent branches of neo-Maussian economic anthropology. Weiner proposes a theory of social value that is rooted in women's social behaviours and that resists exogamy and transcends exchange. Strathern, in contrast, sees women's behaviours and women's bodies as deeply rooted in exchange, but she emphasizes the personification of the objects of exchange in gift cultures, not excluding the exchange of women. When applied to Chaucer's romances, to the Wife of Bath, and to the Wife's own romance, each approach affords potentially valuable insights and, inevitably, limitations.

Part One. Annette Weiner and 'inalienable possessions'

I. Incest, agency and romance

In her influential 1992 study *Inalienable Possessions*, based on her field work in Papua New Guinea, Annette Weiner attempts a very deliberate feminist intervention into some fundamental principles of anthropology, going back to Lévi-Strauss and to Mauss. In particular, she critiques the model of the production of social value that entails not just the exchange of women but 'the a priori essentialism of the norm of reciprocity' in which 'objects are merely the reflections of their transactors' embeddedness in social relations, and the value of an object remains only a consequence of the identity of the exchanger'.[7]

Weiner responds to these paradigms with two main concepts. The first, from which she draws her title, is the idea of 'inalienable possessions'. Certain objects of special value, she argues, are not exchanged between kinship groups, but passed down within groups. Therefore, they are not gifts or commodities but heirlooms. Such 'inalienable' objects, to Weiner, possess not exchange value but 'transcendental' value: they are outside the system of reciprocity underlying exchange. 'Whereas other alienable properties are exchanged one against each other,' Weiner writes, 'inalienable possessions are symbolic repositories of genealogies and historical events, their unique, subjective identity gives them absolute value placing them above the exchangeability of one thing for another.'[8] Such objects are often in the care of women, and they are often objects, particularly types of cloth, that are conventionally made by women, and thereby endowed with special 'procreative power'.[9]

The other, related concept is 'sibling intimacy'. For Lévi-Strauss, the exchange of women between kinship groups, and the concomitant creation and fostering of complex and extended social bonds, is necessitated by the supposed inviolability of the incest taboo. But as Weiner notes, 'Although actual sexuality between brothers and sisters is prohibited in most societies, the cultural recognition of a brother's and sister's socially and economically charged intimacy creates a unique bond that unites them for life.'[10] Through exogamous exchange, women take on the roles of wife and mother, which do have their own value, power and authority. But women can maintain the role of sister, even after marriage, and with it a position of social authority independent of the exchange of women. Despite the presumed universality of the incest taboo and the associated imperative for exogamy, valuable social relations exist within kinship groups, including associations among women and also incestuous relationships, particularly brother-sister intimacy. In the societies she studies, Weiner writes, 'the reproductive power in brother-sister intimacy gives women as sisters an impressive domain of authority and power'.[11] In this endogamous mode of sister, women are analogous to the objects, like specially treasured cloths, that they create and endow with social meaning and power because they do not exchange them with other kinship groups: 'Like inalienable possessions, this ritualized sibling bond remains immovable because in each generation politically salient social identities and possessions are guarded and enhanced through it. Therefore, the incest taboo and sibling ties must be reconceptualized as part of reconfiguring exchange theory.'[12]

Weiner's theories have found some purchase in literary studies. Notably, Maureen Quilligan has applied this line of argument to explore Elizabethan texts, in relation to the political and cultural status of Queen Elizabeth herself, and to investigate 'how and why traditional kinship structure might endow elite females with agency by means of an endogamous halt in what we have come to call "the traffic in women"'.[13] In a wide variety of early modern English texts by both men and women, Quilligan finds female characters forming associations among themselves or fostering intimate relations, literally or symbolically incestuous, with brothers, and thereby resisting patriarchal expectations for exogamous marriage and gaining autonomy for themselves. But she also looks at stories of real or implied father-daughter incest. In her concluding chapter, Quilligan turns to Shakespeare's *King Lear*, seeing in Cordelia's devotion to her father a symbolically incestuous resistance to normative exogamy, which also grants her agency and power:

> Cordelia has the most agency in the play when she comes back
> from France at the head of an army; but that is also when she

is fulfilling Lear's fantasy of rescue and communion. She has the least amount of agency – is banished from the stage in chosen silence – when she seems to us to be enacting her most autonomous independence from her father, [y]et she expresses this seeming 'autonomy' only by her obedience to the rules enjoining the mandatory traffic in women, contenting herself to be the bond 'between men'.[14]

What makes this analysis relevant to our current purposes is not just that Quilligan provides the most extensive application of Weiner's theoretical model to literary criticism, but also that she analogizes *Lear* to Shakespeare's *Pericles, Prince of Tyre*. Quilligan addresses as well that play's partial source, John Gower's 'Apollonius of Tyre' – the incest narrative that Chaucer's Man of Law abjures in his prologue.

The incest plot takes up a relatively small portion of 'Apollonius', but Gower's expansive tale comprises the bulk of Book 8 of *Confessio Amantis*, which is dedicated to the sin of incest. Gower thus acknowledges the importance of the incest motif to his story. The centrality of the incest to Gower's tale was equally apparent to his contemporary Chaucer. In the *Canterbury Tales*, the Man of Law, in his prologue introducing his tale of Custance, explicitly rejects the incest that animates Gower's analogous romance of voyages and marriages. The Man of Law notes that even so indiscriminately prolific an author as Chaucer would never write of such immoral matters as the tale

> of Tyro Appollonius,
> How that the cursed kyng Antiochus
> Birafte his doghter of hir maydenhede,
> That is so horrible a tale for to rede,
> Whan he hir threw upon the pavement.
> And therfore he, of ful avysement,
> Nolde nevere write in none of his sermons
> Of swiche unkynde abhomyncacions,
> Ne I wol noon reherce, if that I may. (II.81–9)

An application of Weiner's theories to this tale would emphasize the endogamous nature of the incest relationship – King Antiochus's killing of his daughter's suitors out of a desire to keep her for himself – as a counter-force to the forces of exchange, embodied in the exogamous exchange of the heroine. In abjuring the 'unkynde abhomynacions' of incest in Gower's tale, the Man of Law is also rejecting the endogamous elements that Quilligan sees as resisting the exchange of women in tales of the Apollonius tradition. The *Man of Law's Tale* therefore consists entirely of the motifs of exogamy and international exchange that predominate in Gower's 'Apollonius'.[15]

In fact, from the beginning of Gower's 'Apollonius', there is tension between Antiochus's desire to retain his daughter and the marriage market that clamours for an eligible young woman:

> Bot fame, which goth every weie
> To sondry regnes al aboute
> The grete beauté telleth oute
> Of such a maide of hih parage:
> So that for love of mariage
> The worthi princes come and sende,
> As thei the whiche al honour wende,
> And knewe nothing hou it stod.
> The fader, whanne he understod,
> That thei his dowhter thus besoghte,
> With al his wit he caste and thoghte
> Hou that he myhte finde a lette.   (8.348–59)[16]

The suitors are drawn to Antioch not for the love of the princess, nor even for the love of her beauty or her lineage, which define her market value, but 'for the love of marriage', as if the principle of exogamy itself were the overriding force driving people around the Mediterranean. The inviolability of this principle is greater even than the patriarchal will of a king and father; Antiochus must devise a stratagem in order to try to circumvent it.

Similarly, Chaucer's Man of Law seems to feel that his tale of Custance's transportation, and her marriage and remarriage, is primarily about mercantile activity and the accumulation of wealth. It may at first seem rather incongruous that the Man of Law, though he is not a merchant and his tale is not explicitly about the accumulation of wealth, apostrophizes the 'hateful harm, condicion of poverte' (II.99) in his prologue, defending the moral and Christian standing of 'richesse' and declaring, 'O riche marchauntz, ful of wele been yee, / O noble, o prudent folk, as in this cas!' (II.122–3). The ensuing tale, however, soon proves to be about trade and wealth even as it is about the travails of Custance. It begins;

> In Surrye whilom dwelte a compaignye
> Of chapmen riche, and therto sadde and trewe,
> That wyde-where senten hir spicerye,
> Clothes of gold, and satyns riche of hewe.
> Hir chaffare was so thrifty and so newe
> That every wight hath deyntee to chaffare
> With hem, and eek to sellen hire ware.   (II.134–40)

These Syrian merchants bring report to their Sultan of the beauty of the daughter of the emperor of Rome. It is as if they are spreading word of the availability and quality of the kinds of luxury goods they trade in, an impression reinforced when the terms of the marriage contract are settled, stipulating that the Sultan 'shal han Custance in mariage, / And certein gold, I noot what quantitee' (II.241–2). When the wedding party is murdered, the Sultaness's councillors set Custance adrift 'in a ship al steerelees' and 'bidde hire lerne saille / Out of Surrye agayn-ward to Ytaille' (II.439–41). Like Gower's 'Apollonius of Tyre', the *Man of Law's Tale* repeatedly sends the heroine sailing along traditional Mediterranean trade routes alongside ships laden with commodities. Chaucer's heroine, though, goes even farther, floating, somehow, all the way to Northumberland, where another exotic marriage awaits. The exogamous nature of the narrative, and of the genre, is heightened by the extreme distance of exchange and by the inter-religious conditions of the marriages, first to the Muslim Sultan, and then to pagan British King Alla.

There may be some basis, then, for applying to these Middle English romances an argument like Quilligan's, which employs Weiner's anthropological theories to demonstrate that incest narratives resist exogamy and the exchange of women, and preserve or generate values outside exchange. But there are also serious problems with this approach. First and most obvious, father-daughter incest is an odd way to figure the resistance to the patriarchal exchange of women.

Father-daughter incest has no place in Weiner's study: her focus throughout is on 'sibling intimacy'. Quilligan takes a broader view of endogamous relations, expanding it to include the kinds of father-daughter relations she sees in Shakespeare's *Lear* and *Pericles*. She cites Gower's tale in order to contrast its representation of the daughter as the unwilling victim of her possessive father to the depiction in *Pericles* of the daughter as a much more willing agent in the incestuous affair. (Hence the potential analogy to Cordelia and Lear.)[17]

Gower's Antiochus is a predator, and to facilitate his predation the text is careful to eliminate the possibility of female associations, and to restrict the options for female agency, leaving no recourse but submission to male domination. Antiochus's daughter cannot resist him because neither her mother nor any other woman is present:

> Sche couthe noght hir maidenhede
> Defende, and thus sche hath forlore
> The flour which sche hath longe bore.
> It helpeth noght althogh sche wepe,
> For thei that scholde hir bodi kepe
> Of wommen were absent as thanne,
> And thus this maiden goth to manne. (8.302–8)

As Maria Bullón-Fernández has argued, incest tales like Gower's 'Apollonius of Tyre' dramatize 'the father's authority over the daughter and the limits of that authority'.[18] Father-daughter incest is the quintessential act of patriarchal domination of the woman's body and will.

In the *Canterbury Tales* as well, despite the Man of Law's protestations (which have the jocular air of a friendly rivalry between poets), patriarchal authority is likely to be exercised through incest, rather than despite it. Yvette Kisor notes that in analogues to the *Man of Law's Tale*, the Custance character is not given in marriage, but rather flees an incestuous father. The Man of Law abjures incest narratives, and Chaucer suppresses that element of this tale, but to Kisor 'the emperor's bestowing of Custance in marriage becomes a less noisome and more socially accepted version of what is at the heart of father-daughter incest: a father asserting control over his daughter's body'.[19] Similarly, in the *Clerk's Tale* Walter performs his ultimate act of humiliation of Griselda by staging his marriage to their daughter.

Furthermore, though incest is by definition endogamous, the father's desire to maintain his control of the daughter's body does not really preserve the woman from a system of exchange. Gower's Antiochus can be said to keep his daughter for himself rather than consenting to exchange her, but it is also true that he has already exchanged for her, because he traded the mother for the daughter. This is the starting point of Gower's tale, which opens with the death of Antiochus's queen:

> The king, which made mochel mone,
> Tho stod, as who seith, al him one
> Withoute wif, bot natheles
> His doghter, which was piereles
> Of beauté, duelte aboute him stille. (8.283–7)

Gower moralizes this 'concupiscence' (8.293) as the fleshly weakness of desiring and taking what is nearest at hand. That is, Antiochus falls into incest because, his wife having died, he is alone but for his daughter. But Antiochus's actions are the fundamental act of the prerogative of the patriarchal will. This is a male fantasy of the death of the wife and the replacement with a younger and more desirable wife, the inevitable judgement of the male gaze and replacement that all women are subject to.

In this, too, Apollonius duplicates Antiochus. When, while at sea, Apollonius's wife 'dies' in childbirth, Apollonius finds her eliminated and replaced by her daughter, a younger version of herself:

> Sche was delivered al be nyhte
> And ded in every mannes syhte;
> Bot natheles for al this wo
> A maide child was bore tho. (8.1055–8)

The elimination of the first wife is total; the sailors insist, due to a superstition that Gower does not feel obliged to explain, that the body must be dumped overboard – and only later are we allowed the salient detail that she is not even dead. Revived in Ephesus, the wife becomes a nun: she is alive, but her agency in the story has been ceded to her daughter, and both Apollonius's mourning for his wife and his reunification with her are overshadowed by the love story of father and daughter. In Gower's version of the tale, this wife is never even given a name. It has become conventional to say that Antiochus and Apollonius converge as characters in their illicit intimacy with their daughters and their reluctance to exchange them through marriage.[20] I think it is truer that they are most alike, and most incestuous, when they exchange their wives for their daughters.

Nonetheless, there are in the *Man of Law's Tale* ostentatious acts that interrupt the system of exogamous exchange. The endogamous interventions, however, are performed not by fathers, but by mothers. The Sultaness murders her own son with his entire wedding party in order to scuttle his inter-religious marriage to the young woman she resents. This mother – an older woman resenting her replacement by the young bride – is depicted as monstrous, but what is most unnatural about her is her resistance to patriarchal prerogative. Custance, in being sent off from Rome to marriage in Syria, acknowledges her father's authority:

> Allas, unto the Barbre nacioun
> I moste anoon, syn that it is youre wille;

> But Crist, that starf for our redempcioun
> So yeve me grace his heestes to fulfille!
> I, wrecche womman, no fors though I spille!
> Wommen are born to thraldom and penance,
> And to been under mannes governance.   (II.281–7)

The Sultaness, on the other hand, is the embodiment of resistant, and therefore evil, womanhood:

> O Sowdanesse, roote of iniquitee!
> Virago, thou Semyrame the secounde!
> O serpent under femynynytee,
> Lik to the serpent depe in helle ybounde!
> O feyned womman, al that may confounde
> Vertu and innocence, thurgh thy malice,
> Is bred in thee, as nest of every vice!   (II.358–64)[21]

The same antagonistic relationship between mother-in-law and daughter-in-law, the older queen and the younger bride, animates the remainder of the tale in the repeated plots of Alla's mother.

Ultimately, then, it is impossible to make an absolute distinction between the exogamy and the exchange of women in the *Man of Law's Tale* and incest and resistance to exchange in Gower's 'Apollonius'.

II. Virginity and exchange

It may be that the genre of romance is inherently exogamous, and that it entertains endogamous motifs only as short-lived counter-forces to the vectors of marriage and exchange that definitively shape it. Perhaps in other genres or modes, poets can offer more sustained representations of incest and endogamy. Genius begins Book 8 of the *Confessio* by observing that brother-sister incest was a natural predecessor of exogamy – literally present at the creation:

> Nature so the cause ladde,
> Tuo douhtres ek Dame Eve hadde,

> The ferste cleped Calmana
> Was, and that other Delbora.
> Thus was mankinde to beginne;
> Forthi that time it was no sinne
> The soster for to take hire brother,
> Whan that there was of chois non other ...   (8.63–70)

Genius explains that before the time of Abraham, 'Thei token thanne litel hiede, / The brother of the sosterhiede / To wedde wyves' (8.95–7).[22] In Book 3 of *Confessio Amantis*, Gower portrays the incestuous love between the siblings Canace and Machaire with considerable sympathy, depicting it as the unfortunate workings of natural desire. When Canace becomes pregnant she is viciously punished by the implacable patriarch Eolus, outraged by the violation of the imperative for exogamy that his authority upholds. This leads Chaucer's Man of Law, before rejecting 'Apollonius', to decry 'thilke wikke ensample of Canacee, / That loved hir owene brother synfully – / Of swiche cursed stories I sey fy!' (II.78–80).

But as other anthropologists have objected, brother-sister incest is not necessarily a model of resistance to the exchange of women, either. David Graeber characterizes the sibling intimacy that Weiner observes in New Guinea as 'the degree to which even after marriage, men refuse to give their sisters up'.[23] This manifests an endogamous impulse, but it does not supplant exogamy, nor does it necessarily break the 'traffic in women'.

In the *Canterbury Tales*, there is in fact a singular instance of explicit brother-sister incest, though its potential as a deliberate strategy of resistance to exigencies of exogamous exchange are perhaps blunted by the fact that this particular sibling intimacy occurs among chickens:

> This gentil cok hadde in his governaunce
> Sevene hennes for to doon al his plesaunce,
> Whiche were his sustres and his paramours,
> And wonder lyk to hym, as of colours;
> Of whiche the faireste hewed on hir throte
> Was cleped faire damoysele Pertelote.   (VII.2865–70)[24]

Chaucer's invocation of brother-sister incest is facetious, and it dissolves instantly into a dramatization of the quotidian affairs of Chauntecleer and Pertelote, which are depicted as a satire of gender roles in normative marriage.

On the other hand, legend and myth afford many stories of sisterly intimacy. Both Gower (*Confessio Amantis* 5.5551–6074) and Chaucer (*Legend of Good Women* 2228–393) tell the story of Philomela and Procne, the sisters who unite to overcome, via metamorphosis, a husband who rapes his sister-in-law. Chaucer's Philomela weaves into her tapestry 'How she was served for hire systers love' (2365).

Chaucer makes little use of incest or other motifs of 'sibling intimacy' in the *Canterbury Tales*, and there is even less suggestion in his romances than there is in Gower's *Confessio* that endogamous strategies might offer agency in resisting the exchange of women.

However, Quilligan observes, if incest is one way to break the exogamous exchange of women, then lesbianism is another, and a third is celibacy.[25] Of these, the last is by far the most accessible to a medieval English author. Weiner's analysis of endogamous relations is based on observations of actual practices among living cultures, and she explains that the brother-sister intimacy she describes can be expressed in a wide array of social and sexual forms: 'Although actual sibling intimacy may be culturally disavowed, it is at the same time, inexorable. My use of *sibling intimacy* encompasses this broad range of culturally reproductive actions, from siblings' social and economic closeness and dependency to latent, disguised, or overt incest.'[26] But in the medieval West generally, and – outside a few persistent classical myths – in Middle English narrative, this form of endogamous social relation is not viable as a counterforce to the real and imagined imperative for exchange and marriage. In contrast, there are limitless narrative opportunities for valorizing virginity. It is in the temple of Diana – decorated with representations of Daphne 'yturned til a tree' (I.2062) to stymie the pursuit of Apollo, and Acteon 'an hert ymaked' (I.2065) and eaten by his own hounds for violating with his gaze the virgin goddess – that Emily prays that the possessive desires of the rival knights might be turned away from her, and that she might be released from the seemingly inexorable obligation to be taken by a man in marriage:

> Chaste goddesse, wel wostow that I
> Desire to ben a mayden al my lyf,
> Ne nevere wol I be no love ne wyf.
> I am, thow woost, yet of thy compaignye,
> A mayde, and love huntynge and venerye,
> And for to walken in the wodes wilde,
> And noght to ben a wyf and be with childe.   (I.2304–10)

While the Man of Law, on Chaucer's behalf, eschews stories of incest, the *Canterbury Tales* is replete with virgins and virginity. The quality is embodied in the character of Virginia in the *Physician's Tale*: 'As wel in goost as body chast was she, / For which she floured in virginitee / With alle humylitee and abstinence' (VI.43–5). Her transcendent value seems manifest in Nature's declaration that she has formed Virginia with a beauty beyond the imitation of men, in accord with the will of God: 'My lord and I been ful of oon accord. / I made hire to the worshipe of my lord' (VI.25–6).

Even Virginia, though, is not intended to remain a virgin. The corrupt judge Apius attempts to use the law to take Virginia from her father Virginius. The moral is to guard young women closely, as the Physician apostrophizes to those who would protect them, be they 'maistresses' that 'knowen wel ynough the olde daunce' (VI.79) or parents: 'Ye fadres and ye moodres eek also, / Though ye han children, be it oon or mo, / Youre is the charge of al hir surveiaunce, / Whil that they been under youre governaunce' (VI.93–6). Virginia is an exemplar not of celibacy but of chastity, which is guarded in order to preserve her status in the economy of marriage: the value of her virginity is linked to her potential to marry.

This conforms to Irigaray's figuration of women's value in the social marketplace. Whereas the married woman is assessed in terms of use value, 'The virginal woman … is pure exchange value. She is nothing but the possibility, the place, the sign of relations among men.'[27]

Similarly, Dorigen in the *Franklin's Tale*, when she faces the prospect of her adulterous assignation with Aurelius, considers following the examples of illustrious women that 'han hemselven slayn / Wel rather than they wolde defouled be' (V.1420–1); like them, she would die to preserve her chastity, because of the value of her marriage.

To truly resist the marriage system, a woman would have to choose not just chastity but celibacy. As Quilligan says, when a woman embraces life in a religious order, the halt in the traffic of women 'is at least named with the terms borrowed from intimate family positions; nuns are traditionally called "sisters"'.[28] Chaucer's Saint Cecilia is the perfect example: her tale dramatizes a series of disruptions of marriage schemes. Like Emily, she prays to be preserved from marriage and to be allowed to remain a virgin: 'O Lord, my soule and eek my body gye / Unwemmed, lest that I confounded be' (VIII.136–7); unlike her, Cecilia is throughout the dominant agent of her own tale. Like Virginia, she is brought before a cruel Roman judge; unlike her, Cecilia audaciously rejects his 'power and auctoritee' (VIII.471). 'What maner womman artow?' (VIII.424) asks Almachius, flummoxed. Certainly, Cecilia employs celibacy as a strategic disruption of the exogamous exchange in women.

This hagiographical celibacy may be the closest thing in the *Canterbury Tales* to the kind of agential breaking of the traffic in women identified by Weiner in Papuan brother-sister incest. But even so radical an opposition as Saint Cecilia's may reveal limitations, not only in the application of Weiner's model to Chaucer's poetry, but in the theoretical framework itself. In Weiner's core concept of 'keeping-while-giving', an individual keeps *some* of what she produces – cloth, for instance – while giving away most. What is kept, Weiner claims, has 'transcendent' value. But it is far from certain that what is kept transcends the patterns of exchange. As David Graeber comments, Weiner's system of value can seem like the mirror image of market values:

> Rather than value being the measure of how much one would like to acquire something one does not possess, in Weiner, it becomes

the measure of how little one would wish to give up the things one does. Objects of transcendent value are simply the very last things one would be willing to part with.[29]

Given the significance of Weiner's claims of the 'transcendent' value of 'inalienable' possessions, claims that challenge the very core of the modern anthropological tradition, Graeber's objection is important to understand. I myself do not do anthropological fieldwork, but I do watch a lot of television, so I personally understand it in terms of an interpretive crux I call 'the *Antiques Roadshow* problem'. As the reader is surely aware (or should be), the undying television series of that name, in British and American incarnations, invites average people to bring their collectibles and heirlooms for on-camera appraisals by experts. Any casual viewer of the show is likely to have seen a segment like this one, so representative that it is archived on the show's website: a woman appears with an antique chair. The appraiser identifies it as deriving from the Federalist era (a period especially coveted, as we regular watchers know, by furniture collectors) and observes that the guest must have 'at least one very distinguished ancestor'. She confirms that the chair belonged to General William Floyd, her husband's 'grandfather seven generations back' and a signer of the Declaration of Independence from New York. The appraiser then provides the details of the chair – a 'garden Windsor' made by William MacBride in New York City in the 1790s. This chair may seem like nothing special to the viewer – that in fact is the show's rationale – but it evinces many of the qualities that Weiner associates with 'inalienable possessions'. It has been in the possession of a single kinship group for eight generations, and it has gained value not by being traded but by being handed down within the family. This is what makes it an heirloom. Its value is connected to the narrative associations it accrues in being passed down, like the story of the ancestor who signed the Declaration of Independence. And it is in the possession of a woman, even though the chair is the legacy of her husband's family; as Weiner notes, it is often women who are the special keepers of heirloom objects. But the most telling element of this segment comes at the end, when the appraiser, having built up tension by reciting the chair's qualities in arcane detail, reveals his estimate of its market value:

> Appraiser: $10,000, okay. Are you surprised?
> Guest: I am, and very pleased.
> Appraiser: Well, you're not going to put it out in your garden, though. You only did that in the 18th century.
> Guest: No, and this is staying in the family. I'm so pleased. That's good news![30]

The owner simultaneously expresses her pleasure and excitement at the market price, and insists that she would never sell it and that it is 'staying in the family'. It is at this point that I, as a viewer, yell at the television my formulation of the critical crux: 'Then why did you bring it on the *Roadshow*!?' But in light of Graeber's critique of Weiner, the answer is obvious: people bring objects like this for appraisal in order to learn exactly how much they are not getting by refusing to exchange them. A guest might consider her object priceless, but the pricelessness of an object is predicated on the existence of a market from which it is being withheld. Therefore, such supposedly 'inalienable' objects do not transcend systems of exchange; they draw their value from the choice of the possessors not to exchange them.

Saint Cecilia's story begins 'whan this mayden sholde unto a man / Ywedded be' (VIII.127–8). It is then that she is lauded for her 'body clene' and her 'unwemmed thoght' (VIII.225); she is 'unwemmed' because she is unwedded. Her sanctity consists in her being undefiled in body and spirit, through which '[t]he world hath wist what it is worth, certeyn, / Devocioun of chastitee to love' (VIII.282–3). Through force of character and devotion, Cecilia preserves her own chastity despite social obligations to marry, and despite judicial enforcement of patriarchal law. But can she properly be said to break the traffic in women, or to transcend exchange value, if the worth of her sacrifice is predicated on a marriage market from which she withholds herself?[31]

III. A woman on the market

Perhaps it is appropriate, therefore, that Weiner's theories find their greatest applicability to the *Canterbury Tales* in the character who is most emphatically not a virgin. The Wife of Bath defines her essential nature in opposition to virginity:

> I nyl envye no virginitee.
> Lat hem be breed of pured whete-seed,
> And lat us wyves hoten barly-breed;
> And yet with barly-breed, Mark telle kan,
> Oure Lord Jhesu refresshed many a man.   (III.142–6)

While the Wife of Bath's heterosexual adventurism may seem contrary to Weiner's vision of female agency, there are elements of her character that strongly recall details of Weiner's model. There is, first, the striking parallel inherent in her profession. In the *General Prologue*, she is introduced as a wife, but her social standing is not determined by her standing as anyone's wife (nor, as some would find conspicuous, to her production of children) but rather to her 'clooth-makyng' (I.447). Cloth-making is for Weiner the activity most emblematic of women's productive powers independent of exchange.

Equally significant are the Wife of Bath's frequent evocations of close female friends and relations, with whom she often shares private information and intense intimacy. In particular, she and her 'gossib' share secrets, both profound and inconsequential, of her husband, infuriating and disempowering him:

> He som tyme was a clerk of Oxenford,
> And hadde left scole, and went at hom to bord
> With my gossib, dwellynge in our toun;
> God have hir soule! Hir name was Alisoun.
> She knew myn herte, and eek my privetee,
> Bet than oure parisshe preest, so moot I thee!
> To hire biwreyed I my conseil al.

> For hadde myn housbonde pissed on a wal,
> Or doon a thyng that sholde han cost his lyf,
> To hire, and to another worthy wyf,
> And to my nece, which that I loved weel,
> I wolde han toold his conseil every deel.
> And so I dide ful often, God it woot,
> That made his face often reed and hoot
> For verray shame, and blamed hymself for he
> Had toold to me so greet a pryvetee.   (III.527–42)

The Wife of Bath stresses her intimacy with her 'gossib' – 'She knew myn herte, and eek my privetee'. The 'gossib' is also named Alison, a peculiar duplication that calls attention to the insularity and self-reflexiveness of the relationship, and echoes its power to disrupt the expectations of heterosexual union and exchange.

It is worth noting that the *-sib* in 'gossib' is the same root as the *sib-* in 'sibling': it means relative or kin, and 'gossib' literally means godparent or godchild, or the child of one's godparent, and thus also close relation, or eventually, as apparently in the *Wife of Bath's Prologue*, close female friend.[32] Chaucer's Parson declares that the spiritual role of a godparent amounts to legal consanguinity, and therefore that sexual relations with a 'godsib' would be incestuous: 'And certes, parentele is in two maneres, outher goostly or flesshly; goostly, as for to deelen with his godsibbes. / For right so as he that engendreth a child is his flesshly fader, right so is his godfader his fader espiritueel. For which a womman may in no lasse synne assemblen with hire godsib than with hire owene flesshly brother' (X.908–9). In the Wife of Bath and her Alison, we have one true instance in the *Canterbury Tales* of 'sibling intimacy' – not identical to the brother-sister incest that Weiner cites, but close to Quilligan's adaptation of the term to describe resistant, feminine strategies of endogamy.

This is apparently only one strand in the Wife of Bath's web of female social relations. She speaks also of her 'dame', and in the passage quoted above she says that she shared her husband's 'privetee' also with 'my nece, which that I loved weel' as well as 'another worthy wyf'. It is not certain that these are all separate individuals: it has been suggested, for instance, that her 'dame' is not her mother but her godmother, and that this is her 'gossib', whom she also refers to as 'dame Alys' (III.548).[33] These ambiguities are probably unresolvable, but what is undeniable is that in her prologue the Wife of Bath describes a series of intimate connections among women who are kin or the social equivalent, with whom she forms a community that serves as a bulwark against the privileges and authority of men.

Yet, again, when Weiner's theoretical model seems most relevant to the *Canterbury Tales*, it also reveals its insufficiencies, or at least its imperfect applicability to the female characters and their narrative roles in Chaucer's works. The cloth is a revealing example: the Wife of Bath, from the moment she is introduced in the General Prologue, enacts her association with that central motif of Weiner's study, the role of women in producing and preserving objects of hallmark social value, often taking the form of textiles. But Weiner's point is that these objects are preserved from and transcendent of systems of exchange outside kinship groups; they are instead passed down as heirlooms, their inalienability marked by the family narratives that accrue to them. The Wife of Bath's cloth-making, though, is mentioned only in the General Prologue, and never at any point in her prologue. And in her General Prologue portrait, her cloth is the furthest thing from an heirloom; it is, rather, a commodity, competing in an international market with other luxury goods: 'Of clooth-makyng she hadde swich an haunt / She passed hem of Ypres and of Gaunt' (I.447–8). She is a wealthy manufacturer of commercial cloth, and she uses the wealth derived from it to elevate her status in her town. No possession could be more alienable than the Wife of Bath's cloth.

The contrast is even more striking in connection to her real and symbolic 'sibling intimacy'. In her prologue, the Wife of Bath represents herself as a 'woman on the market'. She is a 'woman on the market' in the sense of Luce Irigaray's well-known chapter, 'Women on the Market', in which Irigaray argues, using Lévi-Strauss's terms, that capitalist culture is based on the commodification of women, who are traded as objects by men in a system of male desire and competition:

> The exchange of women as goods accompanies and stimulates exchanges of other 'wealth' among groups of men. The economy – in both the narrow and the broad sense – that is in place in our societies thus requires that women lend themselves to alienation in consumption, and to exchanges in which they do not participate, and that men be exempt from being used and circulated like commodities.[34]

The Wife of Bath is also a 'woman *on* the market' in the sense that she expounds her own views on the market in women, which closely parallels those of Irigaray. She spends much of her prologue satirizing men's purchase of women's bodies as commodity through marriage – a barely euphemized system of prostitution:

> What eyleth yow to grucche thus and grone?
> Is it for ye wolde have my queynte allone?
> Wy, taak it al! Lo, have it every deel!
> Peter! I shrewe yow, but ye love it weel;
> For if I wolde selle my *bele chose*,
> I koude walke as fressh as is a rose;
> But I wol kepe it for youre owene tooth. (III.443–9)

But the Wife of Bath is also a woman on the market in the sense that, as a now fortunately rather outdated idiom would have it, she is *on the market* – the marriage market, that is. She announces her theme to be the 'wo that is in mariage' (III.3) and declares herself an expert on the topic based on her own experience, but almost immediately she begins defending multiple marriages. Her network of 'gossibs' would seem to be the kind of endogamous relations that Weiner sees as transcending exogamy, and that Quilligan finds to resist exogamy in early modern literature. But while the Wife of Bath and her female friends and kin do conspire partly to resist male domination, they also work together to further exogamy. From her 'dame' she gets the advice on how to gain Jankyn's affections: 'I bar hym on honde he hadde enchanted me – / My dame taughte me that soutiltee' (III.575–6). After her marriage to Jankyn, none of her gossibs or dames or nieces appear again.

Ultimately, the Wife of Bath commits herself to the marriage system in ways that seem conspicuously to undermine her own interests – by marrying Jankyn and, even more rashly, giving all her title and property to him; by praising her fifth marriage and marriage itself even after her rude awakening; and by aspiring to remarry again in the future. In the beginning of her prologue, she declares that after five marriages she is actively committed to another: 'Welcome the sixte, whan that evere he shal' (III.45). She ends her prologue with wistful memories of a happy marriage, and she ends her tale with a prayer for 'Housbondes meeke, yonge, and fressh abedde, / And grace t'overbyde hem that we wedde' (III.1259–60), with the implication that outliving a husband means taking another.

Certainly, in her prologue and her tale, the Wife of Bath offers an extended critique of power dynamics within marriage, as well as implicit and explicit strategies for challenging that imbalance. It is also true that in insisting on the legitimacy of her own desires, emotions and physical pleasures, she is upending some essential conventions of the marriage market, particularly as conceived by a critic like Irigaray. But considered in the light of Weiner's anthropological model of female agency through endogamous relations, it becomes all the more conspicuous that one of the most consistent elements in the Wife of Bath's self-presentation – which she herself acknowledges is sometimes inconsistent – is her commitment to marriage itself. It is partly on account of her apparent location of her sense of self within a model of marriage and marriageability, that some critics find her overall portrait undercut by delimiting materialism or neurotic submissiveness.[35] The feminist critics who note such limitations are likely to ascribe them to failure of vision on Chaucer's part, but it would also seem then that if our ultimate goal is a coherent and unified justification of the Wife of Bath, Weiner's model of exchange may not do the trick.

Part Two: Marilyn Strathern and the 'gender of the gift'

IV. The Wife of Bath: partible person

In her best-known book, *The Gender of the Gift*, Marilyn Strathern argues that a set of modern, Western preconceptions about personhood, exchange and value has led to misunderstandings of gender and female autonomy in other cultures.[36] For instance, there is the Western tendency to imagine commodity exchange as the natural form of exchange, and any other form of exchange as a variant or ancestor of purchase.

As I touched on in the introduction to this volume, many sociologists and anthropologists studying the gift were long unsatisfied with theories that assumed or posited the essential sameness of gifts and commodities, and were in search of a way to distinguish substantially between the two. An important advance in this project was provided by the anthropologist Christopher Gregory in his 1982 book *Gifts and Commodities*, based on his field work in Papua New Guinea. Beginning with the observation that all societies have both gift exchange and commodity exchange, Gregory seeks to define the qualitative difference between these two types of exchange. What he finds is that the two types of exchange stand for two types of relationships. He concludes: 'Commodity exchange relations are objective relations of equality established by the exchange of alienated objects between independent transactors. Gift exchange relations are personal relations of rank, established by the exchange of inalienable objects between transactors who are related.'[37]

Commodities are fully alienated from the donor at the moment of transaction. Gifts are never alienated from the donor; rather, they always retain their history. By preserving the memory of the transaction, the obligation for repayment is carried into the future, and the result is the establishment of a social bond between the transactors. As a result, objects in exchange are personified. In Papua New Guinea, Gregory insists, objects exchanged between kinship groups, be they pigs, yams or canoes, gain the status of persons and 'are regarded as humans'.[38]

But what if the gift being exchanged is a person? In New Guinea, Gregory says, 'Women as gifts, like things as gifts, are never alienated from their clans, and when they are exchanged against thing-gifts mutual indebtedness, rather than prices, is the outcome.'[39] Strathern adapts Gregory's formula, making it one of the starting points of her analysis: '[I]f in a commodity economy things and persons assume the social form of things, then in a gift economy they assume the social form of persons.'[40]

To many, including Rubin and Irigaray, the primitive exchange of women is the prototype of capitalist exploitation and the subjugation of women in modern society. To some extent this is true: there is a continuity of male domination and exploitation of women across time and cultures. But Strathern, taking up from studies like Gregory's (Strathern's fieldwork is also in Papua New Guinea), argues that the exchange of women in tribal cultures is normally a gift exchange rather than a commodity exchange. The wife can be translated into a commodity, and often is, but the two types of exchange are categorically distinct. When given as a gift, the woman is not alienated from her original family. Like other gifts, she embodies the relationship established between clans in the transaction; she stands for the memory of the donation and the obligation for future repayment. When she produces progeny, the tie between the family groups is solidified and carried into subsequent generations. The woman as gift is, in this sense, personified.

Subjectivity, with its inherent assumptions of a unitary identity, is not only a Western concept but one designed to suit a capitalist economy.[41] Strathern therefore eschews the term. In the gift economies and tribal exchanges of her field studies, she finds that people are most 'personified' when they are 'objectified':

> In so far as people turn one set of relationships into another, they act (as individual subjects) to turn themselves into persons (objects) in the regard of others. They objectify themselves, one might say. And *this* is indeed the point of making themselves active agents; this is their destiny.[42]

This is only one way in which assumptions of unitary identity are encoded in Western language. The use of the word 'individual' to signify each, distinct person implies that the person is a singular, atom-ized, autonomous, intentionally self-motivated actor in a social system. Additionally, it implies that a person is by nature whole and indivis-ible. To Strathern, this seemingly natural conception of the individual is culturally and historically contingent, and foreign to the cultures she studies: 'Far from being regarded as unique entities, Melanesian persons are as dividually as they are individually conceived. They contain a gen-eralized sociality within.' Thus, it is more proper to speak of 'dividual persons', as the person is inherently 'the plural and composite site of the relationships that produced them'.[43]

These ideas are the basis for Strathern's hallmark concept of 'partible personhood'. As personhood itself is constructed through relationships, persons therefore exist initially and primarily as they are perceived by others. As people have multiple relationships and multiple species of relationships, in each of which they perform dif-ferent social roles, personhood must necessarily be multiple, and the person should be defined differently in the enactment of different relationships. A person is 'partible', therefore, in that she or he can be parted into multiple roles or social positions. But a person is also partible in that the person's essence can be embodied in an object given in exchange.

Given all this, I will argue that Chaucer's Wife of Bath may best be understood not as an individual given to inconsistencies, but rather a 'dividual' person constructed as 'the composite site of the relation-ships that produced' her. Since both Gregory and Strathern insist that no culture consists entirely in gift exchange or entirely in commodity exchange, some of these relationships that generate the Wife of Bath's identity are commodity-oriented, but others are gift-oriented.

Granted, in the *Wife of Bath's Prologue* commodity exchange is conspicuously dominant. This is especially true in the earlier portions, in her discussion of her first three husbands. From the start of her prologue, she defends multiple marriage against the received ideal of virginity. She notes that sex is practical and functional: 'And certes, if ther were no seed ysowe, / Virginitee, thanne wherof sholde it growe?' (III.71–2). But she observes further that it is useful:

> I graunte it wel; I have noon envie,
> Thogh maydenhede preferre bigamye.
> It liketh hem to be clene, body and goost;
> Of myn estaat I nyl nat make no boost,
> For wel ye knowe, a lord in his houshold,
> He nath nat every vessel al of gold;
> Somme been of tree, and doon hir lord servyse. (III.95–101)

In this metaphor, virgins are vessels of gold, while wives are vessels of wood. A golden bowl is decorative, valued for its beauty and purity, but functionally it has only exchange value. (This is one of the reasons that gold is used for money.) The wooden bowl, on the other hand, has 'use value', as the wife is valued for sex and reproduction. As Irigaray says, 'Once deflowered, woman is relegated to the status of use value, to her entrapment in private property; she is removed from exchange among men.'[44]

In discussing her first three husbands, the Wife of Bath challenges and sometimes inverts the power relations between herself and her husbands, but marriage remains based on purchase, consumption, and the practical value of use. That is to say, marital and sexual relations are instrumental, as reflected in her euphemisms for sexual organs, both male and female. 'In wyfhod I wol use myn instrument' (III.149), she says, but she also says,

> Why sholde men elles in hir bookes sette
> That man shal yelde to his wyf hire dette?
> Now wherwith sholde he make his paiement,
> If he ne used his sely instrument? (III.129–32)

As she points out, her instrumental conception of sex is authorized by the conventional use of economic terms like 'dette' and 'paiement' to describe marriage obligations. She can therefore refer to a potential husband's sexual organ as his 'nether purs' (III.44b) and to her own 'instrument' as a precious object that her husband will pay dearly for:

> Myn housbonde shal it have bothe eve and morwe,
> What that hym list come forth and paye his dette.
> An housbonde I wol have – I wol nat lette –
> Which shal be bothe my dettour and my thral.   (III.152–5)

Even when the Wife of Bath most forcefully asserts her autonomy in the face of a husband's presumptions to control her – 'Thou shalt nat bothe, thogh that thou were wood, / Be maister of my body and of my good ... / I trowe thou woldest loke me in thy chiste!' (III.313–14, 317) – her terms indicate that what she is asserting is self-ownership. She has learned the rules of a commercial system, and is insisting on her own agential role in it: 'What sholde I taken keep hem for to plese, / But it were for my profit and myn ese?' (III.213–14) And when she describes her method of extracting wealth from her rich, old husbands, she envisions sex and marriage as elements in a broader social world that is entirely commercial:

> I wolde no lenger in the bed abyde,
> If that I felte his arm over my syde,
> Til he had maad his raunson unto me;
> Thanne wolde I suffre hym do his nycetee.
> And therfore every man this tale I telle,
> Wynne whoso may, for al is for to selle.   (III.409–14)

But is all for sale? Does the Wife of Bath herself entirely believe this? In another passage, when she begins to speak of her fifth marriage, she purports to explain her attraction to Jankyn in terms of the capricious nature of women's desires:

> We wommen han, if that I shal nat lye,
> In this matere a queynte fantasye:
> Wayte what thyng we may nat lightly have,
> Therafter wol we crie al day and crave.
> Forbede us thyng, and that desiren we;
> Preesse on us faste, and thanne wol we fle.

> With daunger oute we al oure chaffare;
> Greet prees at market maketh deere ware,
> And to greet cheep is holde at litel prys:
> This knoweth every womman that is wys.   (III.515–24)

It appears at first glance like a page from Adam Smith. 'Greet prees at market maketh deere ware' is a succinct articulation of the principle of supply and demand. But the point of the passage is that there is something perverse, by normal market standards, in the desires of women. A 'queynte fantasye' – curious predilection – leads women to desire objects more when they are more expensive, to sell reluctantly even when prices are high, and to shun purchases (on the market of love, of course) that are offered at too great a bargain. The phrase 'queynte fantasye' also, of course, includes a pun, as 'queynte' is used by the Wife of Bath, and elsewhere by Chaucer, as a less euphemistic term for *bele chose* or *quoniam*. The Wife of Bath thus emphasizes the mysterious and contrary desires of women, emanating from the core of their sexual beings, that confound the normal vectors of market pricing. There are forces other than an invisible hand at work in this market. There is also, it seems, an invisible 'queynte', and its operation is considerably less predictable.

Perhaps, as has been suggested, female desire cannot be accounted for in conventional economic models.[45] As I have argued, I think it is more broadly true that qualities like desire itself are not translatable into economic terms.[46] The Wife of Bath herself encourages us to see this as a caprice, an inexplicable perversity that women are given to. If we take her at her word, then we can resort to those critiques of her character, either for being subject to totalizing economic forces that she cannot fully comprehend nor resist, or for being neurotic and self-defeating in traditionally anti-feminist ways. But I think it is particularly important that even within the hyper-commercialized discourse of the Wife of Bath one can still see language that resists market-based explanations and seems to seek for alternatives. She is here talking about her relationship with Jankyn. As Strathern maintains, modes of exchange – gift or commodity – are distinguished by the kinds of relations formed by the transaction. The Wife of Bath's discourse is exceedingly economic when she is discussing her first three husbands. The fourth and fifth marriages are different because they are realized by a different mode of exchange.

It is surely counter-intuitive to claim about the Wife of Bath's unhappy fourth marriage, as it was when I claimed it about violence in the *Miller's Tale*, that it is rooted in a kind of gift exchange. But part of her inability to explain fully what happened in that marriage or how she feels about it – she never gives his name, and her narrative at this point is especially fragmented and halting – is that the economic meta-phors she had been applying previously no longer function adequately. The fourth husband cheats on her. One might well ask why she should care. She could counsel herself, as she did her previous husbands, 'He is to greet a nygard that wolde werne / A man to lighte a candle at his lanterne' (III.333–4). Some would say that she cares because it forces her to confront the waning power of her own sexuality. Perhaps so, but what matters most, I think, is that she does care. She vows to respond in kind:

> I seye, I hadde in herte greet despit
> That he of any oother had delit.
> But he was quit, by God and by Seint Joce!
> I made hym of the same wode a croce;
> Nat of my body, in no foul manere,
> But certeinly, I made folk swich cheere
> That in his owene grece I made hym frye
> For angre, and for verray jalousye.   (III.481–8)

It is telling that she claims to have 'quit' him. The term can connote, as we have seen, either equivalent repayment, or superfluous payback. The Wife of Bath here seems to intend repayment, for the passage emphasizes her search for equivalence in her response to his philan-dering: she makes him a cross of the same wood; she fries him in his own grease. And yet her lingering anger reveals that this equivalence is insufficient. She is angry not because she has been cheated – an economic notion, for which an economic response might suffice – but because she has been cheated *on*. She arranges for him to feel 'angre' and 'jalousye' because that is what she feels. Whatever the original impetus was for this marriage, it has resulted in relations that are indicative of gift transaction, because, in anthropological terms, it is a transaction that has generated social relations – not positive or happy social relations, but social relations nonetheless.

The Wife of Bath's relations with her fifth husband are even more fraught, but also more clearly rooted in the logic of the gift. She declares that in cases of love she cares nothing whatsoever for compensation: 'I took no kep, so that he liked me, / How poore he was, ne eek of what degree' (III.625–6). She finds Jankyn so attractive, when she sees him carrying her fourth husband's bier, that 'al myn herte I yaf unto his hoold' (III.599). Once they are wed, she says, 'And to hym yaf I al the lond and fee / That evere was me yeven therbifoore' (III.630–1). She *gives* her heart to Jankyn; she *gives* herself to Jankyn in marriage; she *gives* Jankyn her sex; she *gives* Jankyn her wealth. The Wife of Bath does not think she is inverting yet reduplicating a system of commercial exchange by purchasing for herself an object of sexual desire with her acquired wealth. She seems to assume instead that her fifth marriage is substantively different from her first three because it is rooted in a different form of exchange, based on the different expectations of the social relations and obligations thereby generated. It is not that she is inconsistent, but rather that her identity is generated 'multiply' through the different exchanges and through the different modes of exchange, in which she takes part. She is, as Strathern would say, a 'partible' person.

Some of the occasions that the Wife of Bath seems to objectify herself should be reconsidered in light of Strathern's theories. For instance, in a not atypical passage, the Wife of Bath claims that Jankyn, though half her age, should desire her for, among other things, her sexual organ, which her previous husbands have assured her is 'the beste *quoniam* myghte be' (III.608). Has she here internalized a masculine objectification of her own body? Perhaps. She has told previous husbands that they 'shul have queynte right ynogh at eve' (III.332), and that she could if she wished 'selle' her *'bele chose'* (III.447). But among Strathern's more startling assertions is that in New Guinea a variety of partible persons are conceived as already existing within a person, waiting to be 'extracted' and to be potentiated as gifts and personified as relationships.[47] This is especially apparent in the exchange of women as brides: 'The gift (the bride) already exists and must be extracted, and extraction thus activates the very relation which makes the object.'[48] The person, even the person's body, is in reality a nexus of realized and potential relationships: 'The body's features are a register, a site of ... interaction. Consequently, what is drawn out of a person are the social relationships of which it is composed: it is a *microcosm of relations*.'[49] This leads Strathern to explore 'the transactability of what we would regard as sexual attributes.'[50] Objects acquire gender according to the relations formed by their exchange – this is the most elemental form of 'the gender of the gift' – and people understand their own gender in relation to such objects. Ultimately, Strathern asserts that 'the gender of people's sexual organs depends on what they do with them' and that 'it is possible to detach parts of oneself'.[51]

When the Wife of Bath refers to her own sexual organ – and this, of course, is very frequent – she speaks of it as if it is an external, essentially detachable part of herself. But she also seems to think of it as embodying her desire for her lover and her lover's desire for her. It is part of her dividual person, and it variously potentiates her personhood depending on how and to whom she gives it. She threatens to sell her *bele chose*, and thereby indicates to her first three husbands that she considers their relationships commercial transactions in which her sex has been purchased. But she gives her *quoniam* – one that, she is pleased to say, he considers 'the beste *quoniam* myghte be' (III.608), incomparable, and thus beyond the commensurate assessments of the market – to Jankyn, and thereby establishes that her fifth marriage is based on a gift relationship, in which the purpose of exchange is to generate social relations conditioned on obligation.

And, yes, she soon regrets it: 'But afterward repented me ful soore; / He nolde suffre nothyng of my list' (III.632–3). Strathern acknowledges that gift relations are susceptible to 'domination'. (As I repeatedly reiterate in the course of this book that the conditions of the gift are not that it is always pleasant and happy, I take consolation from the fact that anthropological gift theorists feel compelled to do the same.) Sometimes this domination reflects imbalances of power and status between men and women. But Strathern maintains that 'acts of dominance consist in taking advantage of those relations created in the circulation of objects and overriding the exchange of perspectives on which exchange as such rests'.[52] And she insists that this does not indicate an inherent, fundamental inequality in gift exchange. There are features of gift exchange that a man can exploit to dominate the exchange to his own advantage, but, Strathern says,

> *the domination does not stand for anything else* – for culture over nature or whatever – and does not have to engage our sympathy on that score. It is itself. It inheres in all the small personal encounters in which one man finds himself at an advantage because of other men at his back. Among the substitutions available to him, as it were, is the replication of all-male relations in the plural form which enlarges the capacity of each individual.[53]

Strathern is not the most accessible or pellucid of writers; her central meaning can be quite elusive.[54] But the emphasis she places here makes it especially important to try to discern her point. I certainly do not think she means to erase patterns or systems of male domination.[55] The last sentence of the passage quoted above could serve as a concise if idiosyncratic definition of patriarchy. When she says that domination by men in gift exchange *'does not stand for anything else'*, she seems to mean that it is not symptomatic of something compromised within gift exchange itself. Domination is not essential to the meaning of exchange. Gift exchange is not fundamentally and primarily about power, and the exchange of women is not emblematic of all exchange. The exchange of women is not, as in Lévi-Strauss, a Freudian imperative that underlies culture and civilization, nor is it a foundational system of sexual exploitation, nor is it the originary act of material self-interest that leads inexorably to the market and capitalism.

Just as there is a qualitative distinction between the commodity and the gift, there is a qualitative distinction between domination in commodity exchange and domination in gift exchange. Commodity exchange turns human relations into material value, and domination in commercial contexts entails an individual extracting material profit from the exchange. Gift exchange turns objects and people into relations, and therefore domination in gift exchange entails an individual exploiting the symbolic associations generated by the exchange for personal gain. In the context of the first part of her prologue, the Wife of Bath's body is exchanged as a commodity and is gendered as female in the role of wife. When, however, she gives her property and her heart and her *quoniam* to Jankyn, she is motivated by a personal desire that she presumes to be mutual; she does not expect to be gendered as a result of the exchange, but rather expects mutual love and obligation to result. When Jankyn dominates her by recourse to his 'book of wikked wyves' (III.691), a book that derives largely from monastic anti-matrimonial tracts, we can justifiably say that he is resorting to 'the replication of all-male relations in the plural form which enlarges the capacity of each individual'. This is Strathern's definition of domination in gift exchange.

Jankyn's abuse is unjust in ways that reflect historical and social injustices of clerical authority and male dominance, as the Wife of Bath emphatically declares. But the injustice does not inhere in gift exchange itself, nor even in the exchange of women. The proof of this is that when the Wife of Bath, by dint of personal struggle and extensive rhetorical critique, redresses her perceived wrongs, she does not ultimately seek to end the relations formed by exchange, nor to avoid or eliminate the transactions that underlie them. In the end, 'He yaf me al the bridel in myn hond, / To han the governance of hous and lond' (III.813–14). Jankyn gives back her gifts – not, apparently, in order to end relations between them, since the restoration ostensibly preserves their marriage. Rather, the Wife of Bath concludes her prologue by having Jankyn re-establish the conditions for exchange that she perceives as more equitable.

V. The *Wife of Bath's Tale* and the poetics of the gift

Further evidence for the legitimacy and persistence of the gift in the Wife of Bath's discourse is that, while she critiques the commercial exploitation of women's bodies by employing the terms of the market, she responds to the domination of women in gift exchange by employing what has been called 'the poetics of the gift'.

This is a rhetorical strategy particularly well suited to a character so deeply associated with both textuality and exchange. The Wife of Bath is a manufacturer of cloth, and also a weaver of texts and a retailer of stories. The analogy between these two activities is commonly observed. The textiles that the Wife of Bath produces are unquestionably commercial products, but as I have argued she is also capable of imagining gift exchange, distinct from commercial transaction, and of entering into exchanges that are primarily intended to produce social relations rather than profits. This is even more clearly demonstrated in her tale, which manifests 'the poetics of the gift'.

'The poetics of the gift' was formulated by Sarah Kay, in response to R. Howard Bloch's complexly Foucauldian archaeology of medieval literary modes. In *Etymologies and Genealogies*, Bloch distinguishes between epic – in the medieval context, primarily *chansons de geste* – and romance by contrasting the symbol to the sign. The epic mode, and the earlier medieval philosophy of representation, presupposes an immediate and secure link between word and referent; this is the 'symbol'. With the rise of courtly culture and the romances that were its predominant fictional mode, representation comes to be made primarily not through symbols but through 'signs', which mediate between the word and its meaning. The main locus for this culture is the aristocratic household:

> The household presupposes a mode of property which, because of the necessity of division, is necessarily more partible. Such property – alienable, personal, salable, constitutive of the principle of exchange itself – corresponds to the reintroduction into the circuit of human affairs of the mobile form of wealth par excellence: money.[56]

Money, according to Bloch, is a fluctuating sign of wealth and value, and the commercial economy, and romance, are inherently more semiotically indeterminate, more given to ambiguity, uncertainty, self-reflexiveness and play.

Kay, one of the few critics to apply Marilyn Strathern's anthropological theories to medieval literature, observes that Bloch's model fails to recognize the ontological complexities of objects in exchange. 'So dominated is his thought by the conceptions of a commodity economy,' says Kay, 'that he sees only the thing-ness of thing exchanged. He regards money as inherently more ambiguous than wealth objects because they are only themselves whereas money mediates over a range of commodities; his conception of the transaction focuses on the material objects and their material connotations.'[57]

Bloch's underlying assumption – that prior to the rise of the money economy exchange involved merely the transferal of unmediated 'things' – betrays what Strathern calls 'a specific Western root metaphor' that imagines that 'things exist in themselves' and that they have 'intrinsic properties'.[58] Modern Westerners assume that things are the object of exchange, and that people who are exchanged are 'objectified'. But this is because the market culture to which we are habituated renders both objects and people, in their social roles, into objectified commodities, used for material profit but not for generating social life or autonomy. In the gift cultures that she studies, Strathern describes both objects and people in exchange as 'reified': their latent qualities are made real when they activate social relations.

The difference between gift exchange and commodity exchange, in Strathern's neo-Maussian model, is that commodities are 'objectified' things and people, while gifts are 'personified' things and people. Thus Sarah Kay notes an 'indeterminacy of the relation between "things" and "persons", and between participating transactors' in gift culture.[59] And she is therefore able to claim for this system the potential for the kind of semiotic play, the poetics, that Bloch locates in the commodity-centred, market-oriented culture in which he locates romance: 'If the sign, in Bloch's sense, permits play and ambiguity in relation to *things* – i.e. in reference and connotation – then what he calls "symbol" in fact

generates irony and equivocation with regards to persons and relationships – i.e. in politics and ethics.'[60]

This, to Kay, is the context of 'the poetics of the gift'. It is a
valuable insight, and in fact I would say that there is even more
direct support for it in Strathern's analysis than Kay describes. Bloch's
dichotomy of sign and symbol finds a parallel in Strathern's distinction
between 'metonymic' and 'metaphoric' gift.[61] Bloch takes the 'medi-
ating' role of the sign and the analogous role of the sign-system of
money in a commercial economy to be inherently more sophisticated
and ambiguous than the symbolic representation in epic. Strathern,
in contrast, calls gift transactions 'mediated exchange', in that the
object in exchange (which may of course be a person) 'can circulate
between persons and mediate their relationship'.[62] Mauss's original
point was that the gift is conceived as containing some inalienable
portion of the donor. The gift is therefore a part of the donor that
contains his or her identity: it is in this sense a metonym. But in mediated exchange, that potential identity is 'extracted' from the donor.
For the recipient, it stands for the set of social relations enacted by
the exchange and the social status of the object in exchange. Thus,
the 'metonym' becomes a 'metaphor'. This process is most discern-
ible in the circulation of women, as in the marriage exchanges of the
Hagen, the New Guinea highlanders who are the primary focus of
Strathern's fieldwork:

> As an aspect of Hagen men's social identities, women are personi-
> fied as 'female' thereby, circulating as detachable parts of clans
> or persons thereby rendered 'male'. But they do so by virtue of
> the kinship transformation that turns them from sisters to wives
> ... From the point of view of the donors (wife-givers), the sister is
> now a detached part, but she comes to the recipients (wife-takers)
> as an entire representative of her natal kin. This is a switch from
> metonymic to metaphoric gift. It is constituted in the different per-
> spectives that the male participants have of their interaction. Hence
> the necessity that they are in exchange, *for what they exchange
> is their viewpoints*.[63]

This model of gift exchange is a semiotic system. Strathern's long-term anthropological observation allows us to see that it is as complex as any sign-system. It is not based on naive or rudimentary assumptions about symbols, nor it is predicated on direct and unmediated connections between word and a self-determined, pre-existing thing, nor on stable and unitary linkages of symbols and referents.

Kay's primary purpose in applying anthropological gift theory to medieval literature is to defend the *chansons de geste* against a long-standing inclination, by Bloch and many other critics, to assert the greater literary and semiotic sophistication of romance. Central to her project is a revision of the understanding of women in *chansons*: 'A feminist criticism of *chansons de geste* is needed to show the importance of epic women as persons, as political actors, and as articulators of narrative, and not only as objects of oppression or desire.'[64] One of her key claims in this argument is that women are exchanged as gifts in *chansons*, but as commodities in romances. I do not intend to challenge Kay's interpretation of the French romances and *chansons* of the twelfth and thirteenth centuries.[65] For the relevance of her argument to Chaucer, however, it is essential to make one preliminary point: the exchange of women in the romances in the *Canterbury Tales* conforms to the definition of gift exchange, not commodity exchange.

As I noted at the beginning of this chapter, Emily is the focus of exchange throughout the *Knight's Tale*. In the denouement, when Theseus intervenes again to arrange her marriage to Palamon, his explicit purpose is to establish social and political ties between Athens and Thebes:

> Thanne semed me ther was a parlement
> At Atthenes, upon certein pointz and caas;
> Among the whiche pointz yspoken was,
> To have with certein contrees alliaunce,
> And have fully of Thebans obeisaunce.
> For which this noble Theseus anon
> Leet senden after gentil Palamon,
> Unwist of hym what was the cause and why,

> But in his blake clothes sorwefully
> He cam at his comandement in hye.
> Tho sente Theseus for Emelye.   (I.2970–80)

People or objects exchanged in order to generate social relations are by definition gifts.

Theseus obscures this political impetus when he justifies his marrying of Emily to Palamon (significantly, without the expressed consent of either of them).[66] But even in doing so, he claims that the exchange enacted in the marriage is justified, and in fact necessitated, by a universal continuum that locates the human world of social relations with the natural and supernatural order – 'the faire cheyne of love' (I.2988). Theseus's terms are remarkably similar to those Strathern uses to define the goals and results of exchange between social groups, which she calls 'enchainment': 'Enchainment is a condition of all relations based on the gift. The inevitability of enchainment reveals a continuity between kin-based relationships and those of ceremonial exchange.'[67]

This is true of other Chaucerian romances as well. In the *Man of Law's Tale*, Custance is introduced in terms similar to a commodity, but the hallmark feature of her serial weddings is that they entail connections via exogamy between disparate social groups, marked most notably by differences of religion; this is the primary source of the antagonism of her mothers-in-law. Walter in the *Clerk's Tale* is in a position to purchase or to simply take Griselda, to treat her as a commodity. He insists, however, on asking Janicula to consent to be his father-in-law – 'If that thou vouche sauf, what so bityde, / Thy doghter wol I take, er that I wende, / As for my wyf, unto hir lyves ende' (IV.306–8) – and on asking Griselda if she will consent to the marriage as well. Griselda, whose abject poverty, obscurity and humility provide the tale with its core pathos, is personified in this exchange, in part because she takes on the public and agential role of marchioness, and also because accepting and entering into the marriage actualizes her subjective experience, which to this point has been glimpsed only in a partially suppressed desire to see Walter's new bride. True, Walter is doing all this only out of his desire to exercise complete and incontrovertible control of a wife's inner being. But in order to realize this perverse desire, he needs a wife with an activated will that he can dominate.

It should probably be reiterated that acknowledging the conditions of gift exchange in the treatment of women in these romances does not imply that the transactions are inherently good or fair. Powerful and self-serving men like Theseus and Walter – as well as less powerful but equally self-serving men like Jankyn – are not seeking fairness; rather, they are enacting what Strathern calls 'domination'. But domination can occur in any exchange, and the form it takes is different in the case of a gift exchange as opposed to a commercial exchange. As commodity exchange objectifies human relations, domination of such exchanges takes the form of acquiring material profit; as gift exchange uses people and things to generate social relations, domination in these exchanges take the form of the control of symbolic and social connections.[68]

It is in this context that the Wife of Bath makes her intervention into the 'poetics of the gift'. She generates 'irony and equivocation with regards to persons and relationships', in Kay's terms, in a ludic challenge to the masculine domination of 'the connections and dis-connections' created by gift exchange. She does this in her prologue, particularly in the portions relating to Jankyn, in which gifts and obli-gations, power and authority, and masculine and feminine roles are complexly enacted, inverted and reaffirmed. But she performs the strategy even more thoroughly in her tale, engaging the romance trad-ition to explore and test its conventions of exchange and gender. In Chaucerian romances like the *Knight's Tale*, women are exchanged like gifts. The Wife of Bath's choice to tell an Arthurian romance, but a comic one and to some extent a burlesque of the genre, seems intended to engage the inherent gift-logic of the genre and to subject it to the inversion and ironic play of gift-poetics.[69]

The Wife of Bath sets her tale, therefore, 'In th'olde dayes of Kyng Arthour / Of which that Britons speken greet honour' (III.857–8), and simultaneously in the epoch when 'The elf-queene, with hir joly com-paignye / Daunced ful ofte in many a grene mede' (III.860–1). She evokes a time of legendary patriarchal authority, which she endorses, but she also introduces an imagined matriarchal authority whose jollity and dance are the play that challenges received order. Equally important is that she sets the tale in the ancient past – 'manye hundred yeres ago' (III.863) – before, that is, the modernity of her own time, which would include modern political and legal structures, as well as the markets of the late Middle Ages. But she demarcates this earlier era with the arrival of friars – the intrusion of an all-male Christian priesthood pointing to conditions when even an imagined position of social authority becomes remote for women. We might recall Annette Weiner's observations on the potential disruptions to an indigenous gift economy:

> From the perspective of changing world systems, it is not simply Western colonialism and capitalism that destroys traditional modes of production nor is it Christianity that subverts these islanders' cosmological beliefs. Internal changes brought about by competing groups, such as chiefly rivals and the growing power of a priestly hierarchy, can change the technology or alter the meanings of inalienable possessions so that women's presence in political events is decreased and comes under the control of men.[70]

The Wife of Bath is setting her tale in the realm of the gift.

The initial act of the tale, however, is not an exchange at all. The knight's heedless rape of the maiden is recognized immediately by all the Britons as 'oppressioun' (III.889), and following the 'cours of lawe' (III.892) King Arthur condemns him to death. That 'the queene and other ladyes mo' (III.894) then petition Arthur to spare the knight's life has been a persistent problem for many readers, in part because it puts the women of the tale in the position of begging that a rapist be spared, but also because it reduplicates the motif from so many other romances in which women participate in the narrative almost exclusively by beseeching knights for mercy. This relegated feminine role delimits women's agency in the service of allowing men to show mercy to each other without compromising the masculine virtues of strength and justice. It occurs repeatedly in the *Knight's Tale*, for instance, including when Theseus discovers Palamon and Arcite illegally duelling in the grove and declares that they shall be killed:

> The queene anon, for verray wommanhede,
> Gan for to wepe, and so dide Emelye,
> And alle the ladyes in the compaignye ...
> And alle crieden, bothe lasse and moore,
> 'Have mercy, Lord, upon us wommen alle!'
> And on hir bare knees adoun they falle
> And wolde have kist his feet ther as he stood;
> Til at the laste aslaked was his mood,
> For pitee renneth soone in gentil herte.   (I.1748–50, 1756–61)

Where Emily cannot act to achieve any of her own desires, she can – and must – join with other women in begging that men, who think nothing of her aspirations, be spared to pursue their own.

But the scene at the start of the *Wife of Bath's Tale* is fundamentally different. The queen and her ladies do not beg Arthur for mercy. Rather, they ask that the knight be given to them. They 'preyeden the kyng of grace / Til he his lyf hym graunted in the place, / And yaf hym to the queene, al at hir wille, / To chese wheither she wolde hym save or spille' (III.895–8). Arthur makes a gift of the knight to the queen, and the queen 'thanketh the kyng with al hir myght' (III.899). In the Wife of Bath's romance, rather than being relegated to a static symbolic role that defines their gender, women participate in symbolic exchange that generates social roles.

It is particularly significant that in medieval romance, as in aboriginal gift cultures, the objects in exchange are often women. To Kay, the 'uncertain status of women contributes to a "poetics of the gift" in which political and ethical irony and ambiguity are generated and explored'.[71] In the poetic play of the *Wife of Bath's Tale*, a man is made the object of exchange. The transaction is enacted between a king and a queen, between a man and a woman, between the dictum of law and a generalized conception of matriarchal authority. A male body is proffered as a gift, and the conditions of the transaction determine the social standing of the transactors as well as the social meaning of the male body. The status of the donated man is indeterminate: knight; prisoner; condemned; saved; potential husband. But just as in Strathern's model the gender of an object, including the female body, is determined in exchange, so the knight's body is gendered female by its role in exchange between individuals and groups. The main point of the tale, in fact, is that the knight loses masculine authority and faces unfamiliar restrictions: 'He may nat do al as hym liketh' (III.914).

His exchange also gives him a kind of agency within the tale. He must determine the symbolic significance of his own status in exchange. The conditions set by the women of the court manifest Strathern's principle that the main function of gift transactions is the exchange of 'viewpoints'. To Strathern, the exchange of a woman in marriage is the exchange of the participants' views of what the woman represents in her social roles. The knight, passed around for a year among all the women of Britain, is a conduit of inter-subjective exchange. The women essentially use him to trade competing conceptions of female desire.

Eventually the knight makes a pact with the old woman to save his life. This, too, is a gift exchange. Unlike his rape of the maiden, which rendered her a lifeless commodity, his exchange with the old woman entails obligations on both parties, and results in a relationship. The generation and extension of relationships is the point of gift exchange, and it is the intention of the old woman, who only after saving the knight's life reveals that they are to be married, an obligation that the knight must respect despite his personal desires. The wedding scene undermines male desire and agency by mocking conventional masculine perspective, inverting it and juxtaposing it with female perspective. The groom is the one coerced into marriage, dreading the wedding night when he must fulfil the desires of a more authoritative body that he finds repulsive. When the knight complains that his bride is 'so loothly, and so oold also, / And therto comen of so lough a kynde' (III.1100–1), the old woman responds with a long speech that dwells almost entirely on her condition of being low-born. Her defence of the principle of virtue in deeds rather than birth provides the knight with a perspective that, like that of gender, he has been prevented by class privilege from ever recognizing.

The conclusion of the tale is another notorious critical crux. The old woman's granting of the knight's desires by transforming herself into a young, beautiful and faithful bride has been taken as an instance of wish-fulfilment: either of the knight's wishes for his own sexual satisfaction with a pliant wife, or the Wife of Bath's wishes to imagine herself eternally young and desirable, as she acquiesces to generalized male approval in the traditional expectations of women in marriage. But, alternatively, the climax can be seen as the culminating act in the series of gifts that makes up the tale. The old woman makes a gift of herself – her body, her volition – to establish an ongoing relationship with her husband, but as with all gift exchanges it entails obligations on both donor and recipient. The key is that the knight acknowledges his obligation. By receiving the gift he accepts inherent expectations of reciprocity and limitations on his future actions:

> 'My lady and my love, and wyf so deere,
> I put me in youre wise governance;
> Cheseth youreself which may be moost plesance
> And moost honour to yow and me also.
> I do no fors the wheither of the two,
> For as yow liketh, it suffiseth me.'   (III.1230–5)

That this happy marriage is not 'real' – that it is, if not wish-fulfilment, then a fantasy of more egalitarian social relations – does not falsify it, but rather marks it as the imaginative play entailed by the 'poetics of the gift'.

Romance is indeed rooted in the exchange of women. But in the romances in the *Canterbury Tales*, women are exchanged as gifts, not as commodities. Perhaps Bloch's distinction between the semiotic nature of commercial exchange as opposed to the symbolic nature of gift exchange is valid, but the exchange of symbols in gift exchange is still open to uncertainty and play. This ambiguity is particularly affected by the uncertain status of women as gifts. The Wife of Bath therefore tells an Arthurian romance to exploit this inherent ambiguity in the 'poetics of the gift', so as to challenge and critique the roles allocated to women in romance and in society as a whole, to challenge masculine authority and to imagine greater agency for women and more equitable value in marriage.

SACRED COMMERCE:

Clerics, Money and the Economy of Salvation

The language of commerce permeates the *Canterbury Tales*, and its presence is particularly pronounced in the tales and portraits of clerical figures. But as Linda Georgianna has shown, this is due to the fact that metaphors and idioms of market exchange were part of the Christian mythos since its earliest centuries; concepts as fundamental as 'redemption' are at heart commercial. But, Georgianna cautions, this is not to say that Christian salvation is equivalent to market exchange or an extension of commercial values. Although, Georgianna says, 'Pauline distinctions between commercial and spiritual exchanges were often lost on the early church fathers',[1] theologians in the later Middle Ages were cautious to avoid direct analogies between commodity exchange and the achievement of salvation. Chaucer also deliberately distinguishes between a theological metaphor of purchase and price and the potentially corrupting realities of the market economy. 'Chaucer is fully aware of the possibility of confusion inherent in atonement theory and practice', Georgianna writes. 'Unlike many of his critics, however, Chaucer never confuses a corruptible idea with a corrupt one.'[2]

Georgianna intends these distinctions between theological metaphor and commercial practice as a corrective to critical tendencies, particularly in historicist readings, to see Chaucer as either fully embracing a commercial ethos or criticizing the Church itself for its commercial values. But even she acknowledges that the ecclesiastical principles maintaining the purely metaphorical nature of its own commercial idioms were often unstable.

To some, the clerical habit of using commercial language while simultaneously insisting on the Church's fundamentally non-economic nature is the most essential and telling element of ecclesiastical ideology. In a sub-chapter of 'The Economy of Symbolic Goods' headed 'The Laughter of the Bishops', Pierre Bourdieu observes,

> I have been very struck by the fact that each time the bishops used the language of objectification in relation to the economy of the Church, speaking for example, of a 'phenomenon of supply and demand' to describe the pastoral, they would laugh. (An example: 'We are not societies, uh … quite like the others: we produce nothing, and we sell nothing [laughter], right?' – Chancery of the Paris diocese.) Or, at other moments, they invented extraordinary euphemisms. This leads one to think that one is witnessing not a cynical lie, as a Voltairean reading would have it, but rather a gap between the objective truth, repressed rather than ignored, and the lived truth of practices, and that this lived truth, which hides, through agents themselves, the truth brought to light by analysis, is part of the truth of practices in their complete definition. The truth of the religious enterprise is that of having two truths: economic truth and religious truth, which denies the former.[3]

To Bourdieu, while the Catholic Church is 'an enterprise with an economic dimension founded on the denial of economy', it is also 'immersed in a universe where, with the generalization of monetary exchanges, the search for the maximization of profit has become the basis of most ordinary practices, such that every agent – religious or nonreligious – tends to evaluate in money, at least implicitly, the value of his or her work or time in monetary terms'.[4]

Chaucer's Cambridge clerks John and Aleyn are economistic calculators of equivalence – not despite their clerical training and ecclesiastical vocation, but because of it. Chaucer suggests that Church philosophers, who are presumed to seek eternal truths distinct from the contingencies of secular materialism, are more involved than anyone in transactional, utilitarian, economistic reasoning. This line of critique is not limited to the *Reeve's Tale*; it is central to the ecclesiastical satire that runs throughout the *Canterbury Tales*. Chaucer's notoriously unholy representatives of the Church are often taken to be sinners who fall short of the ideals of their orders or of the Church in general. Alternately, they are taken to embody the failure of the clergy as a whole to live up to its own ideals. More accurately, though, they should be seen as embodying the ideals themselves, which, to some degree unconsciously and to some degree intentionally, have been compromised to accommodate the ideology of the marketplace, and as a result have come themselves to be commercial. Greed, materialism, exploitation and profit calculation are no longer failings of the ideals of the Church, but rather have become expressions of them.

In previous chapters, I have tried to show the limitations of Pierre Bourdieu's social theory in attempting to explain the panoply of human motivations and actions in the *Canterbury Tales*. While Bourdieu's totalizing 'theory of practice', by naturalizing economic mentalities and assuming the self-interest of the marketplace to be a universal and transhistorical fact, obscures the persistent reality of alternative forms of social valuation, it is nonetheless indispensable for describing the undeniably real calculations of material and symbolic profit that go on in all contexts. It is particularly useful in revealing the calculation present in 'anti-economic sub-universes', and one of the most prominent of these is the universe of the Church. Chaucer's satires of religious figures offer a general critique of the ecclesiastical economy in the *Canterbury Tales*, and of its reliance on what Bourdieu calls 'the economy of the offering'. In the humour of these satires, we can hear the laughter of the bishops, who deny their economic reality while also embodying it.

I. The unexpected gift: the *Summoner's Tale* and the spirit of money

For some time now, it has been common among Chaucer scholars to assume that we understand the *Summoner's Tale*. In an influential pair of articles in the late 1960s, John Fleming demonstrated 'how Chaucer incorporates traditional antimendicant materials into his most extended satire of the friars', and revealed the friar of the *Summoner's Tale* as 'a kind of "stage friar" who sums up everything that is wrong with the mendicant orders from a fourteenth-century English secular point of view'.[5] As such, the friar embodies the perversion of Francis's apostolic ideals, in his extravagant lechery, his brazen hypocrisy, the theological sophistry of his self-serving 'glosyng', and, centrally to the *Summoner's Tale*, his avarice.

Such exegesis has saved the tale from being dismissed as merely a scurrilous joke, but it has never resulted in greater critical popularity. As Fleming noted in 1983, 'Even a quick survey of criticism of the *Summoner's Tale* reveals its two salient characteristics, paucity and excellence', and to a considerable extent the same remains true today.[6] While interest in their arch-rivals on the other end of the ideological spectrum, the Lollards, has skyrocketed, interest in the friars, about whom Chaucer has vastly more to say, remains stagnant.

Chaucer's *Summoner's Tale* has to some extent been the victim of its explicators' success. That is, criticism has so thoroughly elucidated the symbolic and theological framework of Franciscan ideals and antifraternal invective in the *Canterbury Tales* that the Friar's portrait and the *Summoner's Prologue and Tale* have come to seem completely interpreted and understood, lacking therefore the ambiguity and polyvalence in which literary criticism traffics – in a word, over-determined. The friar of the *Summoner's Tale* grasps at an imagined money bag, and receives an enormous fart. The ancient and widespread equivalence of money to excremental filth, the metonymic use of money as the essence of matter and the opposite of spirit, is here so manifest that it seems hardly to merit critical comment.

Also over recent decades, however, scholarly analysis has demonstrated that money is not a simple thing, and is never reducible to mere material. Money – in theory and in practice, in early Franciscan literature, in fourteenth-century philosophy and in the *Summoner's Tale* in particular – is complex and ambivalent. Most important, far from being grossly material, money is abstract; it is an object of study that rewards sincere contemplation with ever more advanced understanding of the social and natural worlds.

It comes as no surprise that the filthy lucre friars ostensibly reject figures prominently in antifraternal literature like the *Summoner's Tale*. But the representation of money is often just as integral to the writings of the Franciscan intellectual tradition, even works advancing the ideal of religious poverty. A prime example is *Sacrum commercium sancti Francisci cum domina Paupertate*, a brief but beautiful, sophisticated and artful work of Franciscan literature: Fleming has described it as 'perhaps the single most brilliant example of the simple but lapidary allegory which was to become a major mode of spiritual writing in the later Middle Ages'.[7] The authorship and the date of the work are subjects of debate, though the most recent scholarship places it in the late 1230s, a little more than a decade after Francis's death.[8] It would then pre-date the most virulent period of polemics against fraternal materialism and hypocrisy and reactionary counterattacks in defence of absolute poverty, centred in Paris in the mid-thirteenth century. Clearly, though, the *Sacrum commercium* is intended to reaffirm, in the aftermath of the founder's death, the centrality of poverty to Franciscan spirituality. Nonetheless, in articulating these ideals it conspicuously and intentionally invokes commercial and mercantile images and vocabulary.

As its title suggests, the *Sacrum commercium* tells how Francis searches out Lady Poverty in the mountainous wilderness where she lives. In the subsequent dialogue, Lady Poverty explains her history and leads Francis and his brethren to true spiritual enlightenment. At a crucial moment early in the text, Francis exhorts his companions to join him in climbing the mountain of the Lord to find Lady Poverty. 'Mirabilis est, fratres, desponsatio Paupertatis,' he cries to them.[9] 'The espousal of Poverty, brothers, is wonderful.' In six of the eight early manuscripts of the work, however, the word Francis uses here is not *desponsatio*, 'espousal', but rather *dispensatio*, 'dispensation' or 'management'.[10] Francis seems to exclaim that the business of Poverty is wonderful. Francis continues, 'Nullus est qui e regione clamare audeat, nullus qui se nobis opponat, nullus est qui iure hoc salutare commercium prohibere valeat' (p. 137). 'There is no one of our region who would dare to cry out, no one who would oppose us, no one who would be able to prohibit by law this salvific exchange' (p. 533). The word 'commercium' is used here for the only time in the work except in the title. The 'salvific exchange' it refers to is obviously in context a verbal exchange with Lady Poverty, but the word seems deliberately to have been chosen to evoke commercial exchange. Modern translators tend to render the title of the work as the *Sacred Exchange* ... or the *Sacred Covenant between St. Francis and Lady Poverty*, and the various potential connotations of 'commercium' make these valid interpretations. But the most literal translation is equally valid: *Sacred Commerce*. In fact, one fourteenth-century reference gives it the title *Commercium Paupertatis*, or *The Business of Poverty*.[11]

There is, naturally, an element of deliberate inversion in such evocations of commerce. The *sacred* commerce of religious poverty is contrasted to the *profane* commerce of the marketplace, just as in the magnificent climax of the *Sacrum commercium* Lady Poverty and the friars partake of a banquet of poverty. They ceremoniously dine on crusts of barley bread, wild herbs and cold water, after which they are 'exsaturati ... magis ex tante inopie gloria quam essent rerum omnium abundantia' (p. 173) – 'satisfied more by the glory of such want than by an abundance of all things' (p. 552). But this passage depends for its effect on the genuine allure of the true feast, and similarly the work's commercial references depend on the allure of the marketplace and the world of business and money.

Lester Little has shown that the mendicant orders arose from the urbanized, monetized, market-oriented economy of Mediterranean Europe in the twelfth and thirteenth centuries. Francis and his followers were products of Europe's urban centres and their commercial culture. This explains the friars' reaction against the wealth and materialism of the life of the city, but it also informs their theology and their rhetoric. Little notes the friars' 'frequent use of a monetary vocabulary, a practice that gained authority and impetus from that one-time cloth merchant, Francis of Assisi'.[12] More significant are the contributions of scholastic friars in the thirteenth century, including Aquinas, to the moral and intellectual justification of the profit economy and incipient capitalism. Fraternal scholars were naturally interested in questions of profit and usury, but given their mostly urban origins, they also had some understanding of commercial practices and the practical uses of money, and they 'formulated an ethic that justified the principal activities of the dominant groups in urban society'.[13] They took great care in delineating improper practices of, for instance, money-lending and charging fees for intellectual services, but as a result they also identified proper commercial practices. 'The friars, and a few of their contemporaries who were not friars,' Little writes,

> by building on intellectual developments already under way in the schools of the late twelfth century, began to consider the problems of private property, fair prices, money, professional fees, commercial profits, business partnerships, and moneylending. In each case they came up with generally favourable, approving views, in sharp contrast to the attitudes that had prevailed for six or seven centuries right up to the previous generation.[14]

Similarly, Giacomo Todeschini, an even more prolific historian of the subject, says of philosophers like Peter John Olivi and his late thirteenth-century contemporaries,

> These Franciscan masters ... were not able to admit that money, as an inanimate object, was technically sterile. Although the Christian tradition had repeated it over time and the thirteenth-century Latin translation of Aristotle's writings had reaffirmed the concept of the sterility of money, the Franciscan notion of wealth made legitimate, institutionally valid enrichment a concrete manifestation of the human ability to appreciate and exchange the relative value of things.[15]

More broadly, Todeschini asserts that 'the Franciscans' approach to the market reveals that it was the most rigorous Christian religiosity that formed a large part of the vocabulary in western economics, that the

Christian world was never extraneous from the market ... nor was there a clear separation between morality and business'.[16]

In short, it would be much too simplistic, and in many cases entirely opposite to the truth, to characterize Franciscan thought – even in its ideal and theoretical form, as opposed to the local realities or the hyperbolical caricatures of its critics – as reviling money as filth. It may seem that the *Summoner's Tale* does just that, and does so in graphic terms. This constitutes the most conventional way of reading the *Summoner's Tale*: in aspiring for material reward rather than spiritual poverty, the Friar gets what he seeks in the 'unexpected gift'. Money is thus cast as the opposite of spirit and the essence of matter: excrement. In fact, this idea can be found in Franciscan literature as well. Foundational Franciscan texts like the *Early Rule* emphasize that money in general is to be considered *turpe lucrum* – 'filthy lucre'.[17] The *Sacrum commercium* praises 'qui, terrenis omnibus renuntians, omnia velut stercora reputat' (p. 130) – 'those who renounce the things of the earth and consider them all as dung' (p. 529). As Fleming has noted, the *Sacrum commercium* 'is built phrase by phrase with biblical words'.[18] In this case, the words are St Paul's: 'propter quem omnia detrimentum feci, et arbitror ut stercora' (Phil. 3:8) – 'for whom I have suffered the loss of all things, and count but as dung' (Douay-Rheims). But the association of money with excrement can just as easily be found in Freud; it may be as ancient and as widespread as the dualist cast of Western thought itself, though anthropologists have identified it in non-Western cultures as well.[19] A text like the *Summoner's Tale*, therefore, seems to rely for its ironic effect on the opposition of material and spiritual values, of God and Mammon.

I would maintain, however, that both the *Sacrum commercium* and the *Summoner's Tale*, rather than preserving an absolute dichotomy between money and spirituality, analogize the two. Because the fact is that money is not excrement. Gold or wealth or possessions may be conceived as excrement, but even to such a rigorously dualistic moral perspective money is not, because money is not material. I make this flat assertion despite the fact that no one really knows what money is, and even the philosophers who have considered it in greatest depth end up admitting their perplexity in terms very much like those Augustine used when describing time: we are in money, but we know not what money is.[20] But one thing money definitely is not is essentially material. Money, in the Aristotelian conception, is what intercedes so that people do not have to exchange one material directly for another material. There was, theoretically, a time when money had inherent value that allowed it to be traded for a variety of commercial commodities. But, despite elaborate fictions that societies for ages have maintained to make it seem otherwise, money long ago became a mere symbol of relative value rather than an object with inherent value of its own. Significantly, one of the most crucial steps in this process occurred, as Lester Little has shown, in Italy in the twelfth and thirteenth centuries – in the world of St Francis. In the preceding centuries, the economy of medieval society had moved from one in which wealth was hoarded or displayed as ornament to one in which wealth was circulated and used for transactions – the use of money, as Little says, 'as tool instead of as treasure'.[21] But while vast amounts of precious metal were minted into coins and entered circulation in economies throughout Europe, the value of a coin was still determined by its weight and metal content. The innovation of the late twelfth and early thirteenth centuries was the issuance of a great variety of new coins whose values were not intrinsic but were instead set and assured by the city-state or principality that issued them.[22] Other more complex developments soon followed. As money circulated beyond its realm of issuance, its value fluctuated in relation to other currencies. Unlinked from the physical possession of material objects, money could be deposited, borrowed and held on account, laying the groundwork for the rise of banking. Money could be transferred from one account in one city to another account in another city, where its value might in fact be greater in relation to the local currency – the basis for the monetary transaction in the *Shipman's Tale*. As Little notes,

> Banking thus served the new economy in still another way by creating fiduciary money. Such money was never minted by

governments, but on the basis of public confidence in the institutions that said it existed and had value, it was just as useful as if it had been minted.[23]

One can imagine a merchant of the time – perhaps a cloth merchant of a newly wealthy commercial centre in the Apennines – exclaiming, 'The dispensation of money is a wonderful thing!'

All these monetary advancements represent the incremental, but quite accelerated, abstraction of money. Little cites an observation of Max Weber: 'Money is the most abstract and "impersonal" element that exists in personal life.'[24] In Italy at the turn of the thirteenth century, money was transmuted from the material into the insubstantial. This made possible an almost unprecedented accumulation of material wealth among urban dwellers, which is precisely what the early mendicants reviled. But the money itself was a sophisticated philosophical abstraction. The *Sacrum commercium* denigrates wealth, but it also invokes the vocabulary and the concepts of the commercial economy, in order to accrue to poverty – which is really a simple topic and a ubiquitous condition – the abstract and very potent qualities inherent in the operation of money. Lady Poverty, in her sacredness, is the opposite of wealth, but she is simultaneously analogous to money. It is therefore significant that the 'unexpected gift' that Thomas gives the friar in Chaucer's *Summoner's Tale* is not material excrement – a turd. The fart that the friar receives instead is the ideal metonym for money, not because it is material, but on the contrary, because it is insubstantial.[25]

This is not to deny that the *Summoner's Tale* is an antifraternal satire. It quite patently is an epitome of the genre.[26] If, however, we take the object of its satire to be the friar's materialism or his avarice or even his essentially economic imagination, we miss the greater part of its purpose. Chaucer's real target is that arch-vice of the friars in the view of their critics – hypocrisy. The friar stands as the culmination of the entire intellectual project of mendicancy, which seeks to obscure and deny its own economic foundation.

The beleaguered invalid of the tale, 'doubting' Thomas, is often credited for his scepticism and for his robust and ingenious rejection of the friar's importunity, as if he 'sees through' the hypocrisy of the greedy and literal-minded friar. When he manages to get a word in edgewise to the voluble friar, however, Thomas's own thinking is revealed to be remarkably commercial and materialist:

> 'As help me Crist, as I in fewe yeres,
> Have spent upon diverse manere freres
> Ful many a pound; yet fare I never the bet.
> Certayn, my good have I almoost biset.
> Farwel, my gold, for it is al ago!'　　　　　(III.1949–53)

What Thomas doubts is not the value of paid prayer for the deliverance of his soul, but rather the friar's promise of better health in return for his money. This Thomas is as literalistic as his Gospel namesake.

The friar has encouraged this perspective in Thomas by claiming that he and his brothers have been praying unstintingly for Thomas's recovery: 'In our chapitre praye we day and nyght / To Crist, that he thee sende heele and myght / Thy body for to weelden hastily' (III.1945–7). In response to Thomas's complaint, the friar explains that his donations have been too piecemeal to have been institutionally effective – that is, he brazenly asserts, Thomas just has not given enough money to any one friar.

Both Thomas and the friar are breaking the rules of the game. They are violating what Pierre Bourdieu calls 'the taboo of making things explicit'.[27] They are cutting corners in the process by which economic capital is converted into symbolic capital, the process that Bourdieu labels 'euphemization', the elaborate social performances that we all unconsciously engage in, which have the function of disguising the economic bases of social transactions. Examples of this process of obfuscation can be found in any of the rituals surrounding religious donations. These are offered with expectations of compensation, whether in immediate benefit or in more dilated and abstracted terms, but elaborate practices are always developed in order to make the donation seem less like a purchase or commercial exchange. Instead, the donation is euphemized as pure self-sacrifice, and the object of the

gift figured as transcending negotiation. Thus, the recipient of a religious offering – say, a mendicant friar receiving a gift from a penitent
after confession – benefits materially from the transaction, and benefits
symbolically from maintaining the pretence that he is not interested in
any material gain and completely separate from the monetary economy.
Bourdieu terms this 'the economy of the offering'. But he also borrows
from Jacques Gernet a more evocative name for it: 'sacred commerce'.[28]

The butt of the satire of the *Summoner's Tale* is not merely the
friar's avarice. Rather, the prime object is his self-serving role in
obfuscating this 'sacred commerce'. As the tale progresses, his self-
righteousness becomes increasingly extravagant in equal measure to
his ever more desperate greed. As his hypocrisy becomes hilariously
obvious, euphemization of the 'economy of the offering' breaks down
entirely, and Thomas climactically presents him with the unexpected
donation that epitomizes the hidden truth of the enterprise.

Chaucer's friar, therefore, is not precisely ridiculed for his fascination with money as such. The greater fact, borne out throughout the
Canterbury Tales, is that Chaucer himself is fascinated by money and
its operation to a degree equalled by few other authors. Indeed, the
Summoner's Tale is as much about the fascinating qualities of money
as it is about the hypocritical desire for it. These qualities account for
the tale's seemingly desultory structure, which has so often confused
and frustrated readers.

While Thomas's 'unexpected gift' is the obvious climax of the tale,
after this point fully a quarter of the tale remains. This exceptionally
long *denouement* involves the friar's consternation at having to fulfil
Thomas's demand to divide his gift into equal twelfths. Ultimately,
the squire offers the inventive solution of using a wheel with a friar's
nose at the end of each spoke – a bizarre image that has been expli-
cated as a burlesque of the Pentecost.[29] In between, though, come
the odd and unexplained roles of an anonymous lord and lady, who
express, at curious length, shock and confusion at the friar's predica-
ment. The lord in particular seems to give the problem more attention
than it deserves. The friar 'was alwey confessour' (III.2164) to the lord,
but other than that there seems little reason for the lord to take this

preposterous problem seriously. Some readers, therefore, have taken the lord to be a participant in the satire, merely pretending to give the problem of division serious consideration in order to ridicule the friar publicly. The actual words of the lord, however, suggest that, to the contrary, he is genuinely frustrated by the problem presented by the division of flatulence:

> The lord sat stille as he were in a traunce,
> And in his herte he rolled up and doun,
> 'How hadde this cherl ymaginacioun
> To shewe swich a probleme to the frere?
> Nevere erst er now herde I of swich mateere.
> I trowe the devel putte it in his mynde.
> In ars-metrike shal ther no man fynde,
> Biforn this day, of swich a question.
> Who sholde make a demonstracion
> That every man sholde have yliche his part
> As of the soun or savour of a fart?
> O nyce, proude cherl, I shrewe his face!
> Lo, sires,' quod the lord, 'with harde grace!
> Who evere herde of swich a thyng er now?' (III.2216–29)

The lord continues in this vein for another thirteen lines beyond this point. The Riverside edition of the *Canterbury Tales* quoted here, like virtually all modern editions, places open-quotation marks at line 2218 and close-quotation marks at line 2242, the end of the lord's speech, so that the entire passage appears to be spoken aloud by the lord. But Chaucer prefaces the passage by telling us that at first the lord 'sat stille as he were in a traunce, / And *in his herte* he rolled up and doun.' This would seem to indicate that the first part of this passage represents the lord's internal monologue as he ponders the quandary of the division of the fart. Line 2228 – '"Lo, sires," quod the lord' – would then mark when the lord begins to speak aloud to the people assembled in his court. If this is the case, then the lord is not intentionally mocking the friar. Instead, ridiculous though it may seem, he is seriously considering a philosophical problem posed by Thomas's bequest. Specifically, he is contemplating a problem of divisibility and measurement, of how, as the friar says, 'To parte that wol nat departed be / To every man yliche' (III.2214–15). The immediate object of inquiry is Thomas's fart, but by extension it is a problem of money and economy, and it leads to profound speculations in natural philosophy, from arithmetic to acoustics.

The intellectual historian Joel Kaye has tried to construct a social context for a remarkable school of thought in the first half of the fourteenth century. The thinkers of this school are known today as the 'Oxford Calculators', or as the 'Merton School', since many of the most prominent members – including Thomas Bradwardine, William Heytesbury, John Dumbleton, Richard Swineshead and Walter Burley – were fellows of Merton College. These scholars, along with contemporaries at the University of Paris, engaged in a range of studies of measurement and quantification of a wide variety of social and natural phenomena.[30] Their work constitutes, according to John Murdoch, a 'near frenzy to measure everything imaginable'.[31] Yet there has never been a satisfactory explanation for the source of this development, nor any major claims for its intellectual legacy. Kaye seeks to provide both. The impetus for this 'measuring mania', he demonstrates, was money.

Scholars were already engaged in debates on Aristotelian theories of money, business and ethics, as well as problems of measurement of a physical universe they conceived as existing along series of continua not divisible into discrete units. Their practical experience with money in the commercial economy exposed them to a system that made equivalencies among widely disparate objects and ideas – commodities and products; time and effort; labour and expertise; scarcity and demand. Further, although the value measured by money clearly existed on a continuum, practical use of money broke values down into units. These units were often extremely small – standing for no circulating coins of real value – but they allowed for very exact and very flexible measurement. Kaye maintains that a particularly important quality of money for these fourteenth-century scholars was that, in its practical use, it was essentially abstract – the same quality that facilitated thirteenth-century commerce and engaged the imaginations of early Franciscans. By the early fourteenth century, 'money of account' was in common use in Western Europe. 'Money of account,' Kaye explains, 'functioned as an idealized monetary scale of artificially fixed ratios of named coins that were often no longer in circulation, against which the actual value of the coin in circulation was measured.'[32]

Despite little precedent for the formal study of economics as well as its dubious moral status, these schools of philosophers in Oxford and Paris produced treatises of considerable subtlety and complexity, which they then shared and debated. Most important, such economics inspired these scholars to analyse a range of phenomena and systems in the social and natural worlds, applying from economics methods of measurement with abstract but discrete units. 'Every "quality" capable of increase or decrease, whether physical or mental, came to be visualized as a divisible, continuous magnitude in the process of expansion or contraction,' Kaye explains. 'In Oxford and Paris, elaborate logical and mathematical languages were devised to describe and conceptually measure quantified qualities now conceived as divisible continua.'[33] This application of analytical measurement to the natural world, Kaye concludes, laid the foundation for the scientific advances of subsequent centuries.

Chaucer, of course, was no 'Oxford Calculator'. He did not attend university; he was a layman and a secular poet; he wrote in the second half of the fourteenth century. On the other hand, as J. A. W. Bennett has demonstrated, Chaucer was deeply familiar with contemporary Oxford – as an institution, as a cultural force, as a repository of knowledge and as a geographical location – and he had personal and intellectual associations specifically with Merton College. 'Philosophical' Ralph Strode was a Merton logician before becoming a London lawyer. Chaucer mentions Bradwardine alongside Boethius and Augustine in the *Nun's Priest's Tale* (VII.3241–2). This reference, granted, is in a jocose vein, but Bradwardine's influential mathematical analysis was developed as a gloss on Boethius's *Ars Metrica*, which Chaucer also alludes to in the 'ars-metrike' (III.2222) of the *Summoner's Tale*.[34] To Bennett, Chaucer's citations and references suggest that his learning resembled that of the most sophisticated of his contemporaries, and that it therefore reflects what was being read and taught at the time at Oxford, and would have been informed by Merton scholars.[35]

But even if Chaucer were not directly familiar with the mathematical and scientific analysis of the Merton School, the mechanism that Kaye posits for the initiation of economic thought among the earlier fourteenth-century scholastic philosophers applies thoroughly to Chaucer as well. Although university scholars were presumably removed from the world of the marketplace, these thinkers could not help being immersed in the thoroughly monetized society of the thirteenth and fourteenth centuries.[36] Kaye demonstrates the degree to which college and university administration, and its exigencies of accounting and commerce, dominated the careers of scholars like Nicole Oresme at Paris and Bradwardine at Merton.[37] Kaye concludes:

> As inhabitants of bustling cities and market towns; as account keepers, tax assessors, fee collectors, and treasurers within the university; as victuallers to their fellow students; as benefice holders and office seekers within religious and civic bureaucracies – scholars of the fourteenth century were required to experience, comprehend, and often accommodate their thinking to the insistent realities of money and market exchange ... Bureaucratic techniques developed to impose order on social life, and generally recognized as being successful in doing so, became part of the intellectual arsenal of the scholar seeking to find order in nature.[38]

It is hard to miss the parallels in this description to the professional career of Chaucer, who served the royal administration in roles very similar to those in the academic bureaucracy occupied by the scholars. While writing his poetry, Chaucer served in a series of bureaucratic positions involving bookkeeping and purchasing, from custom-keeper for the port of London to Clerk of the King's Works. Indeed, the eagle of the *House of Fame* claims that Chaucer's two kinds of labour are hardly distinguishable:

> For when thy labour doon al ys,
> And hast mad alle thy rekenynges,
> In stede of reste and newe thynges
> Thou goost hom to thy hous anoon,
> And, also domb as any stoon,
> Thou sittest at another book
> Tyl fully daswed ys thy look. (652–8)

This passage prefaces the lengthy disquisition on acoustics.[39] This is one of the many occasions in Chaucer's poetry when he demonstrates his interest in science, technology and the measurement of natural phenomena. Another conspicuous instance is the *Treatise on the Astrolabe*. (Bennett notes that Merton was in Chaucer's time a significant centre for the study of astronomy in general and of the astrolabe in particular.)[40]

Just as evident in Chaucer's work as his interest in science and measurement is his fascination with the world of money and commerce, and economic transactions both everyday and abstruse, as for instance in the *Shipman's Tale*. In the *Summoner's Tale*, these two interests merge. When Thomas complains that all his gold has not purchased him better health, the friar responds that this is a problem of division:

> Youre maladye is for we han to lyte.
> A, yif that covent half a quarter otes!
> A, yif that covent foure and twenty grotes!
> A, yif that frere a peny, and lat hym go!
> Nay, nay, Thomas, it may no thyng be so!
> What is a ferthyng worth parted in twelve? (III.1962–7)

That last line, of course, contains a pun, and a brilliant foreshadowing of the conclusion, in which the friar will have to part a 'farting' in twelve. It is also an example of the tale's attention to the divisibility of money. There is an obvious, literal answer to the friar's rhetorical question: a farthing parted in twelve is one forty-eighth of a penny. The friar is perfectly aware of this, not only because the farthing – a quarter of a penny – was a common unit for small, local commercial exchanges, but also because this kind of monetary division, real and imagined, is something the friar would do every day, as part of his communal life. Note that the friar imagines Thomas giving another convent 'foure and twenty grotes' (III.1964). He reflexively imagines monetary donations in amounts easily divisible among a convent of twelve friars. When the friar is offered a gift of what he imagines to be money on the condition that he divide it evenly into twelfths, he readily agrees: 'Lo, heer my feith; in me shal be no lak' (III.2139).

When the friar asks, 'What is a farthyng worth parted in twelve?' what he means, of course, is that such a small donation is of too little value to merit his consideration. He is therefore so focused on material wealth that any potential problem of abstract division is not of philosophical interest to him. The obligation to divide the fart into twelfths infuriates him as an insult and as an impossible abstraction. Not so the lord. He falls into a 'traunce' (III.2216) as he contemplates the 'ymaginacioun' (III.2218) that invented such a problem: 'In ars-metrike shal ther no man fynde, / Biforn this day, of swich a question' (III.2222–3). 'Ars-metrike' is another of Chaucer's rich puns, but it also encapsulates the method of the tale. Thomas's challenge is simultaneously scatological, economical, arithmetical and physical – a thought experiment of arse-measuring.

Thus, the problem of dividing a fart among the twelve friars is, like economics, a social phenomenon involving equal dispensation: 'That every man sholde have yliche his part' (III.2225). In recognizing this, the lord realizes that the problem is one of physics and acoustics, requiring the division of 'the soun or savour of a fart' (III.2226). But like money, the fart seems to be pure abstraction, the echoing of empty air: 'The rumblynge of a fart, and every soun, / Nis but of eir reverberacioun' (III.2233–4). As such, its changes seem to occur along an endless and indivisible continuum that defies measurement: 'And evere it wasteth litel and litel awey. / Ther is no man kan deemen, by my fey, / If that it were departed equally' (III.2235–7). The nature of the task Thomas has set the friar challenges the lord's understanding of the physical universe, which is not at all naive, but rather quintessentially Aristotelian. In this conventional model, Kaye explains, 'quantities were composed of parts and were divisible. Qualities, though admitting of variation in degree, were not in themselves composed of parts and therefore not divisible, either conceptually or actually.'[41] The lord therefore dismisses Thomas's challenge a priori as 'an inpossible; it may nat be' (III.2231). So unorthodox a philosophical challenge leads the lord to characterize Thomas as a 'demonyak' (III.2240).

The answer provided by the squire is indeed a burlesque of the Pentecost and a profane insult of the friar. At the same time, though, it intentionally mimics the equal distribution of wealth among a cell of friars. Further, as the squire emphasizes, it is an empirical demonstration of the divisibility into equal measure of intangible qualities and physical phenomena:

> 'And ye shul seen, up peril of my lyf,
> By preeve which that is demonstratif,
> That equally the soun of it wol wende,
> And eke the stynk, unto the spokes ende.'   (III.2271–4)

This demonstration is persuasive. In the end, Thomas is praised as a man of brilliant insight, and the squire whose clerical philosophizing he has inspired is hailed as a new genius of empirical observation and scientific measurement:

> The lord, the lady, and ech man, save the frere,
> Seyde that Jankyn spak, in this matere,
> As wel as Euclide [dide] or Ptholomee.
> Touchynge the cherl, they seyde, subtiltee
> And heigh wit made hym speken as he spak;
> He nys no fool, ne no demonyak.   (III.2287–92)

All of this is undeniably satirical and comical. But what is the object of the satire? Not primarily, I believe, the proto-science of the lord's and the squire's responses. The friar is humiliated through his reception of the sound and stink of a fart and for the image of his providing the same in equal measure to his brethren. But the tale's complex economics and natural philosophy stand in opposition to the friar's shallow fixation on material wealth and his hypocritical commitment to conventional social euphemisms that obscure the economic nature of his vocation. The other characters in the tale, objectively regarded, are just as important, and to them the observation of economic processes reveals a world of comprehensible social and natural systems.

Flatulence is indeed a metonym for money in the tale, but as such it is not the opposite of spirituality but in some essential regards analogous to it. Wealth is the friar's object of misplaced desire, but money, and the wonder of its dispensation, is something that, like spirituality, he ultimately fails to grasp.

II. The Pardoner's intentions

The close correspondences between monetary transactions and human interactions in the *Pardoner's Prologue and Tale*, like those in the *Shipman's* and *Summoner's Tales*, can seem simplistic and over-determined. The rioters seek Death, and find money; in finding money, they destroy their lives and their souls. The Pardoner himself provides the obvious and unavoidable moral: *Radix malorum est Cupiditas*. And one of the most commonplace critical glosses on the texts asserts that the Pardoner corrupts the spiritual and material economies.

But the actual functioning of money and economy in the prologue and tale is much too complex to be so simply or moralistically stated, and much of the complexity derives from the Pardoner's own emphasis on intention. The Pardoner and his performance as a whole foreground questions of intention: is it possible, as the Pardoner insists, for an immoral man to tell a moral tale? Is the tale's value ultimately corrupted by the teller's foul intentions? But the intention that the Pardoner is most interested in is his own intention to win profit – it is, he says again and again, his sole motivation:

> Of avarice and of swich cursednesse
> Is al my prechyng, for to make hem free
> To yeven hir pens, and namely unto me.

For myn entente is nat but for to wynne,
And nothyng for correccioun of synne.
I rekke nevere, whan that they been beryed,
Though that hir soules goon a-blakeberyed!
For certes, many a predicacioun
Comth ofte tyme of yvel entencioun ...   (VI.400–8)

What is most striking in this passage is that the Pardoner is not insisting that he does not care if his victims' souls go to hell; rather, he is insisting that he does not care if their souls go to heaven. Why is the Pardoner so adamant that, while his preaching may cause his listeners to free themselves from their avarice and become open-handed, speeding their progress toward salvation, this is not his intention? Coming from the Pardoner, that most honest of hypocrites, the problem may be philosophical and rhetorical. Or the answer may lie in the inexhaustibly fascinating realm of this character's psychology, and perhaps, as has been most thoroughly examined in recent decades, in his sexual identity. But I would propose that we take this passage as a sincere expression of astonishment at the workings of his moral and material world. The Pardoner here is articulating a genuine sense of wonder that, despite his own corruption and avarice, he is able to make people generous in a way that improves their souls. His intention to profit, then, is sufficient to secure his own profit, and it does not interfere with the goals of others to be saved – in fact, in some manner that the Pardoner cannot explain but can only marvel at, the transactions that pass between the Pardoner and his gullible audience somehow facilitate the achievement of the desires of both parties.

Intention is integral to scholastic economic principles. Medieval philosophy inherited ancient Christian antipathies toward money and profit, but scholastic philosophy also inherited Aristotelian economic thought, which contains notorious self-contradictions. Essentially, it recognizes the value of money as a means for facilitating exchange, but it takes an ethical position against money as an end of accumulation. This was expressed most clearly in usury analysis. From the twelfth century on, based on scriptural authority, the taking of interest on a loan was expressly forbidden by papal decree.[42] This flat prohibition, however, led to a vast number of complications and juridical questions when applied to the practice of an already complex mercantile economy. By the thirteenth century, the most common answer to these problems was to apply a test of intention: did one party intend inequality in the transaction?[43] Pure commercial transactions – exchanges or purchases – were generally less vexed morally than were loans. But philosophers and canonists were still engaged in a process of accommodation – not just of commerce to Christian morality but of Aristotelian ethics to Aristotelian economics. There was anxiety, for instance, about the *superabundantia* that seemed magically to accrue when a merchant bought a commodity at one price and sold it at a higher price. Invoking Aristotle's view that 'human need', which could be equated to demand, was the most natural measure of value, scholastics linked 'just price' to market value. But market value was conceived not as a numerical equivalent arrived at through the technological functioning of a monetized market, but rather as a kind of consensus of informed actors. To seek a profit too much above market price was immoral and illegal, and to enforce this standard merchants could be polled to deduce the proper market price.[44] Furthermore, when they intersected, as they often did, usury analysis trumped market value. It was, for instance, illegal to sell for credit at above market price. And in all such cases, it was the test of intention that was most often applied. As Kaye notes, 'The new emphasis on *intentio*, where guilt was assessed in the internal forum of conscience, allowed clerical theorists to continue to assert an absolute ideal of arithmetic equality, even as the complexity of commercial transactions made such an equality increasingly difficult either to define or to enforce.'[45] Or, as R. Howard Bloch has written, 'As in the areas of sin, penance, and criminal responsibility, intention became the basis of business ethics.'[46]

This context helps to reveal the significance of the economic thought of the fourteenth-century schools of Oxford and Paris. As Kaye demonstrates, they observed that money, operating technologically in a market context, functions efficiently to assign relative values to any object or concept when the data inputs are individual desires, regardless of external morality. A notion was emerging, Kaye says, 'of a market that functioned and ordered itself according to its own principles rather than in conformance to normative expectations or requirements'.[47] The Pardoner is making a similar observation when he insists on his selfish intentions:

> But shortly myn entente I wol devyse:
> I preche of no thyng but for coveityse.
> Therfore my theme is yet, and evere was,
> *Radix malorum est Cupiditas.*
> Thus kan I preche agayn that same vice
> Which that I use, and that is avarice.
> But though myself be gilty in that synne,
> Yet kan I maken oother folk to twynne
> From avarice and soore to repente.
> But that is nat my principal entente;
> I preche nothyng but for coveitise.
> Of this mateere it oghte ynogh suffise. (VI.423–434)

To say that the Pardoner's greed corrupts the material economy is to miss the Pardoner's own point, which is that 'coveityse' *is* the material economy. In market economies, *everyone's* 'entente is nat but for to wynne', but the internal logic of the technological form of money in exchange mediates conflicting desires to generate, ideally, roughly equivalent values.

We are, moreover, in danger of missing Chaucer's point if we dismiss the Pardoner's economic philosophy as the self-justifying musings of a crook. The Pardoner here is very close to Gordon Gecko, insisting that 'Greed, for lack of a better word, is good.' But the power of that character, the only lastingly memorable part of Oliver Stone's *Wall Street*, is that his honesty about his intentions lays bare the hypocrisy of a system that denies that it is based entirely on selfish pursuit of individual gain. That film represents a moment in the mid-1980s when neo-liberalism boldly asserted its ascendancy and declared to the world that unbridled free-market economics was the single greatest force for good in world history. As Kaye notes, the fourteenth-century conception of money as a continuum and a technological system extends from this point to Ludwig von Mises's *Theory of Money and Credit*, a foundational text of economic neo-liberalism.[48] At the risk of hyperbole as extravagant as Oliver Stone's, I believe that Chaucer's Pardoner is an early advocate of this tradition. He rejects as irrelevant the *internum forum*, the internal forum of conscience, that was the focus of scholastic ethics. Like a classical economist, he insists that the only intention that matters, the only intention that is even intelligible, is material self-interest – 'greed, for lack of a better word'.

What, then, of the corruption of the spiritual economy? Here, too, the Pardoner insists that he is not a corrupt exception to a moral order but rather an exemplar of a functioning economic system.

A. J. Minnis has shown that churchmen defending pardons were at pains to distinguish the dispensation of pardons from the sale of commodities and from the actual commercial economy, and to use language to mark this matrix of salvation off from a market system. Minnis concludes that the Pardoner is not representative of the indulgence system, but a corrupt exception to it. The Pardoner, Minnis says,

has made a market of the divine mercy, thus realizing some of the schoolmen's worst fears. I cannot believe that the poet is offering any excuses for such behaviour. At this moment on the road to Canterbury, the spiritual economy is in the ascendant, being allowed its full value and ultimate power.[49]

Bourdieu would encourage us to ask, however, whether the 'schoolmen's worst fears' were not just the corruption of the 'spiritual' and 'material' economies, but also that the spiritual economy might be revealed to be an actual economy. Was it one? On the matter of pardons, R. N. Swanson, in his magisterial study of the topic, is unequivocal: 'Indulgence distribution clearly functioned along lines which can be considered proto-capitalist: a perceived need was being exploited – perhaps even created – for financial gain, with clear marketing strategies and profit motivation.'[50] The protestations of the churchmen that the indulgence economy is not really an economy and should never have anything to do with the material economy is precisely what Bourdieu is referring to as 'the laughter of the bishops'.

One of the clearest manifestations of this phenomenon is what Bourdieu calls the 'economy of the offering', in which 'exchange is transfigured into self-sacrifice to a sort of transcendental entity'.[51] Theologians recognized the economic nature of their enterprise, but responded by denying that nature or by euphemizing it as fundamentally non-economic or anti-economic. In fact the system of granting pardons does function as an economy. It is an economy in which religious donation is transfigured through religious mystification into spiritual capital. It is simultaneously a highly developed and highly lucrative component of the material economy, employing the resources of capital production and the methods of the market to garner wealth for the Church. Most important, it accrues a symbolic profit, absolutely essential to its operation, by denying that it is a part of any economic system at all.

The 'economy of the offering' equally describes the Pardoner's modus operandi. As he declares to us, he pursues his own economic advantage by persuading his listeners to do what is against their own economic interest, generally by transfiguring these donations into self-sacrifice to a transcendental entity. They are still transactions, since the donors expect something for their offerings, particularly the speeding of their souls through Purgatory. Of course, from his own examples it is clear that such transfiguration is not always necessary. Sometimes a less euphemized and more explicit transaction is allowable, since the donor, inspired by his or her own self-interest, desires something less transcendental, like a fertile field, or a prosperous hand, or simply the symbolic profit of appearing generous. So, despite the frequent assertions that the Pardoner corrupts the spiritual and material economies, in fact the opposite is true. He embodies the spiritual and material economies, which are in fact inseparable.

Chaucer is obviously not sympathetic to the Pardoner, at least not to his motivations or actions, and he certainly does not endorse the Pardoner's economic vision. The Pardoner is still, as Kittredge said, 'the one lost soul of the pilgrimage', the summa of corruption and depravity. That his conception of the workings of the market economy are insightful and to some degree empirically accurate is not an exculpation of the Pardoner but rather an indictment of the market. A proper understanding of the Pardoner and his economic views in the late medieval context works against the tendency to exclude his exploitative self-interest as the vice-ridden exception to 'normal' economic behaviour. Equally, it precludes excusing his greed as an exceptional corruption of ecclesiastical economy of salvation. His viciousness makes unavoidable the underlying fact that the Church is part of the market economy, and that the Church's own 'economy of salvation' functions as a market economy, and that the market economy is essentially a social expression of individual, competitive self-maximization.

Nor does Chaucer offer an alternative economic model to the technological workings of the market. We have to wait for Marx to supply a fully formed critique of capitalist economic valuation, demonstrating how the market promotes false value by obscuring the production value of commodities, extracting surplus wealth from producers, and fetishizing the commodity at the point of exchange. But Chaucer nonetheless provides a critique of false values.

The imagination of classical economics assumes that the pursuit of individual profit is the state of nature and the rational and inevitable motivation of *homo economicus*. In recent years, some critics have seen this as Chaucer's position as well; they see Chaucer as endorsing or abetting the rise of capitalism and the bourgeois subject by dramatizing the inevitability, ubiquity and universality of individual self-maximization in a market context. In fact, though, the *Pardoner's Tale* devolves into conflict and chaos. The Host's intervention and rejection of the Pardoner, unprecedented elsewhere in the *Canterbury Tales*, has been taken, with justification, as an expression of personal antipathy toward the Pardoner, his physical nature and his embodiment of sexual ambiguity. But the Host's angry rejection is also aimed at the Pardoner's values, or rather at his oleaginous invitation to enter into a false value system. Ultimately, Chaucer insists that even in a monetized world, individuals, like the Host, remain moral agents, capable of rejecting the 'technological form of money in exchange' when they sense that it is being exploited to create false equivalencies. So the most significant effect of technology on social relations in the fourteenth century, for Chaucer, is its limitation: individuals retain moral and ethical agency, even in a socially technologized world.

In the *Summoner's Tale*, the ultimate object of satire is not the religious figures' greed or even the failure of the representatives of the Church to live up to clerical ideals, but rather it is their refusal to recognize that those ideals have themselves become utilitarian and economistic. The Pardoner, an honest hypocrite, acknowledges, shamelessly, that the Church's economy of salvation mirrors the commercial economy of the secular world. In fact, he recognizes them as the same economy, and marvels at the expansive prospects of increased profit that the fast-evolving systems of exchange seem to promise. The Pardoner sees, as his fellows the friar and the priest might if they were less deluded by their vanity and greed, that the imagination of the Church, by first accommodating and then justifying the commercial economy, is also merging with it, and that the economy of salvation is becoming indistinguishable from the world of the market. This insight is the heart of Chaucer's anticlerical satire as a whole.

6

'FY ON A THOUSAND POUND!'

Debt and the Possibility of Generosity
in the Franklin's Tale

I. Chaucer, Derrida, and the gift (Yes, there is one)

Having begun my discussion of the gift in the *Canterbury Tales* with the portrait of the Franklin in the General Prologue, I conclude now with the *Franklin's Tale*. The delay has been strategic: of the tales told on Chaucer's pilgrimage, the Franklin's may be the one that most explicitly and extensively dramatizes the gift. It is, the Franklin tells us, a Breton lay – a short romance, usually focusing on a crisis in the course of a love affair. In the *Franklin's Tale*, the crisis arises from a series of promises, exchanges and gifts. Unlike many Breton lays, including most of the famous examples by Marie de France, the *Franklin's Tale*, upon arriving at crisis, resolves itself in a cascade of seemingly self-less donations. And it concludes with the Franklin's famous *demande* ending, in which he asks the Canterbury pilgrims, and the reader, to weigh and evaluate the generosity of the characters: 'Lordynges, this question, thanne, wol I aske now, / Which was the mooste fre, as thynketh yow?' (V.1621–2)

This, in addition to the characterization of the Franklin himself, who is considered in his country to be the embodiment of St Julian, the patron saint of hospitality, means that discussions of the gift in Chaucer invariably lead to the *Franklin's Tale*. But a common critical reaction to the tale – one that seems to have become even more prominent in recent years – has been to conclude that there is no real generosity in the tale, and no actual gifts.

D. W. Robertson argued that none of the characters could be truly generous because none gives anything that truly belongs to them, and they are motivated not by generosity but by earthly desire, the very structures of courtly love itself being, to Robertson, merely expressions of cupidity and physical passion. Robertson saw the tale as Chaucer's ironic depiction of the mentality of the Franklin, who is in reality an embodiment of bourgeois materialism, an Epicurean whose ostentatious generosity is meant to obscure the class anxiety of a grasping social climber: '[W]hat the Franklin actually wants is a marriage which avoids the image of the sacrament ... The fact that the Franklin desires such an arrangement is consistent with his class outlook and his Epicureanism, and these factors also account for the "modernity" of his views.'[1] In his time – primarily the 1960s – Robertson converted only a minority of Chaucerians to his views, but that, to him, was further proof of their validity.[2] He fashioned himself in opposition to the New Criticism, and if his contemporaries were inclined to see true generosity in the Franklin or his tale, it was because they were bourgeois materialists, too. 'Chaucer', Robertson complained, 'had no way of knowing that the spiritual descendants of the Franklin would one day rule the world.'[3]

Yet Robertson's concerns were perhaps misplaced. Many critics over the years have doubted the sincerity of the Franklin's final question because they have questioned whether any of the characters in the tale are truly generous. Some of the most recent analyses of the *Franklin's Tale* have gone further by asserting, following Jacques Derrida, that there is no true generosity in the tale because generosity is itself impossible.

Derrida grounds his gift theory in a critique of Mauss and in an absolute opposition of gifts and the economic. Economic exchange is defined by reciprocity; the gift must be the opposite: 'For there to be a gift, there must be no reciprocity, return, exchange, countergift, or debt.'[4] For a gift to be truly generous, then, it would have to be purely altruistic and purely voluntaristic – given with no obligation, and with no expectation of reciprocation. It would have to be entirely 'beyond calculation'. But, Derrida shows, these are temporal impossibilities. Every gift actually reciprocates a gift already given in the past, and every giver necessarily anticipates reciprocation in the future. The gift cycle is therefore predicated on a hopeless quest for forgetting past and future obligations. Derrida declares,

> As the condition for the gift to be given, this forgetting must be radical not only on the part of the donee but first of all, if one can say here first of all, on the part of the donor. It is also on the part of the donor 'subject' that the gift not only must not be repayed but must not be kept in memory, retained as symbol of a sacrifice, as symbolic in general. For the symbol immediately engages one in restitution. To tell the truth, the gift must not even appear or signify, consciously or unconsciously, *as* gift for the donors, whether individual or collective subjects.[5]

Going by this definition, the gift would seem to be under erasure. The gift – '*if there is any*', in Derrida's repeated formulation – cannot be removed from a cycle of reciprocity, and that reciprocity is, to Derrida, the antithesis of the gift. 'It is perhaps in this sense that the gift is the impossible,' Derrida writes. 'Not impossible but *the* impossible. The very figure of the impossible.'[6]

Derrida's gift theory, like so much of his philosophy, has been enormously influential throughout criticism, and it has informed Chaucer studies, as for instance in Britton Harwood's article on the *Squire's* and *Franklin's Tales*, which advertises its Derrideanism in its title: 'Chaucer and the Gift (If There Is Any)'. In Harwood's reading, in these two tales, which together comprise the Fifth Fragment of the *Canterbury Tales*, Chaucer tries 'to erase unproductive expenditure … by safely framing and containing it by economy and exchange'.[7] Analogizing Cambyuskan's feast in the *Squire's Tale* to potlatch – he is 'like a Kwakiutl chief on his own scale'[8] – Harwood argues that the feast 'economizes itself' and that 'Genghis's immense expenditures almost immediately appear not as the effluents of self-subsistence, but rather as calculating and productive, differing only in scale from, say, the outlays of the merchant in the *Shipman's Tale* on his wife's clothing.'[9] The other gifts in the *Squire's Tale* are equally 'calculating and productive'. Harwood goes on to show that in each of the exchanges in the *Franklin's Tale* both parties simultaneously respond to previous donations and anticipate reciprocity, so that there are in the tale no gifts and no generosity. For instance, vows, like the ones that Arveragus and Dorigen base their marriage on, cannot be gifts, because vows are exchanged: 'No matter the content of vows the very exchange of them … returning one given word for another, falls under the sign of the gift.' And in the gestures that conclude the tale there is only a 'competition of non-gifts'.[10]

The Derridean critique of the gift employed by Harwood has been taken up and advanced by Kyle Mahowald. Noting the response of the friar in the *Summoner's Tale* to Thomas's command that the fart be divided into twelve portions – 'It is an inpossible; it may nat be' (III.2231) – Mahowald argues that in that tale 'the impossibility of the fart serves as an analogue for the impossibility of the friar's obtaining money as a gift in exchange for heavenly rewards', and furthermore that the tale 'raises a broader question as to the possibility of the gift in general'.[11] Proceeding to the *Franklin's Tale*, Mahowald finds that a tale that seems to be about gifts contains no gifts at all: 'More extensive analysis of *The Franklin's Tale* reveals that Chaucer sees economic exchange pervading even the most seemingly legitimate generosity.'[12]

Harwood, like Robertson, concludes that the Franklin's *demande* at the end of the tale is a non-question with no legitimate answer:

> The closure that seems to claim a neatness inspiring the question, 'Which was the mooste fre?' in fact comprises three incommensurable and nongenerous acts and leaves the reader unsatisfied. The unsatisfactoriness is the fragment's own suggested response to its having evoked unproductive expenditure only to tame and displace it.[13]

Mahowald concurs: 'Because of these contradictions that undermine all the tale's gifts, the Franklin's final question as to "which was the mooste fre" rings hollow.'[14]

I would posit as a rule that when exegetical and Derridean readings converge, it may to be time to re-evaluate our hermeneutic assumptions. In this case, I believe that literary criticism runs a risk when it relies so heavily on one philosopher's interpretation of a social phenomenon like the gift. Among sociologists and anthropologists, as well as some philosophers, there is considerable resistance to Derrida's gift theory.[15] Pierre Bourdieu objected to it out of disciplinary difference, but also on grounds of abstraction and impracticality:

> The purely speculative and typically scholastic question of whether generosity and disinterestedness are possible should give way to the political question of the means that have to be implemented in order to create universes in which, as in gift economies, people have an interest in disinterestedness and generosity, or, rather, are durably disposed to respect these universally respected forms of respect for the universal.[16]

But the underlying problem with Derrida's theory of the gift, what makes its value questionable when applied to literature, lies not in its practicality, but in its definition. Here is Mauss's declaration of his subject in the first paragraph of *The Gift*, following immediately on his epigraph from the *Edda*: 'In Scandinavian civilization, and in a good number of others, exchanges and contracts take place in the form of presents; in theory, these are voluntary, in reality they are given and reciprocated obligatorily.'[17] And here, on the other hand, is Derrida's definition of the gift at the start of *Given Time*: 'For there to be a gift, there must be no reciprocity, return, exchange, countergift, or debt … For there to be a gift, *it is necessary* [*il faut*] that the donee not give back, amortize, reimburse, acquit himself, enter into a contract, and that he never have contracted a debt.'[18] If Mauss defines the gift as entailing obligation and reciprocity, why does Derrida insist that it is self-evidently, axiomatically necessary that the gift be entirely voluntary and selfless, that it have no intention or expectation of reciprocation or even consciousness of the possibility, that it exist entirely outside exchange? And why would Derrida presume to have deconstructed Mauss's essay, and to have revealed the aporia of the gift, by demonstrating the inevitability of reciprocity, when Mauss says from the outset that reciprocity is a defining feature of the gift?

The answer lies in what Mauss and Derrida each think is entailed by reciprocity, exchange and economy. Derrida's assumptions are in evidence in a much-noted passage near the beginning of *Given Time*:

> Now the gift, *if there is any*, would no doubt be related to economy. One cannot treat the gift, this goes without saying, without treating this relation to economy, even to the money economy. But is not the gift, if there is any, also that which interrupts economy? That which, in suspending economic calculation, no longer gives rise to exchange? That which opens the circle so as to defy reciprocity or symmetry, the common measure, and so as to turn aside the return in view of the no-return? If there is gift, the *given* of the gift … must not come back to the giving (let us not already say to the subject, to the donor). It must not circulate, it must not be exchanged, it must not in any case be exhausted, as a gift, by the process of exchange, by the movement of circulation of the circle in the form of return to the point of departure. If the figure of the circle is essential to economics, the gift must remain *aneconomic*.[19]

Gifts are exchanged, and Derrida takes it as self-evident ('no doubt … this goes without saying') that exchange is economic, and that the economy of any exchange is homogenous 'even to the money economy'.

What does not seem evident to Derrida is that there might be different categories of exchange, and that there might be substantive differences between a gift economy and a market economy. In a market context, all participants are assumed to be individual agents calculating and trading for maximum individual profit. So Derrida further assumes that a gift exchange, like any exchange, is motivated by the value of the return. Derrida recognizes that Mauss imagines the gift to disrupt the market economy.[20] Thus Derrida can only figure Mauss's ideal of the gift as the opposite of his (Derrida's) definition of exchange, that is, as completely un-self-interested – voluntary, unmotivated, altruistic.

Despite Bourdieu's criticism of Derrida's approach to the gift, they share this limited vision of the potential modes of exchange. Their responses to Mauss are in both cases marked by the assumption of homology between gift and commodity, as has been observed and succinctly expressed by the political philosopher Camil Ungureanu:

> Derrida shares with Bourdieu a focus on the ambiguity of gift, albeit they interpret it differently. Bourdieu's economic interpretation implausibly reduces the ambiguity of gift to interest maximization, and inconsistently aims to enhance solidarity by the institutionalization of collective hypocrisy. In turn, by interpreting gratuity as pure unconditionality, Derrida dramatizes the ambiguity of gift, and turns it into 'maddening' paradox and an impossible possibility.[21]

Derrida, like Bourdieu, failed to take note in his analysis of gift the work of neo-Maussian sociologists and anthropologists in their long-standing effort to establish a substantive distinction between gift and commodity. A common point among the neo-Maussians is that the reception of *The Gift* over the decades has been hampered by a misunderstanding of Mauss's core political intentions. Such misimpression is particularly evident in Derrida's insistence on the gift's inherent and essential altruism and voluntarism. Neither of these terms is generally recognized even as a universal category by most contemporary anthropological theorists. They are, rather, generally seen as Eurocentric concepts, which presuppose a market economy to which any act not determined by individual economic self-interest is anomalous. Altruism is seen not as the opposite of market relations but as a fantasy invented by commercial society to normalize market relations, by making the commercial transaction and the contract the natural conditions of human association, and altruism as the impossible and idealized exception that proves the rule. But this is a false binary, and according to anthropologists Chris Hann and Keith Hart, 'Mauss wrote his essay to refute the bourgeois opposition of commercial self-interest to the altruism of the gift.'[22] Or as Graeber says, the obligation to return gifts

> cannot be explained *either* by the market ideology of self-interest
> or by its complement, selfless altruism … Mauss emphasized that
> our accustomed sharp division between freedom and obligation
> is, like that between interest and generosity, largely an illusion
> thrown up by the market, whose anonymity makes it possible
> to ignore the fact that we rely on other people for just about
> everything.[23]

An inescapable cycle of indebtedness, the very condition that to Derrida signals the aporia of the gift, binds people together in permanent relationships. Commercial transactions, on the other hand, are defined by the establishment of equivalent values; no indebtedness results from them, and so no relationship extends beyond their culmination. 'Equivalence represents the death of the gift,' write Alain Caillé and Jacques Godbout. 'It is a way to "put to an end" the chain of the gift, to strip it of that tension which is its dynamic. By the same token, the absence of equilibrium spells the end of a mercantile relationship.'[24] The Baudelaire story that is the touchstone of Derrida's book and lends it its subtitle, 'Counterfeit Money', involves first a purchase at a tobacco shop, and then a donation of a coin to a beggar. Part of Derrida's point is that both transactions are economic. He's right: they are. But from the anthropological perspective, neither is a gift: Baudelaire's friend does not expect to have any further relations with either the tobacconist or the beggar.

A similar contrast in interpretation to that of altruism underlies the other central concept in Derrida's analysis: time. Time is necessary to the gift, Derrida says, because there must be a term when the participants forget, or try to forget, or act as if they forget the obligation to reciprocate: 'As the condition for a gift to be given, this forgetting must be radical not only on the part of the donee but first of all, if one can say here first of all, on the part of the donor.'[25] But 'in time', there must be reciprocation. The 'temporalization' of the gift is just its 'temporization', an enforced time gap before the exchange is completed by countergift. And this proves to Derrida that the gift is simply exchange, and therefore simply economic, and effort to render it otherwise is temporary and ultimately impossible:

> The identity between gift and exchange would not be immediate and analytical. It would have in effect the form of an *a priori* synthesis: a synthesis because it requires temporization and *a priori* – in other words necessary – because it is required at the outset by *the thing itself*, namely by the very object of the gift, by the force or the virtue that would be inherent to it. Here is, it seems the most interesting idea, the great guiding thread of *The Gift*: For those who participate in the experience of the gift and countergift, the requirement of restitution 'at term,' at the delayed 'due date,' the requirement of the circulatory difference *is inscribed in the thing itself* that is given or exchanged.[26]

Again, though, Derrida recognizes no distinction between modes of exchange. If the gift enters into exchange, then it is economic, and thus no gift at all. In contrast, here is how Mauss talks about the importance of time to the gift:

> [I]n every possible form of society it is in the nature of a gift to impose an obligatory time limit. By their very definition, a meal shared in common, a distribution of *kava*, or a talisman that one takes away, cannot be reciprocated immediately. Time is needed in order to perform any counter-service. The notion of a time limit is thus logically involved when there is question of returning visits, contracting marriages and alliances, establishing peace, attending games or regulated combats, celebrating alternative festivals, rending ritual services of honour, or 'displaying reciprocal respect' – all the things that are exchanged at the same time as other things that become increasingly numerous and valuable, as these societies become richer.[27]

Mauss says nothing here about an existentially necessary and simultaneously impossible requirement to forget the donation. He emphasizes instead value – that time is a particularly essential component of exchanges that are held important and that increase in value through exchange. Contemporary economic anthropologists explain that the importance of the caesura between the gift and the reciprocation is that it temporally extends the obligation to return, and therefore the social bond that is the purpose of the exchange in the first place. Mauss also stresses in this passage that this is true of the gift in 'every possible form of society'. The logic of this is borne out when we manage to note elements of donation and dilation not just in Melanesian feasts but in our own everyday practices. If I have lunch with a friend, and she picks up the check, I know that I owe her a lunch. My knowing this does not negate the gift; on the contrary, because I know it, I feel obligated to get the check next time we have lunch, which means that I feel obligated to have lunch with her again, and *that* is the purpose of the gift: to extend obligation into the future in order to generate and sustain relationships. Time is indeed essential: if it were not, then I could just pay my friend cash for my part of the check as soon as she hands the waiter her credit card. But *that* would negate the gift. In this sense, forgetting is part of the gift, but so is remembering: if I do not remember my obligation, that would also negate the gift. Finally, if the reciprocation were as 'economic' as Derrida insists, then I would have to insist that my friend and I revisit the same restaurant and order exactly the same meal – I would have to seek, as in economic exchange, equivalence. But that is the last thing I would do, because gift exchange is different from commercial exchange in that it does not seek but rather eschews equivalence. It seeks disparity, it requires inequality, so that the accounts are never balanced and obligation always persists into the future, as does the sociality that it generates – one of us is always going to be obligated to buy the other person a lunch.

So it is true that time is the condition of the gift. Time lets the gift be the gift. And some would say that Derrida, in insisting on the impossibility of the gift, is not declaring the inexistence of the gift, but rather illuminating the complex existential position required to sustain it.[28]

Caillé and Godbout note that 'the third term in the famous Maussian trilogy, "to give, to receive, to reciprocate," cannot exist' – in the sense that the gift can never be fully and perfectly reciprocated, or it ceases to exist. But, unlike Derrida, they also note that the circular exchange of the gift is different from the circle of commodity exchange:

> It is a strange, essentially paradoxical circle. It is not an economic circle, even if it constantly approaches the economic, even if it's shot through in varying degrees with considerations of self-interest, prestige, and so on that can't fail to have their effect on the donor – for she's no fool and she knows perfectly well that the gift pays off. But she can't let that be the primary motive.[29]

All this is to say that the real problem in the application of Derrida to Chaucer comes when the critic claims that it demonstrates the impossibility of the gift, as when Mahowald says of the *Franklin's Tale* that 'even a tale purportedly *about* "gentilesse" and "being fre" negates the gift'.[30] An assertion like that leads me to give vent to a *cri de coeur* – not my own *cri*, though it is close to my own *coeur*, but David Graeber's:

> In the Anglophone world, the MAUSS group has been almost entirely ignored. Those who like to think of themselves as engaged in cutting-edge critical theory have instead come to read Mauss through Jacques Derrida, who in *Donner le Temps* examined Mauss['s] concept of the gift to discover – surprise! – that gifts, being acts of pure disinterested generosity, are logically impossible. I suppose this is what one would have to conclude, if one believed that there is something called 'Western discourse,' and that it is incapable of referring to anything other than itself. But even those of us who believe that anthropology is, in fact, possible often seem to miss the point that Mauss was not dealing primarily with discourses but with moral principles that he felt were to some extent embodied in the practice, if not the high theory, of *all* societies.[31]

In this spirit, I will claim that the *Franklin's Tale* is very much about 'being fre', and far from negating the gift, it substantiates and affirms it. What the tale brings forth in order to negate is debt, and that is something related to the gift but quite distinct from it.

II. The perversion of a promise

The Franklin's Tale is among Chaucer's tales that are most often read through the lens of the 'dramatic principle'. Since the Franklin has so commonly been seen as middle class, his tale has frequently been interpreted as betraying a conflicting set of values. A chivalric romance told by a wealthy commoner, it is seen to contain aristocratic values within a bourgeois perspective. So, for instance, Robert R. Edwards finds that 'the repeated insistence on *trouthe* in the *Franklin's Tale* grows out of the blurred boundary between aristocratic and mercantile worlds, of the capacity of one system to be translated by the language of another'.[32]

The *Franklin's Tale* does invoke a number of different types of ideals, and from the start it seems designed to dramatize their possibly inevitable conflicts. Arveragus articulates several of them at the beginning of the tale, when Dorigen accepts his marriage proposal:

> And for to lede the moore in blisse hir lyves,
> Of his free wyl he swoor hire as a knyght
> That nevere in al his lyf he, day ne nyght,
> Ne sholde upon hym take no maistrie
> Agayn hir wyl, ne kithe hire jalousie,
> But hire obeye, and folwe hir wyl in al,
> As any lovere to his lady shal,
> Save that the name of soveraynetee,
> That wolde he have for shame of his degree. (V.744–52)

Arveragus simultaneously commits himself to an ideal of egalitarian marriage (which some might link to a hardly universal notion that the goal of marriage is to live 'in blisse'), to courtly ideals of the duty of the lover to his lady (possibly hinting at his profound commitment later in the tale to the chivalric virtue of *trouthe*), and to aristocratic principles of rank and reputation. The subsequent events of the tale may suggest that one cannot consistently maintain all these ideals – or at least, that Arveragus cannot.

But I would suggest that in a broader sense, the central conflict in the *Franklin's Tale* is not between or among sets of values, but rather between modes of determining value. The ideals expressed by Arveragus, and other ideals that are introduced by other characters in the tale, do come into conflict, but they are all ideals – that is, they are conceived by their adherents to be beyond compromise, measurement or calculation. What strikes me as most difficult in the tale, therefore, is not the question of whether the characters live up to their ideals. Mostly, they are not able to, either because of their own fallibility, or because of inherent flaws in the ideals, or because of inevitable conflicts between and among the ideals. Instead, what seems most relevant is how a tale that begins with characters committed to ideals – principles to which individuals must devote themselves for reasons of honour and shame and symbolic obligation, and not for any economic motivation or calculation – arrives by its climax with most of those same characters locked in positions of contractual obligation and monetary debt. The question of the *Franklin's Tale*, in other words, is how debt emerges from non-economic systems of obligation. That is also the question that David Graeber asks in his magnum opus, *Debt: The First 5,000 Years*.

Given that debt is such a ubiquitous and powerful condition of modern society, it is not surprising that its origins are uncertain and that there are many theories to explain it. One especially familiar answer is provided by theories of natural law, in the Lockean tradition elaborated as the field of economics by Adam Smith. This would maintain that the necessity and propensity for economic exchange are inherent to the human condition, and that markets and money and therefore credit and debt were inevitable and desirable developments of civilization.[33] This is the bedrock principle of the ideology underlying global capitalism, economic neo-liberalism and political Libertarianism, despite the fact that almost no one who studies the problem in an informed and systematic way, except for a small portion of professional economists, believes it. Its inaccuracy and inutility are consistently demonstrated, as for instance by the *Franklin's Tale*, in which all the characters are motivated from the start not by any natural inclination to truck and barter but rather by incalculable ideals of symbolic value.

An alternative answer is provided by 'primordial debt theory'. This theory argues that debt is not a natural condition of humankind but a historical condition of the development of societies. Debt, it is maintained, grows out of the obligations that all members of society owe to all others. These obligations are deeply ancient, pre-dating the development of money and markets, and were originally expressed in the form of religious sacrifices, which were meant to represent the incalculable debt we owe to a universal creator on account of our very creation. Eventually, much later in the history of society, these obligations are assumed by the state, in the form of credit; this is the 'state-money theory' of economic history.[34] This theory has much to recommend it: for instance, as Graeber says, 'If the king has simply taken over guardianship of that primordial debt we all owe to society for having created us, this provides a very neat explanation for why the government feels it has the right to make us pay taxes. Taxes are just a measure of our debt to a society that made us.' But, he further notes, this kind of cosmic life-debt is absolute and incalculable; ritual sacrifices actually function only to acknowledge the impossibility of paying it back, except with one's death. So we are still left with the problem of 'how to turn a moral obligation into a specific sum of money'.[35]

In the course of his expansive book, Graeber endeavours to provide another explanation. It begins with the fact that societies are and always have been based on webs of obligation that are based in relationships. These cannot be precisely measured, but while one person owes another person they are in that other person's debt. Such debt is symbolic, however. It can be important – as important as life and death, in fact. But it is only a matter of honour or shame; no literal slavery or subjugation results from the perpetuation of the debt. When the reciprocation is made, it cannot be precisely calculated, but can only result in a new obligation to reciprocate in turn. The change comes when any of those individual obligations are monetized, assigned a specific amount that, however large or small, represents the total obligation in the relationship. When this happens, the debt is no longer in the abstract and symbolic realm of honour and shame. The obligation to pay can be encoded in law as contract obligation. Such contractual debt, since it is legal, can be enforced by the power of the state and the threat of punishment, rooted ultimately in the potential to exercise violence. In this condition, an unpaid debt results in inequality, servitude and even slavery.[36]

That is a thumbnail version of a global and transhistorical vision of the course of social relations. Graeber traces epochal changes in the understanding and the structure of debt and does not pin the transition from obligations to debt to any one period, but he does observe that '[i]t was really in the period of about 1400–1600 that everything came to be framed as debt, presumably reflecting the first stirrings of possessive individualism, and attempts to reconcile it to older moral paradigms'.[37] In this, Graeber is influenced by the historian Delloyd Guth, who has labelled the three centuries prior to the English Civil War as 'the Age of Debt'.[38] This is also the era, obviously, of the *Franklin's Tale*.

At the critical moment in the tale, Aurelius confesses his love to Dorigen, and she rebuffs him bluntly. 'Taak this for a fynal answere as of me' (V.987), she says. Then Chaucer adds,

> But after that in pley thus seyde she:
> 'Aurelie,' quod she, 'by heighe God above,
> Yet wolde I graunte yow to been youre love,
> Syn I yow se so pitously complayne.
> Looke what day that endelong Britayne
> Ye remoeve alle the rokkes, stoon by stoon,
> That they ne lette ship ne boot to goon –
> I seye, whan ye han maad the coost so clene
> Of rokkes that ther nys no stoon ysene,
> Thanne wol I love yow best of any man;
> Have heer my trouthe, in al that evere I kan.'   (V.988–98)

Dorigen ends her speech by telling Aurelius, 'Have heer my trouthe'. Is the concept of *trouthe* so binding that Dorigen is held to her promise even when it is explicit that she offered it 'in pleye'? If *trouthe* is a matter of obligations between people, a recognition that one must be good to one's word in order to retain the trust and respect of another, as opposed to some sort of magical formula that sets the speaker under transcendent obligation, then it would seem to matter if Aurelius understands that Dorigen means to make the suggestion in earnest or in game. It is significant, then, that when Aurelius shows her the Breton coastline apparently voided of rocks, he does not treat her vow as the 'pleye' in which it was intended, nor even as an oath of honour; he knows, after all, that he has fulfilled her request only with 'an apparence a clerk may make' (V.1157). He treats it, rather, as a contract, as an oath that takes on binding quality by the formula in which it is uttered. He forces her attention not just to the term *trouthe* but also to the fact that she said it. He repeats it several times, forcing her to acknowledge her utterance, almost as if she were under oath and he were examining her, and even citing legalistically the time and location of the original statement:

> For, madame, wel ye woot what ye han hight –
> Nat that I chalange any thyng of right
> Of yow, my sovereyn lady, but youre grace –
> But in a gardyn yond, at swich a place,
> Ye woot right wel that ye behighten me;
> And in myn hand youre trouthe plighten ye
> To love me best – God woot, ye seyde so,
> Al be that I unworthy am therto.   (V.1323–30)

In recalling Dorigen's precise words and holding them before her, Aurelius is treating her *trouthe* less like a virtue of keeping her word than like a statement she made under oath. He is treating it as contractual and legalistic.

In debunking the belief in the universality and naturalness of market relations, Marcel Mauss was also critiquing their twin, contractual relations. Instead, Mauss's essay offers a case for society being based fundamentally – in its origins and, though unrecognized, in all its continuing forms – on webs of exchange and obligation that are neither selfless and unmotivated nor commercial and contractual. 'Mauss's chief conclusion,' Hann and Hart write, 'was that the attempt to create a free market for private contracts is utopian and just as unrealizable as its antithesis, a collective based solely on altruism. Human institutions everywhere are founded on the unity of individual and society, freedom and obligation, self-interest and concern for others.'[39]

The agreement between Aurelius and the clerk is even more explicitly a contract for services. Although it is the first mention of money in the tale, and a rather incongruous intrusion of market pricing into a chivalric romance, the clerk broaches the topic with a conventional pretence that his initial price is non-negotiable: 'He made it straunge, and swoor, so God hym save, / Lass than a thousand pound he wolde nat have, / Ne gladly for that somme he wolde nat goon' (V.1223–5). But in response, Aurelius does not even acknowledge the potential for negotiation:

> Aurelius, with blisful herte anoon,
> Answerde thus: 'Fy on a thousand pound!
> This wyde world, which that men seye is round,
> I wolde it yeve, if I were lord of it.
> This bargayn is ful dryve, for we been knyt.
> Ye shal be payed trewely, by my trouthe!'   (V.1226–31)

Aurelius reacts to the clerk's price with the terms of romantic idealization. He dismisses the demanded amount as meaningless in comparison to the value of love, which is greater than the whole world. But at the same time, he declares that the 'bargayn' is settled and that he and the clerk are 'knyt' in their agreement. In accepting the price of a thousand pounds, Aurelius is fixing his obligation to the clerk at a precise and calculable money value. When Aurelius agrees, 'Ye shal be payed trewely, by my trouthe!' he is assuring the clerk of his creditworthiness. The concept of *trouthe* is fully subsumed into a context of contractual obligation.

Chaucer uses pounds as the currency of the debt, despite the tale's ostensible setting in ancient Armorica, and despite his tendency elsewhere to use monetary units specific to the setting. He also chooses an amount that is exorbitant but not unimaginable; by delivering to the clerk all the money in his coffer, 'The value of fyve hundred pound' (V.1573), Aurelius covers half of the obligation with his initial payment. It is a real debt that must be repaid, precisely, in full, and at term. And Aurelius must pay it whether he achieves his amatory goals with Dorigen or not. When he eventually faces the reality of this debt, he realizes that its real effect will be his bankruptcy: 'I se namoore but that I am fordo. / Myn heritage moot I nedes selle, / And been a beggere' (V.1562–4). He gives the clerk all the money he has and asks him to 'graunte hym dayes of the remenaunt' (V.1575) – an extension of time on the debt – so that he can arrange his affairs:

> Maister, I dar wel make avaunt,
> I failled never of my trouthe as yit.
> For sikerly my dette shal be quyt
> Towardes yow, howevere that I fare
> To goon a-begged in my kirtle bare.   (V.1576–80)

Although rank and degree are extremely important to the characters in the *Franklin's Tale*, when they make their exchanges and agreements they act as if the differences in rank between them are irrelevant. As Graeber maintains, the kinds of obligations generated in exchange can arise only between equals. It is the debt that puts the transactors into a state of inequality, presumably temporarily. Since people are always doing things for each other, there is always a period of time when one is indebted to another, and this is a source of inequality. 'Thus does mutual aid slip into inequality,' Graeber says. He adds, 'It seems to me that this agreement between equals to no longer be equal (at least for a time) is critically important. It is the very essence of what we call "debt".'[40] That is why an unpaid debt can be so shameful. 'During the time that the debt remains unpaid,' writes Graeber, 'the logic of hierarchy takes hold. There is no reciprocity … [D]ebtor and creditor confront each other like a peasant before a feudal lord.'[41] But this is all still in the context of honour-based obligations. In the context of monetized, contractual and legal debt, these obligations to return become enforced economic conditions. A person who cannot pay off his debt risks entering into a position of permanent servitude. This is debt in the modern sense. It is the origin of the true subject of Graeber's study, the global debt that oppresses large portions of the world's population, and that dictates that billions of the poorest people on earth are permanently indebted to a handful of the richest. 'The story of the origins of capitalism,' Graeber concludes,

> is not the story of the gradual destruction of traditional communities by the impersonal power of the market. It is, rather, the story of how an economy of credit was converted into an economy of interest; of the gradual transformation of moral networks by the intrusion of the impersonal – and often vindictive – power of the state.[42]

This, though it is submerged in a Breton lay and depicted in an inchoate form in the amatory misadventures of a hapless squire, is the position that Aurelius finds himself in. While still speaking in terms of 'trouthe' and thinking of the shame to his own status and to his family, he is compelled to commit his life to the repayment of a 'dette' incurred by a deceptive clerk and employed for his own disreputable purposes. It will place him in a position of poverty and beggary and permanent debt servitude, not for an abstract concept, but for a five hundred pound balance on an invoice for services rendered. This is how monetization turns obligations into systematic inequality and servility. 'What is a debt, anyway?' Graeber ultimately asks. 'A debt is just the perversion of a promise. It is a promise corrupted by both math and violence.'[43]

Transitively, the thousand pounds that Aurelius owes the clerk link all the obligations in the tale to a system of monetized debt. Not that all the debts are converted to contractual money payments – Arveragus will still insist that out of devotion to the abstract and absolute principle of truth Dorigen must go to her liaison with Aurelius. But the introduction of the monetized debt, which has been substituted for ideals just as abstract – love, service, devotion, desire – indicates that everything could be converted to this precise system of measure. Graeber has defined the global market economy as 'the single greatest and most monolithic system of measurement ever created, a totalizing system that would subordinate everything – every object, every piece of land, every human capacity or relationship – on the planet to a single standard of value'.[44] The *Franklin's Tale* begins with overlapping and conflicting patterns of honour-based ideals, ossifies them in contractual terms, and eventually homogenizes them in a system of measurable monetary values, calculated in pounds. In that sense, the *Franklin's Tale* is a fable of nascent globalization.

This is why it is so important to recognize the agency in the characters' concluding choices in the tale, and the validity of their generosity. Up to the fraught apparent climax of the tale, the relationships are fundamentally contractual. But then, in a series of spontaneous gestures, contracts are voided and debts are forgiven, reversing the course of the tale and allowing for a resolution that seemed impossible. When Dorigen tearfully meets Aurelius, he releases her from her obligation:

> Madame, seyth to youre lord Arveragus
> That sith I se his grete gentillesse
> To yow, and eek I se wel youre distresse,
> That him were levere han shame (and that were routhe)
> Than ye to me sholde breke thus youre trouthe,
> I have wel levere evere to suffre wo
> Than I departe the love bitwix yow two.
> I yow relesse, madame, into youre hond
> Quyt every serement and every bond
> That ye han maad to me as heerbiforn ...
> Thus kan a squier doon a gentil dede
> As wel as kan a knyght, withouten drede.   (V.1526–35, 1543–4)

Aurelius becomes aware of two types of superfluity – two elements of human motivation that exceed the demands of contractual debt. He notes, first, Dorigen's suffering, and secondly, the cost in honour to Arveragus himself in allowing her to meet him. And recognizing these excesses, he turns to terms of 'gentillesse' – which means gentility of birth, but also signifies, in almost all romantic contexts, virtuous action that would indicate a noble sensibility, regardless of blood or station of birth. The 'gentil dede' that the squire performs – an act of generosity open equally to all people – is a rejection of a contractarian relationship in favour of a more fundamental basis for human interaction.[45]

Next, when Aurelius tells the clerk of Arveragus's 'gentillesse' and the sorrows of Dorigen, as well as his own reciprocation and his own future suffering, both romantic and pecuniary, the clerk, continuing the domino effect of generosity, nullifies the contract and walks away:

> Leeve brother,
> Everich of yow dide gentilly til oother.
> Thou art a squier, and he is a knyght;
> But God forbede, for his blisful myght,
> But if a clerk koude doon a gentil dede
> As wel as any of yow, it is no drede!
> Sire, I releesse thee thy thousand pound,
> As thou right now were cropen out of the ground,
> Ne nevere er now ne haddest knowen me.
> For, sire, I wol nat taken a peny of thee
> For al my craft, ne noght for my travaille.
> Thou hast ypayed wel for my vitaille.
> It is ynough, and farewel, have good day!   (V.1607–19)

Those readers disinclined to see these actions as genuinely generous are likely to see the squire's and the clerk's assertions of equal 'gentillesse' to those of higher degree as evidence that their true motivations are one-upmanship – that this is simply competition in the symbolic field of charitability. That Aurelius frames his action in reaction to Arveragus's own acts of gentility and his knightly status, and that the clerk uses precisely the same terms to figure his release of Aurelius as a response to a knight's and a squire's actions, does certainly suggest that these gestures are profoundly agonistic. But there is no necessity to conclude, by way of Derrida, that they are not therefore gifts, nor, by way of Bourdieu, that their agonistic elements are their defining if not sole quality. When Aurelius says, 'Thus kan a squier doon a gentil dede / As wel as kan a knyght' (V.1543–4), and the clerk in turn says, 'But God forbede, for his blisful myght, / But if a clerk koude doon a gentil dede / As wel as any of yow' (V.1610–12), they are both certainly betraying their competitiveness, but they are also revealing that their individual acts are *not* spontaneous, un-self-motivated and gratuitous. They both fully acknowledge, and in fact emphasize, that their gestures are brought forth in a context of preceding gestures, that their generosity is made obligatory by the series of corresponding gestures that went before. According to Derrida, this infinite regress of obligation is an instance of *mise en abyme*, and the proof of the impossibility of the gift. To Graeber, and I think to Aurelius and to the clerk, this supposed aporia of the gift is in fact its precondition.

Aurelius and the clerk, furthermore, do not claim that their acts of generosity grant them superiority or power over other men or other ranks. They claim, rather, that their gestures give them access to equal status. In the terms set out by Graeber, these claims that clerks, squires or knights have equal access to a condition of 'gentillesse' through generous deeds are simply reassertions of the state of equality that is the precondition of all exchange that entails obligation. In both cases, Aurelius and the clerk are declaring that they are returning conditions to their original, debt-free state. The clerk further emphasizes that the voiding of the contract marks the complete severance of the relationship: it is, he says, as if they had never known each other, and never will again.

In some regards, that is the opposite of the purpose and function of the gift. But it is the hallmark of an equally important element of exchange: debt forgiveness. Graeber argues that one of capitalism's greatest successes has been to persuade us all that debt is sacrosanct, and that there is moral and even metaphysical necessity in fulfilling its obligations. In actuality, he shows, the cancellation of debt is deeply ingrained in the origins and history of civilization. In response to 'primordial debt theory', Graeber notes that when the early rulers of Mesopotamian city-states acted in the capacity of gods to affect the lives of their subjects, 'they did not do it by imposing public debts, but rather by canceling private ones'.[46] Debt amnesty persisted as a primary goal of political rebellions through millennia: 'Through most of history, when overt political conflict between classes did appear, it took the form of pleas for debt cancellation.'[47] Like Aurelius's and the clerk's claims of the equalizing capacities of generous donation possessed by individuals of different ranks, debt amnesties by their nature consist first of acknowledging the infinitely receding series of past obligations that have been allowed to ossify into legal, public debts and perpetual inequality, and secondly of returning relations to a prior state of equitability. It is important to note that forgetting has nothing to do with it; on the contrary, if preceding obligations were not remembered and acknowledged, then the slate could never be wiped clean.

Forgiveness of debt is not only a real gift, it is in some sense the realest gift, because it is an act of forgiveness. To Caillé and Godbout, 'Forgiveness is a fundamental gift, a gift of passage (as in 'rites of passage') from the system of violence to the gift system.'[48] If we do not always see the gift in forgiveness, it is, I think, because we do not always see the violence in debt.

What, then, is the answer to the Franklin's *demande*? Personally, I would accept an answer of 'none of the above'. Certainly, all the characters are deeply compromised morally. (All the male characters, anyway. I always maintain in my classes that Dorigen is conspicuously more generous and less compromised than any of the men – though I seldom manage to convince many of my students of this.) What I do not think is an acceptable response is to obviate the question entirely by saying that no generosity exists in the tale because no generosity can possibly exist in the tale. The generosity is as real and as present, and as possible, as any of the less savoury motivations the tale dramatizes. Critics have, in a Derridean way, been placing generosity under erasure in the *Franklin's Tale* based on a definition rooted in an idealized, perhaps intentionally impossible, selflessness. But the *fredom* that Chaucer offers, while based on obligation and reciprocity, is the opposite of a purely contractual relationship, in that the exchanges exist to engender and nurture relationships, instead of the other way around. It matches closely, therefore, with the alternative definitions of generosity being developed by our contemporary social theorists. When Graeber says that 'debt is only the perversion of a promise', he could be describing the plot of the *Franklin's Tale*, in which promises are perverted into contractual obligations, backed by legalism and the unyielding logic of the marketplace. When we deny the existence of true generosity in the tale, I fear we do so because we are now so much subsumed into the world Graeber describes – a world in which contract and debt have become so sacrosanct that any alternative is perceived as inconceivably unrealistic – that the squire's and clerk's simple acts of debt forgiveness and contract nullification are dismissed as fanciful or meaningless.

The better answer to the *demande*, though, might emerge from interpreting the Franklin's term 'fre' not as generosity but as 'freedom'. Barrie Ruth Strauss reminds us that the term 'franklin' means 'freed man', and that to be 'fre' also means 'to be free, at liberty, unbound'.[49] Similarly, Graeber argues that freedom itself is best understood in terms of generosity. He notes that in the ancient Near East it was a matter of course for a new king, on assuming power, to issue an amnesty on debt: 'In Sumeria, these were called "declarations of freedom" – and it is significant that the Sumerian word *amargi*, the first recorded word for 'freedom' in any known human language, literally means 'return to mother' – since this is what freed debt-peons were finally allowed to do.'[50] The origins are similar for the biblical Law of Jubilee, a regularly occurring 'Sabbath year' when debts were erased: '"Freedom" in the Bible, as in Mesopotamia, came to refer above all to release from the effects of debt.'[51] The freedom at stake here is not just that of the debtor, but also that of the debtee. After concluding that a debt is 'a promise corrupted by both math and violence', Graeber adds a last word: 'If freedom (real freedom) is the ability to make friends, then it is also, necessarily, the ability to make real promises.'[52] The Franklin, in his *demande*, may be asking not just who displays a free spirit, a propensity for liberality and generosity, but also who is most free *to be* generous – that is, which of the characters is most liberated to envision a way out of ostensibly inescapable social bonds of debt and repayment, and to envision and act on impulses that are more socially positive and productive. I don't have a specific answer to that question, either, but I know that it is a legitimate question.

CONCLUSION

The economic anthropology that has guided me in this project is deeply political in its intentions. One of the unifying principles of neo-Maussian economic anthropology is that in writing *The Gift* Marcel Mauss had fundamentally political aims, primarily the goal of elaborating a more ethical theoretical basis for social relations than that offered by neo-liberal economics and industrial capitalism. In returning to Mauss's text now, these theorists intend, and often say so explicitly, to revive a critique of the neo-liberal ideologies that underlie much of contemporary globalized capitalism. In some cases, the political goals are more immediate and precise: in his book *Debt: The First 5,000 Years*, David Graeber is making a moral, historical, social and philosophical case for Third World debt relief.

I have tried to make it clear that my intentions in this book are, at a much more modest scale, political as well. In particular, I have tried to show that, in light of the work of contemporary sociologists and anthropologists, much of the social theory that Chaucerians and other literary critics have been relying on is grounded in assumptions that are neither philosophically necessary nor politically desirable, and that can have the effect, presumably unintentionally, of naturalizing market relations and of representing neo-liberal economic forces as universal and inevitable, when they are neither of these things.

Nonetheless, I do not wish to leave the impression that I am interested in the *Canterbury Tales* solely as a medium through which to make sociological arguments, and that the texts themselves and the experience of reading them are of secondary importance. The main reason for developing a politically and socially accurate critical apparatus is that without doing so we cannot read and understand literary texts accurately.

The crucial point is that literary criticism must be informed by social theory because literature is a social phenomenon. No author could have been more acutely aware of this than was Chaucer, who framed his collection with a narrative in which disparate members of society form a community around the telling of stories. The *Canterbury Tales* represents not just the telling of tales or the reading of tales but also the exchange of tales – the ways in which stories are received, and the ways in which new stories are generated and in response – as constitutive simultaneously of the social and the literary. The sociological and the literary-critical are inseparable.

This is why it is so essential that criticism apply a capacious and flexible model of exchange. If exchange can be envisaged only as commerce, then one will necessarily see the trading of stories in the *Canterbury Tales* as fundamentally commercial. When the medieval intellectual historian Joel Kaye, whose groundbreaking work I have cited frequently in this study, turns to Chaucer's work for evidence of 'monetary and market consciousness' in the fourteenth century, he is influenced by Chaucerians like R. A. Shoaf, who claims that 'Chaucer posits economics, "quiting," as the structure of relations in the *Canterbury Tales*', and Patricia Eberle, who argues that Chaucer's implied audience 'will bring a commercial outlook to the tales'.[1] Therefore, when Kaye looks at the Host and his introduction of a regimen of tale exchange for the pilgrimage, he sees the tyranny of the bourgeoisie:

> What is the ordering principle to be? Who should naturally lead or 'govern' this confraternity? The good Parson, the Priest, the Monk, the Knight, all might have claim to be the 'natural' choice to lead. But it is the energy of the publican Host, the burgess of Cheapside, that shapes and commands the enterprise. It is the Host that organizes the tale-telling on the principle of 'quiting' or 'repaying.' It is the Host who has himself chosen as absolute 'governour,' who

appoints himself judge of 'heigh and lough,' who determines the prize (supper at his own tavern!), and who assesses the pecuniary punishment for anyone 'whoso be rebel to my juggement.'[2]

Everything Kaye says about the Host here is true. But it is also true that, from the beginning, the Host envisions the pilgrims not only as competing through tales but also as contributing tales for collective enjoyment:

> Ye goon to Caunterbury – God yow speede,
> The blisful martir quite yow youre meede!
> And wel I woot, as ye goon by the weye,
> Ye shapen yow to talen and to pleye;
> For trewely, confort ne myrthe is noon
> To ride by the weye doumb as a stoon;
> And therfore wol I maken yow disport,
> As I seyde erst, and doon yow som confort.   (I.769–76)

The Host figures the tales as the glue in the pilgrims' 'felaweshipe', as the principle that will sustain 'so myrie a compaignye' (I.764), the spontaneous society that forms at his tavern and that he proposes to preserve on the road. There is obligation to contribute a tale, but that is, as is sometimes said of taxes, the price of a civil society.

Therefore, the Host is always looking for the next good tale. He is impatient with anything he considers 'sermonyng' (I.3899), like the *Reeve's Prologue*, which apparently dwells too long on complaint and does not move swiftly enough to narrative diversion. He enjoys predicting the nature of each person's contribution, and he calls on pilgrims for tales even when no compulsion to 'quite' any other pilgrim is immediately obvious. This is most striking in the case of Chaucer himself, who has gone unnoticed as a member of the pilgrimage until the Host plucks him from obscurity and demands that he contribute: 'Sey now somwhat, syn oother folk han sayd; / Telle us a tale of myrthe, and that anon' (VII.705–6). Chaucer owes no payback to anyone: the Host instead says that his tale is his share of the collective creative project of the traveling community. When the Canon and his Yeoman suddenly ride up to the pilgrims, and when the Canon just as abruptly departs, the Host encourages the Yeoman to tell his tale as well. The Host tells him to ignore the past threats of the Canon – 'Ye … telle on, what so bityde. / Of al his thretyng rekke nat a myte" (VIII.697–8) – and says nothing of any competition. Finally, in the *Parson's Prologue*, the Host becomes quite desperate in his request that the Parson donate a story. The Parson has as much 'quiting' to do as anyone: the Host has accused him of being a 'Lollere' (II.1173), and he takes exception to the moral condition and deportment of his fellow travellers. But the Host's injunction to him is he be 'fructuous' (X.71), and that he make the final contribution, now that 'every man, save thou, hath toold his tale' (X.25). It is a generalized obligation.

Just as the obligation to contribute tales is shared, so is the critical assessment of the tales. Despite the authority claimed by the Host in the General Prologue for his own 'juggement', the pilgrims respond freely, both negatively and positively, both individually and collectively – 'In al the route nas ther yong ne oold / That he ne seyde it was a noble storie' (I.3110–11) – to the various tales. There is exchange in the critical responses as well, and obligation, and certainly agonistic competition. A community of readers perhaps by its nature fosters competition. (I can be a pretty competitive reader myself.) But this kind of exchange hardly conforms to a market model. It is, for one thing, too open-ended: no transaction can ever be said to be settled. The collective spirit of interpretation is more clearly represented in the broadening gesture of the Knight at the end of the first part of his tale: '"Yow loveres axe I now this questioun: / Who hath the worse, Arcite or Palamoun?"' (I.1347–8). It is even more manifest in the Franklin's question at the end of his tale: '"Which was the mooste fre, as thynketh yow? / Now telleth me, er that ye ferther wende"' (V.1622–3). The *demande* ending is directed simultaneously by the Franklin to the pilgrims and by Chaucer to a limitless community of readers across time. The invitation implies an obligation to respond, but each reader is free to react with the range of possible responses demonstrated by Chaucer's pilgrims – hostility, boredom, frustration, spiritual inspiration, moral disapprobation, comic appreciation or even drunken indifference. This interpretive freedom indicates that the exchanges between author and reader, or within the community of interpreters, are not bound by a system of equivalent response, of tit-for-tat or *do ut des*. Whatever responses we offer enter into and extend the sociality engendered by the literary exchange. Why, then, should we as critics intervene by insisting that no free response is possible? On the grounds of transcendent moral standards by which all the characters and all readers are abjectly fallen and capable only of fallible judgement? On the grounds of an inherent obligation to win at the game of storytelling or interpretation? On the grounds that the obligation to respond negates an imagined prerequisite of absolute voluntarism? These are not necessary or beneficial. Most of all, they are just not the right way to respond to a gift.

NOTES

Introduction: Chaucer's Commodities, Chaucer's Gifts

1. All quotations of the *Canterbury Tales* are drawn from *The Riverside Chaucer*, general editor Larry D. Benson (Boston: Houghton Mifflin, 1987).

2. Lee Patterson, *Chaucer and the Subject of History* (Madison: University of Wisconsin Press, 1991), p. 32.

3. Derek Brewer, 'Class Distinction in Chaucer', *Speculum*, 43 (1968), 304; Brewer's emphasis.

4. Alcuin Blamires, 'Chaucer the Reactionary: Ideology and the General Prologue to *The Canterbury Tales*', *Review of English Studies*, new series, 51, 204 (2000), 538–9.

5. Aldo D. Scaglione, 'Boccaccio, Chaucer, and the Mercantile Ethic', in David Daiches and Anthony Thorlby (eds), *Literature and Western Civilization, II: The Mediaeval World* (London: Aldus, 1973), p. 582.

6. David Aers, *Chaucer* (Atlantic Highlands, NJ: Humanities Press International, 1986), p. 24; Aers's emphasis.

7. Aers, *Chaucer*, pp. 35–6.

8. Patterson, *Chaucer and the Subject of History*, p. 324.

9. Patterson, *Chaucer and the Subject of History*, p. 366.

10. Helen Fulton, 'Mercantile Ideology in Chaucer's *Shipman's Tale*', *Chaucer Review*, 36 (2002), 311.

11. Craig E. Bertolet, '"Wel bet is roten appul out of hoord": Chaucer's Cook, Commerce, and Civic Order', *Studies in Philology*, 99 (2002), 230.

12. Lianna Farber, *An Anatomy of Trade in Medieval Writing: Value, Consent, and Community* (Ithaca: Cornell University Press, 2006). See also Roger A. Ladd, *Antimercantilism in Late Medieval English Literature* (New York: Palgrave Macmillan, 2010); Jonathan H. Hsy, *Trading Tongues: Merchants, Multilingualism, and Medieval Literature* (Columbus: Ohio State University Press, 2013).

13. For important examples of the application of economics and economic thought to literature and critical theory, see Marc Shell, *The Economy of Literature* (Baltimore: Johns Hopkins University Press, 1978), and *Money, Language, and Thought* (Baltimore: Johns Hopkins University Press, 1982).

14. Christopher Gregory, *Gifts and Commodities* (London: Academic Press, 1982), p. 71. See also Gregory, *Savage Money: The Anthropology and Politics of Commodity Exchange* (Amsterdam: Harwood Academic Publishers, 1997), particularly pp. 41–70.
15. See David Graeber, *Toward an Anthropological Theory of Value: The False Coin of Our Own Dreams* (New York: Palgrave, 2001), p. 36; Marilyn Strathern, *The Gender of the Gift: Problems with Women and Problems with Society in Melanesia* (Berkeley: University of California Press, 1988), p. 134.
16. See Alain Caillé, *Critique de la raison utilitaire: Manifeste du MAUSS* (Paris: La Découverte, 1989).
17. Alain Caillé, 'Gift', in Keith Hart, Jean-Louis Laville and Antonio David Cattani (eds), *The Human Economy: A Citizen's Guide* (Cambridge: Polity Press, 2010), p. 181.
18. David Graeber, *Debt: The First 5,000 Years* (Brooklyn, NY: Melville House, 2011), p. 391.

Chapter 1: The Franklin's Potlatch and the Plowman's Creed: The Gift in the General Prologue

1. John Dryden, 'Preface' to *Fables Ancient and Modern*, in *The Poems and Fables of Dryden*, edited by James Kinsley (London: Oxford University Press, 1962), p. 531.
2. Patricia J. Eberle, 'Commercial Language and the Commercial Outlook in the *General Prologue*', *Chaucer Review*, 18 (1983), 163.
3. Eberle, 'Commercial Language', 171.
4. Craig E. Bertolet, '"Wel bet is roten appul out of hoord": Chaucer's Cook, Commerce, and Civic Order', *Studies in Philology*, 99 (2002), 233. Bertolet expands his reading of the Franklin, with emphasis on the transformation of material capital into symbolic capital, in *Chaucer, Gower, Hoccleve and the Commercial Practices of Late Fourteenth-Century London* (Burlington, VT: Ashgate, 2013), pp. 62–9. See also E. C. Ronquist, 'The Franklin, Epicurus, and the Play of Values', in Robert Myles and David Williams (eds), *Chaucer and Language: Essays in Honor of Douglas Wurtele* (Montreal: McGill-Queen's University Press, 2001), pp. 44–60.
5. Robert Kilburn Root, *The Poetry of Chaucer: A Guide to Its Study and Appreciation* (Boston: Houghton Mifflin, 1906), p. 273.
6. Jill Mann, *Chaucer and Medieval Estates Satire: The Literature of Social Classes and the General Prologue to the* Canterbury Tales (Cambridge: Cambridge University Press, 1973), pp. 152–9.
7. D. W. Robertson, Jr., *A Preface to Chaucer: Studies in Medieval Perspectives* (Princeton: Princeton University Press, 1962), p. 276. See also Hugh T. Keenan, 'The General Prologue to the *Canterbury Tales*, Lines 345–346: The Franklin's Feast and Eucharistic Shadows', *Neuphilologische Mitteilungen*, 79 (1978), 36–40.

8. Johan Huizinga, *The Autumn of the Middle Ages*, translated by Rodney J. Payton and Ulrich Mammitzsch (Chicago: University of Chicago Press, 1996), particularly chapter 12, 'Art in Life', pp. 294–328.

9. Stephen Mennell, *All Manners of Food: Eating and Taste in England and France from the Middle Ages to the Present* (Oxford: Blackwell, 1985), p. 58.

10. See David Graeber, *Toward an Anthropological Theory of Value: The False Coin of Our Own Dreams* (New York: Palgrave, 2001), pp. 188–210.

11. Mennell, *All Manners of Food*, p. 58.

12. It would be difficult enough, as well as controversial, to try to say precisely what potlatch is itself, even in terms of the field of anthropology. It has been recognized since the mid-twentieth century, for instance, that some of the most distinctive features of potlatch as observed by white ethnographers, particularly the ostentatious and competitive destruction of property, in reality emerged or were exaggerated in reaction to repressive practices of Canadian colonial authorities. See Helen Codere, *Fighting with Property: A Study of Kwakiutl Potlatching and Warfare, 1792–1930* (Seattle: University of Washington Press, 1950). Others doubt whether an objective outside perspective of the practice is readily available to anthropological analysts. Isabelle Schulte-Tenckhoff ('Misrepresenting the Potlatch', in Caroline Gerschlager (ed.), *Expanding the Economic Concept of Exchange: Deception, Self-Deception, and Illusion* (Dordrecht: Kluwer Academic Publishers, 2001), pp. 167–88) finds that 'the potlatch has served as a mirror for economic imperialism that naturalises or essentialises the characteristic features of our own ideology and social order' (p. 168). Others have argued that the practice itself is really a product of the colonial forces that have sought to restrict, control and define it. See Christopher Bracken, *The Potlatch Papers: A Colonial Case History* (Chicago: University of Chicago Press, 1997).

13. Britton J. Harwood has compared the feasting in the *Squire's Tale* to potlatch and remarks that Cambyuskan is 'like a Kwakiutl chief on his own scale'. 'Chaucer and the Gift (If There Is Any)', *Studies in Philology*, 103 (2006), 28–9.

14. See Schulte-Tenckhoff, 'Misrepresenting the Potlatch', pp. 172–5; Chris Hann and Keith Hart, *Economic Anthropology: History, Ethnography, Critique* (Cambridge: Polity Press, 2011), pp. 42–8.

15. See Graeber, *Theory of Value*, p. 191.

16. Quotations from the French text of Mauss's essay are taken from *Essai sur le don: Forme et raison de l'échange dans les sociétés archaïques* (Paris: Presses Universitaires de France, 2007). The English translations are from *The Gift: The Form and Reason for Exchange in Archaic Societies*, translated by W. D. Halls (New York: Norton, 1990).

17. Mauss, *The Gift*, p. 6.

18. Mauss, *The Gift*, p. 7; Mauss's emphasis.

19. See, among others, Georges Bataille, 'The Gift of Rivalry: "Potlatch"', in *The Accursed Share: An Essay on General Economy*, translated by Robert Hurley (New York: Zone Books, 1988), pp. 63–77; Claude Lefort, 'L'échange ou la

lutte des hommes', *Les Temps modernes* (1951), 1404–17. As Florence Weber observes, 'Leur lecture est pessimiste: tout échange est lutte, toute lutte de générosité est lutte pour le pouvoir, et le don n'est qu'un processus de destruction qui ne connait pas de limites.' 'Préface à l'édition "Quadrige"', in Mauss, *Essai sur le don*, p. 20.

20. Jacques Derrida, *Given Time: I. Counterfeit Money*, translated by Peggy Kamuf (Chicago: University of Chicago Press, 1992), p. 12.

21. Derrida, *Given Time*, p. 37.

22. Mauss, *The Gift*, p. 37.

23. Derrida, *Given Time*, p. 46.

24. Pierre Bourdieu, *Outline of a Theory of Practice*, translated by Richard Nice (Cambridge: Cambridge University Press, 1977), p. 194; Bourdieu's emphasis.

25. Pierre Bourdieu, *Practical Reason: On the Theory of Action* (Stanford: Stanford University Press, 1998), p. 100.

26. Martha C. Howell, *Commerce before Capitalism in Europe, 1300–1600* (Cambridge: Cambridge University Press, 2010), p. 149. See also Gadi Algazi, 'Introduction: Doing Things with Gifts', in Gadi Algazi and Valentin Groebner and Bernhard Jussen (eds), *Negotiating the Gift: Pre-modern Figurations of Exchange* (Göttingen: Vandenhoek & Ruprecht, 2003), pp. 9–27.

27. Howell, *Commerce before Capitalism*, pp. 157, 159–71.

28. Howell, *Commerce before Capitalism*, p. 153; Bourdieu, *Outline of a Theory of Practice*, p. 14. Does this mean, then, that the gift changed and became essentially agonistic at this point, influenced by and in imitation of the commercial transactions within which it was embedded? Or, as Bourdieu would have it, was the gift always everywhere motivated by competitive self-interest and the desire for profit and domination? Howell chooses not to decide. 'My study takes the pragmatic approach', she writes. '[I]t does not ask whether the *dons, prosenten, gifte*, and the like that people then distributed were "really" gifts according to some abstract model' (p. 157).

29. Susan Crane, 'The Franklin as Dorigen', *Chaucer Review* 24 (1990), 240. See also Robert P. Miller, 'It Snewed in His Hous', *English Language Notes*, 22 (1985), 14–16; Henrik Specht, *Chaucer's Franklin in the Canterbury Tales* (Copenhagen: Akademisk Forlag, 1981), particularly pp. 30–1; Paul Strohm, *Social Chaucer* (Cambridge, MA: Harvard University Press, 1989), pp. 107–8; Peter Cross, 'The Franklin', in Stephen H. Rigby and Alastair J. Minnis (eds), *Historians on Chaucer: The 'General Prologue' to the* Canterbury Tales (Oxford: Oxford University Press, 2014), pp. 227–46.

30. See Peter Goodall, 'Chaucer's "Burgesses" and the Aldermen of London', *Medium Aevum*, 50 (1981), 284–91; Britton J. Harwood, 'The "Fraternitee" of Chaucer's Guildsmen', *Review of English Studies*, 39 (1988), 413–17; Brian Gastle, 'Chaucer's "Shaply" Guildsmen and Mercantile Pretensions', *Neuphilologische Mitteilungen*, 99 (1998), 211–16.

31. Graeber, *Theory of Value*, p. 160. Graeber has also found some fundamental errors in Mauss's interpretation of potlatch; see 'Debt, Violence, and

Impersonal Markets: Polanyian Meditations', in Chris Hann and Keith Hart (eds), *Market and Society: The Great Transformation Today* (Cambridge: Cambridge University Press, 2009), pp. 112–13.

32. Mauss, *The Gift*, p. 7.

33. Quoted in Martin Treml, 'On Mauss and Myths: Exploring Different Forms of Exchange', in Caroline Gerschlager (ed.), *Expanding the Economic Concept of Exchange: Deception, Self-Deception and Illusions* (Dordrecht: Kluwer Academic Publishers, 2001), p. 150.

34. Mauss, *The Gift*, p. 69.

35. On the symbolic plowman, see Stephen A. Barney, 'The Plowshare of the Tongue: The Progress of a Symbol from the Bible to *Piers Plowman*', *Mediaeval Studies* 35 (1973), 261–93.

36. Mann, *Estates Satire*, p. 73.

37. G. Stilwell, 'Chaucer's Plowman and the Contemporary English Peasant', *ELH*, 6 (1939), 285–90 (285).

38. Stephen Knight, *Geoffrey Chaucer* (Oxford: Blackwell, 1986), pp. 79–80.

39. Alcuin Blamires, 'Chaucer the Reactionary: Ideology and the General Prologue to *The Canterbury Tales*', *Review of English Studies*, new series, 51, 204 (2000), 530.

40. Max Weber, 'The Social Psychology of World Religions', in *From Max Weber: Essays in Sociology*, ed. and translated by H. H. Gerth and C. Wright Mills (1946; New York: Oxford University Press, 1970), p. 273.

41. Bourdieu, *Practical Reason*, p. 114; Bourdieu's emphasis.

42. See, for instance, David Aers, *Chaucer* (Atlantic Highlands, NJ: Humanities Press International, 1986), p. 35.

43. Mann, *Estates Satire*, p. 71.

44. Judith Bennett figures the Plowman as essentially one of these common people, 'a generic toiler in the fields' accustomed to working 'in cooperation with a group of tenants'. 'The Curse of the Plowman', *Yearbook of Langland Studies*, 20 (2006), 219.

45. Christopher Dyer, '*Piers Plowman* and Plowmen: A Historical Perspective', *Yearbook of Langland Studies*, 8 (1995), 161. See also Mark Bailey, 'The Ploughman', in Rigby and Minnis (eds), *Historians on Chaucer*, pp. 352–67.

46. Dyer, '*Piers Plowman* and Plowmen', 167–8.

47. Dyer, '*Piers Plowman* and Plowmen', 168.

48. Mauss, *Essai sur le don*, p. 71; Mauss's emphasis.

49. *Le Grand Robert*, 'prestation': 'I.4 (V. 1930). Admin. Allocation en espèces que l'État verse au travailleur pour l'aider dans certaines circonstances prévues par la loi.'

50. Hann and Hart, *Economic Anthropology*, p. 50.

51. *Le Grand Robert*, 'prestation': 'I.2. Dr. féod. Fourniture, redevance due au seigneur part son sujet.'

52. Graeber, *Theory of Value*, p. 162.

53. Graeber, *Theory of Value*, pp. 218–19.

54. Karl Polanyi, *The Great Transformation: The Political and Economic Origins of Our Time* (1944; Boston: Beacon Press, 1957). More than seventy years after the publication of *The Great Transformation*, 'Polanyi's stock as a social thinker is rising', according to Keith Hart and Chris Hann, 'Introduction: Learning from Polanyi', in Keith Hart and Chris Hann (eds), *Market and Society: The Great Transformation Today* (Cambridge: Cambridge University Press, 2009), p. 4. Evidence for this comes not just from the discipline of social theory but also from medieval history. Jacques Le Goff, in his recent book, cites Polanyi as his 'principal inspiration for the avoidance of anachronism and the understanding of the functioning of "the economic" in medieval society', in *Money and the Middle Ages*, translated by Jean Birrell (Cambridge: Polity, 2012), p. 128.

55. Polanyi, *Great Transformation*, p. 188.

56. Polanyi, *Great Transformation*, p. 75. See also Hann and Hart, *Market and Society*, p. 5.

57. Polanyi, *Great Transformation*, p. 187.

58. See Polanyi, *Great Transformation*, pp. 35–7.

59. Dyer, '*Piers Plowman* and Plowmen', 163. Piers Plowman himself serves as a reeve late in the poem (B.19.258–61), but Dyer notes that Piers may at this point be a 'servile tenant' and may be required to take a turn as his lord's reeve.

60. 'Second Shepherds Play', in Martin Stevens and A. C. Cawley (eds), *The Towneley Plays*, Early English Text Society (Oxford: Oxford University Press, 1994), lines 48–65.

61. See David Lepine, 'The Parson', in Rigby and Minnis (eds), *Historians on Chaucer*, pp. 334–51.

62. See Karl Polanyi, 'The Economy as Instituted Process', in Karl Polanyi, Conrad Arensberg and Harry W. Pearson (eds), *Trade and Market in the Early Empires* (New York: The Free Press, 1957), pp. 250–6.

63. See Polanyi, *Great Transformation*, pp. 49–50. See also Hann and Hart, *Market and Society*, p. 7.

64. 'Redistribution' is a key term for Polanyi. Generally, it signifies a common mode of political economy in centralized societies before the institution of the market, when all that is produced is given to a figure of central authority, who then redistributes it. See *Great Transformation*, pp. 49–55; *Trade and Markets*, pp. 250–6.

65. Quoted in Le Goff, *Money and the Middle Ages*, p. 128. On Polanyi's key concept of 'embeddedness', see Jens Beckert, 'The Great Transformation of Embeddedness: Karl Polanyi and the New Economic Sociology', in Hann and Hart (eds), *Market and Society*, pp. 38–55.

66. Lee Patterson, *Chaucer and the Subject of History* (Madison: University of Wisconsin Press, 1991), p. 31.

67. Mann, *Estates Satire*, p. 73.

Chapter 2: The Lack of Interest in the *Shipman's Tale*: Chaucer and the Social Theory of the Gift

1. E. Talbot Donaldson, *Chaucer's Poetry: An Anthology for the Modern Reader* (New York: Ronald Press Company, 1958), pp. 931–2.
2. Helen Fulton, 'Mercantile Ideology in Chaucer's *Shipman's Tale*', *Chaucer Review*, 36 (2002), 318–19.
3. William E. Rogers and Paul Dower, 'Thinking about Money in Chaucer's Shipman's Tale', in Robert G. Benson and Susan J. Ridyard (eds), *New Readings of Chaucer's Poetry* (Cambridge: D. S. Brewer, 2003), p. 132.
4. Lee Patterson, *Chaucer and the Subject of History* (Madison: University of Wisconsin Press, 1991), p. 361.
5. Lianna Farber, *An Anatomy of Trade in Medieval Writing: Value, Consent, and Community* (Ithaca: Cornell University Press, 2006), p. 69. See also Roger A. Ladd, *Antimercantilism in Late Medieval English Literature* (New York: Palgrave Macmillan, 2010); Craig E. Bertolet, *Chaucer, Gower, Hoccleve and the Commercial Practices of Late Fourteenth-Century London* (Burlington, VT: Ashgate, 2013), pp. 83–104. Bertolet concludes, 'The greatest sin in the tale is not adultery but the failure to repay a debt' (pp. 103–4).
6. Pierre Bourdieu, *Practical Reason: On the Theory of Action* (Stanford: Stanford University Press, 1998), p. 75. Chapter 4, 'Is a Disinterested Act Possible?' is translated by Randal Johnson.
7. Bruce Holsinger has placed Mauss's influence on Bourdieu alongside the surprisingly deep influence of Erwin Panofsky's medievalism in the development of Bourdieu's concept of the *habitus*. See 'Indigineity: Panofsky, Bourdieu, and the Archaeology of the *Habitus*', in Bruce Holsinger, *The Premodern Condition: Medievalism and the Making of Theory* (Chicago: University of Chicago Press, 2005), pp. 94–113.
8. The word 'interest' derives from the Latin *inter esse* – that which comes between. See John Thomas Noonan, *The Scholastic Analysis of Usury* (Cambridge, MA: Harvard University Press, 1957), pp. 104–5. The use of the Latin *interesse* to mean payment on a loan is traceable at least to the Bolognese lawyer Azo in the early thirteenth century. (Lester K. Little, *Religious Poverty and the Profit Economy in Medieval Europe* (Ithaca: Cornell University Press, 1978), p. 180.) The *Oxford English Dictionary* cites the first usage of 'interest' in English for money paid beyond principle on a loan to 1529. The Middle English equivalent of *interest* is *intress(e)*, meaning both concern and legal claim or right. Chaucer does not use the word in the *Canterbury Tales*, but both the *OED* and the *MED* cite Chaucer's short poem 'Fortune' (*c.*1387–8) as the first recorded usage of the word in the legal sense. See also David Graeber, *Debt: The First 5,000 Years* (Brooklyn, NY: Melville House, 2011), pp. 322, 446 n. 58.
9. See Raymond de Roover, *Money, Banking and Credit in Mediaeval Bruges: Italian Merchant Bankers, Lombards, and Money-Changers* (Cambridge, MA: Medieval Academy of America, 1948), p. 151; Peter Spufford, *Money and*

Its Use in Medieval Europe (Cambridge: Cambridge University Press, 1988), p. 254. See also J. L. Bolton, *Money in the Medieval English Economy, 973–1489* (Manchester: Manchester University Press, 2012).

10. de Roover, *Money, Banking*, p. 151.

11. de Roover, *Money, Banking*, p. 305.

12. On the development and utilization of the bill of exchange, see Edwin S. Hunt and James M. Murray, *A History of Business in Medieval Europe, 1200-1550* (Cambridge: Cambridge University Press, 1999), p. 72, as well as de Roover, *Money, Banking*, pp. 48–67, and Spufford, *Money and Its Use*, p. 395. On the use of the bill of exchange by the merchant of the *Shipman's Tale*, see Kenneth S. Cahn, 'Chaucer's Merchants and the Foreign Exchange: An Introduction to Medieval Finance', *Studies in the Age of Chaucer*, 2 (1980), 88–9.

13. Fulton, 'Mercantile Ideology', 318.

14. Cahn, 'Chaucer's Merchants', 88.

15. See J. A. Burrow and V. J. Scattergood's explanatory notes to the *Shipman's Tale* in *The Riverside Chaucer*, general editor Larry D. Benson (Boston: Houghton Mifflin, 1987), pp. 910–13; see also Cahn, 'Chaucer's Merchants', 85. My thanks to Derek Pearsall for pointing out to me this difference of scale between the two loans.

16. Mary Braswell claims that 'a loan does not appear in any of the analogues to the story – these are concerned with *gifts* instead' (*Chaucer's 'Legal Fiction': Reading the Records* (Madison, NJ: Fairleigh Dickinson University Press, 2001), p. 85). This is true in so far as in some of the analogues an object is exchanged rather than money. But the closest analogues to the *Shipman's Tale* – Boccaccio's *Decameron* 8.1 and Sercambi's *Novelliero* 19 – include monetary loans, and Sercambi refers explicitly to the charging of interest. In *Novelliero* 19, the suitor Bernardo asks the husband Pircosso for two hundred florins to complete a transaction, adding, 'And when I have my first pay, I will return them to you with whatever interest you say (*con quello merito mi dirai*).' When Pircosso says that he is going out of town on business, Bernardo slyly says, 'If what has been promised me should not be fulfilled, do you wish me to return these florins (*questi fiorini*) to your wife?' Pircosso answers, 'Yes, return this money (*questi dinari*).' Larry D. Benson and Theodore M. Andersson (eds), *The Literary Context of Chaucer's Fabliaux* (Indianapolis: Bobbs-Merrill, 1971), pp. 314, 315. Sercambi's emphasis on 'these florins' seems to indicate that Bernardo will repay only the principal if his anticipated transaction falls through while Pircosso is out of town.

17. See Odd Langholm, *Economics in the Medieval Schools: Wealth, Exchange, Value, Money and Usury according to the Paris Theological Tradition, 1200–1350* (Leiden: Brill, 1992), pp. 306, 408.

18. Langholm, *Economics in the Medieval Schools*, p. 337.

19. Noonan, *Scholastic Analysis*, pp. 104–5.

20. Mauss, *The Gift: The Form and Reason for Exchange in Archaic Societies*, translated by W. D. Halls (New York: Norton, 1990), p. 3.

21. For the theoretical and historical contexts of Mauss's development of his views on the gift, see Beate Wagner-Hasel, 'Egoistic Exchange and Altruistic Gift: On the Roots of Marcel Mauss's Theory of the Gift', in Gadi Algazi, Valentin Groebner and Bernhard Jussen (eds), *Negotiating the Gift: Pre-Modern Figurations of Exchange* (Göttingen: Vandenhoeck & Ruprecht, 2003), pp. 141–71. For a review of applications of gift theory to medieval history, see Arnoud-Jan A. Bijsterveld, 'The Medieval Gift as Agent of Social Bonding and Political Power: A Comparative Approach', in Esther Cohen and Mayke B. de Jong (eds), *Medieval Transformations: Texts, Power, and Gifts in Context* (Brill: Leiden, 2001), pp. 123–56. For a consideration of recent developments in gift theory and their relevance to the study of late medieval culture, see Martha C. Howell, *Commerce before Capitalism in Europe, 1300–1600* (Cambridge: Cambridge University Press, 2010), especially chapter 3: 'Gift Work', pp. 145–207. Two interdisciplinary anthologies collecting excerpts from influential gift theorists are also particularly useful: Aafke E. Komter (ed.), *The Gift: An Interdisciplinary Perspective* (Amsterdam: Amsterdam University Press, 1996); Alan D. Schrift (ed.), *The Logic of the Gift: Toward an Ethic of Generosity* (New York: Routledge, 1997).

22. Pierre Bourdieu, 'Marginalia – Some Additional Notes on the Gift', in Schrift (ed.), *The Logic of the Gift*, p. 231.

23. Graeber, *Toward an Anthropological Theory of Value: The False Coin of Our Own Dreams* (New York: Palgrave, 2001), p. 28.

24. Pierre Bourdieu, *The Logic of Practice*, translated by Richard Nice (Stanford: Stanford University Press, 1980), pp. 112–13.

25. Bourdieu, *Practical Reason*, p. 84.

26. Graeber, *Theory of Value*, p. 29.

27. Graeber, *Theory of Value*, p. 28.

28. Many theorists maintain that no culture is based exclusively on gift relationships or exclusively on commodity exchange, claiming instead that these two systems co-exist. See, notably, Christopher Gregory, *Gifts and Commodities* (London: Academic Press, 1982).

29. Howell, *Commerce before Capitalism*, p. 153; Bourdieu, *Outline of a Theory of Practice*, p. 14.

30. See, for instance, Rogers and Dower, 'Thinking', p. 135.

31. Graeber, *Theory of Value*, p. 29.

32. Graeber, *Theory of Value*, p. 218. On Mauss's concept of *'prestation totale'*, see also Patrick J. Geary, 'Gift Exchange and Social Science Modeling: The Limitations of a Construct', in Algazi, Groebner and Jussen (eds), *Negotiating the Gift*, pp. 129–40.

33. Graeber, *Theory of Value*, p. 218.

34. Graeber, *Theory of Value*, p. 218.

35. Cathy Hume, 'Domestic Opportunities: The Social Comedy of the *Shipman's Tale*', *The Chaucer Review*, 41 (2006), 156–7.

36. Holly Crocker, 'Wifely Eye for the Manly Guy: Trading the Masculine Image in the *Shipman's Tale*', in T. L. Burton and John F. Plummer (eds), *'Seyd in Forme and Reverence': Essays on Chaucer and Chaucerians in Memory of Emerson Brown, Jr.* (Provo, UT: Chaucer Studio Press, 2005), p. 60. See also William F. Woods, 'A Professional Thyng: The Wife as Merchant's Apprentice in the *Shipman's Tale*', *Chaucer Review*, 24 (1989), 139–49.

37. Bourdieu, *Practical Reason*, p. 106. On gift theory and marriage, see also Jane Fair Bestor, 'Marriage Transactions in Renaissance Italy and Mauss's *Essay on the Gift*', *Past & Present*, 164 (1999), 6–46.

38. Elizabeth Edwards has argued that the economics of fabliau in general are unable to subsume female sexuality and pleasure. See 'The Economics of Justice in Chaucer's Miller's and Reeve's Tales', *The Dalhousie Review*, 82 (2002), 106–12.

39. Thus Crocker ('Wifely Eye', p. 60) concludes that when the wife engages in the economy of the tale, 'the currency is masculinity itself'.

40. See Thomas Hahn, 'Money, Sexuality, Wordplay, and Context in the *Shipman's Tale*', in Julian N. Wasserman and Robert J. Blanch (eds), *Chaucer in the Eighties* (Syracuse: Syracuse University Press, 1986), p. 243.

41. This impression has been voiced by previous readers, notably Derek Pearsall, in *The Canterbury Tales* (London: George Allen & Unwin, 1985), p. 217.

42. Bourdieu, *Practical Reason*, p. 76.

43. Bourdieu, *Practical Reason*, p. 78.

44. Pierre Bourdieu, *Outline of a Theory of Practice*, translated by Richard Nice (Cambridge: Cambridge University Press, 1977), p. 178.

45. Graeber, *Theory of Value*, p. 260.

46. Jacques T. Godbout, in collaboration with Alain Caillé, *The World of the Gift*, translated by Donald Winkler (Montreal: McGill-Queen's University Press, 1998), p. 176.

47. Godbout and Caillé, *The World of the Gift*, p. 184.

48. Godbout and Caillé, *The World of the Gift*, p. 173.

49. Godbout and Caillé, *The World of the Gift*, p. 177.

50. Godbout and Caillé, *The World of the Gift*, p. 181.

51. Patterson, *Chaucer and the Subject of History*, p. 352.

Chapter 3: Giving Evil: Excess and Equivalence in the Fabliau

1. The earliest instances recorded by the *Middle English Dictionary* refer to payment of ransom, but from the late fourteenth century there are numerous examples of the word's uses in all these senses. *Middle English Dictionary*, 'quiten'.

2. R. A. Shoaf, *Dante, Chaucer, and the Currency of the Word: Money, Images, and Reference in Late Medieval Poetry* (Norman, OK: Pilgrim Books, 1983), pp. 167–68.

3. Joseph Bédier, *Les Fabliaux: Études de littétature populaire et d'histoire littéraire du moyen âge* (Paris: É. Bouillon, 1893). Charles Muscatine, 'The Social Background of the Old French Fabliaux', *Genre*, 9 (1976), 1–19.

4. Muscatine, 'Social Background', 18.

5. Simon Gaunt, *Gender and Genre in Medieval French Literature* (Cambridge: Cambridge University Press, 1995), p. 285.

6. Patricia J. Eberle, 'Commercial Language and the Commercial Outlook in the *General Prologue*', *Chaucer Review*, 18 (1983), 185.

7. Charles Muscatine, *Chaucer and the French Tradition* (Berkeley: University of California Press, 1957), p. 59.

8. Thomas D. Cooke, *The Old French and Chaucerian Fabliaux: A Study of Their Comic Climax* (Columbia: University of Missouri Press, 1978), p. 171.

9. Paul A. Olson, 'The *Reeve's Tale*: Chaucer's *Measure for Measure*', *Studies in Philology*, 59 (1962), 17.

10. Marcel Mauss, *The Gift: The Form and Reason for Exchange in Archaic Societies*, translated by W. D. Halls (New York: Norton, 1990), pp. 81–2.

11. Christian Sheridan, 'Conflicting Economies in the Fabliaux', in Holly A. Crocker (ed.), *Comic Provocations: Exposing the Corpus of Old French Fabliaux* (New York: Palgrave Macmillan, 2006), p. 97.

12. Sheridan, 'Conflicting Economies', p. 109.

13. Sheridan, 'Conflicting Economies', p. 99. Sheridan cites Bourdieu, 'The Work of Time', in Aafke E. Komter (ed.), *The Gift: An Interdisciplinary Perspective* (Amsterdam: Amsterdam University Press, 1996), pp. 135–47.

14. Sheridan, 'Conflicting Economies', p. 101.

15. Carl von Clauswitz, *On War*, translated by Michael Howard and Peter Paret (Princeton: Princeton University Press, 1987), p. 84.

16. Claude Lévi-Strauss, *The Elementary Structures of Kinship*, edited and translated by James Harle Bell, John Richard von Sturmer and Rodney Needham (Boston: Beacon Press, 1969), p. 67.

17. Mark Rogin Anspach, 'Violence Deceived: Changing Reciprocities from Vengeance to Gift Exchange', in Caroline Gerschlager (ed.), *Expanding the Economic Concept of Exchange: Deception, Self-Deception and Illusions* (Dordrecht: Kluwer Academic Publishers, 2001), pp. 213–24.

18. Anspach, 'Violence Deceived', p. 216.

19. Anspach, 'Violence Deceived', p. 215; Anspach's emphasis.

20. Anspach, 'Violence Deceived', p. 216; Anspach's emphasis.

21. Anspach, 'Violence Deceived', p. 217.

22. 'Noah', in Martin Stevens and A. C. Cawley (eds), *The Towneley Plays*, Early English Text Society (Oxford: Oxford University Press, 1994), lines 313–21.

23. Absolon's injury of Nicholas is, indeed, a parody of anal rape. See Kathleen A. Bishop, 'Queer Punishments: Tragic and Comic Sodomy in the Death of Edward II and in Chaucer's *Miller's Tale*', in Kathleen A. Bishop (ed.), *The Canterbury Tales Revisited – 21st Century Interpretations* (Newcastle: Cambridge Scholars Press, 2008), pp. 16–24.

24. Alain Caillé, 'Gift', in Keith Hart, Jean-Louis Laville and Antonio David Cattani (eds), *The Human Economy: A Citizen's Guide* (Cambridge: Polity, 2010), p. 182.

25. Jacques T. Godbout, in collaboration with Alain Caillé, *The World of the Gift* (Montreal: McGill-Queen's University Press, 1998), p. 179.

26. Marginal notes in several manuscripts gloss Oswald's line with the Latin dictum from which it derives: 'Licitum est vim vim repellere'. See Douglas Gray's explanatory note in the *Riverside Chaucer*, general editor Larry D. Benson (Boston: Houghton Mifflin, 1987), p. 849, as well as Franz Montgomery, 'The Reeve's reference to repelling force with force is a well-known maxim of the law of England', *Philological Quarterly*, 10 (1934), 404–5; Louis McCorry Myers, 'A Line in the Reeve's Prologue', *Modern Language Notes*, 49 (1934), 222–26.

27. Mary Flowers Braswell, *Chaucer's 'Legal Fiction': Reading the Records* (Madison, NJ: Fairleigh University Press, 2001), p. 83. The *Corpus Iuris Civilis* is the sixth-century compilation of Roman civil law that found wide use in the later Middle Ages for establishing legal principles. On legal elements of the *Reeve's Tale*, see also Joseph L. Baird, 'Law and the Reeve's Tale', *Neuphilologische Mitteilungen*, 70 (1969), 679–83, and Olson, 'The *Reeve's Tale*'.

28. Robert Worth Frank, Jr., 'The Reeve's Tale and the Comedy of Limitation', in Stanley Weintraub and Philip Young (eds), *Directions in Literary Criticism* (University Park: Penn State University Press, 1973), pp. 58, 59.

29. On *ingegno* – cleverness – particularly that of clerks, as a driving motive of fabliau, see Frank, 'Limitation', p. 59.

30. J. A. W. Bennett, *Chaucer at Oxford and at Cambridge* (Toronto: University of Toronto Press, 1974).

31. Odd Langholm, 'The Medieval Schoolmen (1200–1400)', in S. Todd Lowry and Barry Gordon (eds), *Ancient and Medieval Economic Ideas and Concepts of Social Justice* (Leiden: Brill, 1998), p. 491.

32. Lester K. Little, *Religious Poverty and the Profit Economy in Medieval Europe* (Ithaca: Cornell University Press, 1978), p. 174.

33. See Joel Kaye, *A History of Balance, 1250–1375: The Emergence of a New Model of Equilibrium and Its Impact on Thought* (Cambridge: Cambridge University Press, 2014).

34. R. Howard Bloch, *Etymologies and Genealogies: A Literary Anthropology of the French Middle Ages* (Chicago: University of Chicago Press, 1983), p. 170.

35. Bloch, *Etymologies and Genealogies*, p. 171.

36. Acts 8:20 (Douay-Rheims translation).

37. Elizabeth Edwards, 'The Economics of Justice in Chaucer's Miller's and Reeve's Tales', *Dalhousie Review*, 82 (2002), 109.

38. Edwards, 'Economics of Justice', 112.

39. This is assuming that there is any female pleasure in the *Reeve's Tale*. As Chaucerian criticism has in recent years begun to more fully acknowledge the representation of non-consensual sex in the *Reeve's Tale* and elsewhere,

it is becoming more common to see Symkyn's wife and especially Malyne as victims of rape. See, for instance, Nicole Nolan Sidhu, '"To Late for to Crie": Female Desire, Fabliau Politics, and Classical Legend in Chaucer's *Reeve's Tale*', *Exemplaria*, 21 (2009), 3–23; Heidi Breuer, 'Being Intolerant: Rape is Not Seduction (in "The Reeve's Tale" or Anywhere Else)', in Kathleen A. Bishop (ed.), *The Canterbury Tales Revisited – 21st Century Interpretations* (Newcastle: Cambridge Scholars Press, 2008), pp. 1–15.

40. Lee Patterson, *Chaucer and the Subject of History* (Madison: University of Wisconsin Press, 1991), p. 349.

41. Godbout and Caillé, *The World of the Gift*, pp. 182–3.

42. Godbout and Caillé, p. 180.

43. Graeber, *Theory of Value*, p. 260.

Chapter 4: The Exchange of Women and the Gender of the Gift

1. Roberta Krueger, 'Love, Honor, and the Exchange of Women in *Yvain*: Some Remarks on the Female Reader', *Romance Notes*, 25 (1985), 306.

2. Claude Lévi-Strauss, *The Elementary Structures of Kinship*, edited and translated by James Harle Bell, John Richard von Sturmer and Rodney Needham (Boston: Beacon Press, 1969), p. 115.

3. Gayle Rubin, 'The Traffic in Women: Notes on the "Political Economy" of Sex', in Raya R. Reiter (ed.), *Toward an Anthropology of Women* (New York: Monthly Review Press, 1975), p. 175.

4. Rubin, 'Traffic in Women', p. 176.

5. Karen Newman, 'Directing Traffic: Subjects, Objects, and the Politics of Exchange', *differences*, 2 (1990), 247.

6. Luce Irigaray, 'Women on the Market', in *This Sex Which Is Not One*, translated by Catherine Porter (Ithaca: Cornell University Press, 1985), pp. 170–2.

7. Annette B. Weiner, *Inalienable Possessions: The Paradox of Keeping-While-Giving* (Berkeley: University of California Press, 1992), p. 14.

8. Weiner, *Inalienable Possessions*, p. 33.

9. See Weiner, *Inalienable Possessions*, p. 95.

10. Weiner, *Inalienable Possessions*, p. 67.

11. Weiner, *Inalienable Possessions*, p. 18.

12. Weiner, *Inalienable Possessions*, pp. 67–8. Weiner emphasizes that the intimacy and potential incest that she is speaking of are primarily, and almost exclusively, between brothers and sisters. See p. 171, n. 1.

13. Maureen Quilligan, *Incest and Agency in Elizabeth's England* (Philadelphia: University of Pennsylvania Press, 2005), p. 1.

14. Quilligan, *Incest and Agency*, p. 216.

15. Gower also tells the 'Tale of Constance' in *Confessio Amantis* II.587–1598. Chaucer's primary source for the *Man of Law's Tale*, however, was the French prose 'De la noble femme Constance' from *Les Cronicles* of Nicholas

Trevet (or Trivet). See Margaret Schlauch, 'The Man of Law's Tale', in W. F. Bryan and Germaine Dempster (eds), *Sources and Analogues of Chaucer's Canterbury Tales* (New York: Humanities Press, 1958), pp. 155–206; Robert M. Correale, 'The Man of Law's Prologue and Tale', in Robert M. Correale and Mary Hamel (eds), *Sources and Analogues of the Canterbury Tales*, vol. II (Cambridge: D. S. Brewer, 2005), pp. 277–350. Another Middle English analogue (though not apparently one that Chaucer knew) survives as *Le Bone Florence of Rome*. See the edition of Jonathan Stavsky (Cardiff: University of Wales Press, 2017).

16. All quotations of John Gower's *Confessio Amantis* are taken from the edition of Russell A. Peck, vols 1–3 (Kalamazoo, MI: Medieval Institute Publications, 2000–4).

17. See Quilligan, *Incest and Agency*, pp. 217–19. Similar connections among *King Lear*, *Pericles* and Gower's 'Apollonius' have been drawn by Larry Scanlon in 'The Riddle of Incest: John Gower and the Problem of Medieval Sexuality', in Robert F. Yeager (ed.), *Re-Visioning Gower* (Asheville: Pegasus Press, 1998), pp. 93–128. I refer here to Shakespeare's *Pericles*, as does Quilligan, but she also acknowledges (p. 215) that the incest narrative in that play appears in the earlier acts now widely taken by critics to have been written by a different playwright.

18. Maria Bullón-Fernández, *Fathers and Daughters in Gower's* Confessio Amantis: *Authority, Family, State, and Writing* (Cambridge: D. S. Brewer, 2000), p. 2.

19. Yvette Kisor, 'Moments of Silence, Acts of Speech: Uncovering the Incest Motif in the *Man of Law's Tale*', *Chaucer Review*, 40 (2005), 141–62. See also R. A. Shoaf, '"Unwemmed Custance": Circulation, Property, and Incest in the Man of Law's Tale', *Exemplaria*, 2 (1990), 287–302.

20. See Diane Watt, *Amoral Gower: Language, Sex, and Politics* (Minneapolis: University of Minnesota Press, 2003), pp. 138–40.

21. On the 'incestuous poetics' of the *Man of Law's Tale*, see also Diane Cady, 'Damaged Goods: Merchandise, Stories, and Gender in Chaucer's *Man of Law's Tale*', *New Medieval Literatures*, 17 (2017). On the Man of Law's comparison of the Sultaness to Semiramis, Cady notes that among the legends that contributed to Semiramis's notoriety was a story of her having married her son.

22. See Scanlon, 'The Riddle of Incest', pp. 107–12.

23. Graeber, *Toward an Anthropological Theory of Value: The False Coin of Our Own Dreams* (New York: Palgrave, 2001), p. 265, n. 14.

24. The Nun's Priest's seemingly gratuitous remark about Chauntecleer's flock of sisters may recall comments by Genius in his discourse on incest and marriage at the start of Book 8 of the *Confessio*:

> For love, which is unbesein
> Of all reson, as men sein,

> Thurgh sotie and thurgh nyceté,
> Of his voluptuosité
> He spareth no condicion
> Of ken ne yit religion,
> Bot as a cock among the hennes,
> Or as a stalon in the fennes,
> Which goth amonges al the stod,
> Riht so can he no more good,
> Bot takth what thing comth next to honde. (8.153–63)

As Larry Scanlon says, 'These two concluding similes, the cock among the hens, and the stallion among the stud obviously connect human erotic resistance to irrational nature, but they do so in a way that also affirms human regulatory control' ('Riddle of Incest', p. 111). By analogy, Chaucer may make Chauntecleer the incestuous husband of his sisters in order to play on themes of masculine rationality and sexual weakness that animate the tale.

25. Quilligan, *Incest and Agency*, p. 13: 'Theoretically, there are three ways to halt the traffic in women. One is incest, where women make an erotic choice within their own close kin. Two is celibacy, either personal spinsterhood or institutional vocation, the latter when a woman enters a religious order … And, as adumbrated by Rubin, there is a third way out of the traffic – a choice that would in theory root out all kinship system – and that is a lesbian desire that does not comply with the compulsory heterosexuality required by the exchange of women.'

26. Weiner, *Inalienable Possessions*, p. 68.

27. Irigaray, 'Women on the Market', p. 186. Portions of the quotation are italicized in the source.

28. Quilligan, *Incest and Agency*, p. 13.

29. Graeber, *Theory of Value*, p. 35.

30. 'William MacBride Windsor Armchair, ca. 1790' *www.pbs.org/wgbh/roadshow/season/4/tampa-fl/appraisals/william-macbride-windsor-chair--199901A32* (accessed 3 February 2017).

31. In a chapter entitled 'Virginity and the Gift' in *Saints' Lives and Women's Literary Culture, c. 1150–1300: Virginity and Its Authorizations* (Oxford: Oxford University Press, 2001), pp. 56–90, Jocelyn Wogan-Browne considers the virgin martyr in relation to the gift, but primarily in terms of 'the virgin's "dotality", her capacity to be given and to give' (p. 57). That is, Wogan-Browne finds as much significance in the virgins' agency as gift-givers as in their role as gifts themselves: 'Women's gift-giving powers, and their patronage, continue as a significant strand in the representation of virgin martyr lives' (p. 88).

32. 'god-sib(be', Middle English Dictionary, University of Michigan; 'gossip, n.' *OED Online*, Oxford University Press, June 2016.

33. See, for example, Peter G. Beidler's note to line 530 (p. 62) in *The Wife of Bath* (Boston: Bedford, 1996).

34. Irigaray, 'Women on the Market', p. 172.

35. An example of the former would be Laurie Finke, 'Al is for to selle', in Beidler (ed.), *The Wife of Bath*, pp. 171–88. Finke sees the Wife of Bath's serial marriages as emblematic of Marxist 'primitive accumulation': '[T]hey function as a chain of substitutions, her desire to accumulate wealth reducing them to so many interchangeable commodities ... The fifth simply reverses the pattern without substantially altering it' (p. 178). An example of the latter would be Elaine Tuttle Hansen, '"Of his love daungerous to me": Liberation, Subversion, and Domestic Violence in the Wife of Bath's Prologue and Tale', in Beidler (ed.), *The Wife of Bath*, pp. 273–89: 'Despite their obvious love of speaking and their fluency with words, paradoxically, both Chaucer and the Wife of Bath also seem to share a fantasy of silent submission to higher forces' (p. 285).

36. The contrast that I am setting up here between Weiner's and Strathern's theories is recognized and acknowledged by the authors themselves. Weiner sees Strathern as accepting the conventional anthropological theory of the exchange of women: 'Strathern presumes to move beyond positivist theory by beginning with indigenous notions of person identity and then showing the types of social relations that are their concomitants. She uses the terms "detachability" and "transformation" to discuss exchange events, but the processes she describes still are tied to a Lévi-Straussian model of reciprocal exchange. Therefore, objects are merely the reflections of their transactors' embeddedness in social relations, and the value of an object remains only a consequence of the identity of the exchanger' (*Inalienable Possessions*, p. 14). Strathern acknowledges the legitimacy of both 'ceremonial exchange' – the meaning-generating exchange of gifts between groups – and 'production and reproduction' – the essentially female-based generation of value within a kinship group – and she suggests at several points that the latter form is a parallel between her model and Weiner's: 'Weiner has supplanted interpretations that rest on notions of reciprocity derived from *The Gift* (Mauss 1954) with a modeling of Massim exchange as a species of reproduction ... Reciprocity in exchange cannot be taken as an independent social form. As will become apparent, my later arguments dovetail with hers in so far as I attempt to elucidate different types of productivity' (Marilyn Strathern, *The Gender of the Gift: Problems with Women and Problems with Society in Melanesia* (Berkeley: University of California Press, 1988), pp. 144–5). But Strathern acknowledges that her model of 'ceremonial exchange' is essentially different from Weiner's views: 'Ceremonial exchange activity of the Hagen kind is set off from domesticity and from production and reproduction in household relations, as it is from the demands of personal kin ties' (p. 159).

37. Christopher Gregory, *Gifts and Commodities* (London: Academic Press, 1982), p. 71. See also Christopher Gregory, *Savage Money: The Anthropology and*

Politics of Commodity Exchange (Amsterdam: Harwood, 1997), pp. 41–70; Graeber, *Theory of Value*, p. 36.

38. Gregory, *Gifts and Commodities*, p. 45.

39. Gregory, *Gifts and Commodities*, pp. 66–7.

40. Strathern, *Gender of the Gift*, p. 134. This sentence is italicized in Strathern's text. Strathern is frequently credited with originating this idea of personification through gift and objectification through commodity, but she herself clearly asserts that the concept derives from Gregory's *Gifts and Commodities*: 'The contrast sustained in this book between commodity systems and gift systems of exchange is taken directly from Gregory's work' (p. 18). See also pp. 144–5.

41. See Strathern, *The Gender of the Gift*, pp. 55–9.

42. Strathern, *The Gender of the Gift*, pp. 313–14.

43. Strathern, *The Gender of the Gift*, p. 13. Strathern (p. 348, n. 7) attributes the term 'dividual' to McKim Marriott, 'Hindu Transactions: Diversity without Dualism', in B. Kapferer (ed.), *Transactions and Meaning* (Philadelphia: ISHI Publications, 1976).

44. Irigaray, 'Women on the Market', p. 186.

45. See Elizabeth Edwards, 'The Economics of Justice in Chaucer's Miller's and Reeve's Tales', *Dalhousie Review*, 82 (2002).

46. See Graeber, *Theory of Value*, pp. 257–61.

47. See Strathern, *The Gender of the Gift*, pp. 225–40.

48. Strathern, *The Gender of the Gift*, p. 230.

49. Strathern, *The Gender of the Gift*, p. 131; Strathern's emphasis.

50. Strathern, *The Gender of the Gift*, p. 111.

51. Strathern, *The Gender of the Gift*, pp. 211, 212.

52. Strathern, *The Gender of the Gift*, pp. 326–7.

53. Strathern, *The Gender of the Gift*, pp. 327–8. The emphasis, importantly, is Strathern's.

54. This is not a unique view: even other economic anthropologists, like David Graeber, can be daunted by Strathern's prose: 'Perhaps the main thing that has limited her work's appeal is that most of it is written in an incredibly difficult language, largely of her own invention – one which seems to have an endless capacity to slip away almost as soon as the reader thinks she's grasped it. It can be very frustrating to read' (*Theory of Value*, p. 35).

55. 'Feminism' is a problematic term for Strathern, and her own place within Western feminist thought, as well as her position as a feminist and an anthropologist, are complex issues that she addresses directly and at length. See 'A Place in the Feminist Debate', *The Gender of the Gift*, pp. 22–40.

56. R. Howard Bloch, *Etymologies and Genealogies: A Literary Anthropology of the French Middle Ages* (Chicago: University of Chicago Press, 1983), p. 164.

57. Sarah Kay, *The* Chansons de geste *in the Age of Romance: Political Fictions* (Oxford: Clarendon Press, 1995), p. 42.

58. Strathern, *The Gender of the Gift*, p. 134.

59. Kay, Chansons de geste, p. 48.
60. Kay, Chansons de geste, p. 42.
61. See Strathern, 'Relations Which Separate', *The Gender of the Gift*, pp. 191–224.
62. Strathern, *The Gender of the Gift*, p. 178.
63. Strathern, *The Gender of the Gift*, pp. 229–30. Again, the emphasis is Strathern's.
64. Kay, Chansons de geste, p. 15.
65. Kay also acknowledges that in some classic romances, the woman's role is much more like that of a gift in exchange, and she concedes that the 'difference between commodity and gift is one of emphasis and perspective' (Chansons de geste, p. 223).
66. I have explored the dynamics of power and representation in this tale in '"With many a floryn he the hewes boghte": Ekphrasis and Symbolic Violence in the *Knight's Tale*', *Philological Quarterly*, 85 (2006), 49–68.
67. Strathern, *The Gender of the Gift*, p. 161.
68. See Strathern, *The Gender of the Gift*, p. 167: 'The appropriation of surplus product is central to a commodity economy; those who dominate are those who determine the manner of appropriation. In a gift economy, we might argue that those who dominate are those who determine the connections and disconnections created by the circulation of objects.'
69. Of course, Gower also tells an analogue of the *Wife of Bath's Tale* as *The Tale of Florent* in *Confessio Amantis* I.1407–1861.
70. Weiner, *Inalienable Possessions*, pp. 96–7.
71. Kay, Chansons de geste, p. 48.

Chapter 5: Sacred Commerce: Clerics, Money and the Economy of Salvation

1. Linda Georgianna, 'Love So Dearly Bought: The Terms of Redemption in the *Canterbury Tales*', *Studies in the Age of Chaucer*, 12 (1990), 90.
2. Georgianna, 'Love So Dearly Bought', 88–9.
3. Pierre Bourdieu, *Practical Reason: On the Theory of Action* (Stanford: Stanford University Press, 1998), pp. 113–14. The parentheses, brackets and ellipses are in the original.
4. Bourdieu, *Practical Reason*, pp. 112–13.
5. John V. Fleming, 'The Antifraternalism of the *Summoner's Tale*', *Journal of English and Germanic Philology*, 65 (1966), 688, 700; 'The Summoner's Prologue: An Iconographic Adjustment', *Chaucer Review*, 2 (1967), 95–107. See also Arnold Williams, 'Chaucer and the Friars', *Speculum*, 28 (1953), 499–513; Arnold Williams, 'Two Notes on Chaucer's Friars', *Modern Philology*, 54 (1956), 117–20; Jill Mann, *Chaucer and Medieval Estates Satire: The Literature of Social Classes and the General Prologue to the* Canterbury Tales (Cambridge: Cambridge University Press, 1973), pp. 37–54; Penn R. Szittya, *The Antifraternal Tradition in Medieval Literature* (Princeton: Princeton University Press, 1986), pp. 231–46.

6. John Fleming, 'Anticlerical Satire as Theological Essay: Chaucer's *Summoner's Tale*', *Thalia*, 6 (1983), 5–22.

7. John Fleming, *Introduction to the Franciscan Literature of the Middle Ages* (Chicago: Franciscan Herald Press, 1977), p. 78.

8. Translations of the *Sacrum commercium* are taken from 'The Sacred Exchange between Saint Francis and Lady Poverty', in Regis J. Armstrong, J. A. Wayne Hellmann and William J. Short (eds), *Francis of Assisi: Early Documents*, vol. 1: *The Saint* (New York: New City Press, 1999), pp. 529–54. In their introduction to the text (pp. 526–7), Armstrong, Hellman and Short make the case for a date of 1238 and for the authorship of Caesar of Speyer.

9. *Sacrum commercium sancti Francisci cum domina Paupertate*, edited by Stefano Brufani (Assisi: Edizioni Porziuncola, 1990), p. 137.

10. 'Sacred Exchange', p. 533, note b.

11. Lester K. Little, *Religious Poverty and the Profit Economy in Medieval Europe* (Ithaca: Cornell University Press, 1978), p. 200.

12. Little, *Religious Poverty*, p. 200.

13. Little, *Religious Poverty*, p. 216.

14. Little, *Religious Poverty*, p. 181.

15. Giacomo Todeschini, *Franciscan Wealth: From Voluntary Poverty to Market Society*, translated by Donatella Melucci (St Bonaventure, NY: Franciscan Institute, 2009), pp. 139–40.

16. Todeschini, *Franciscan Wealth*, pp. 7–8.

17. See Michael F. Cusato, O.F.M., 'The Early Franciscans and the Use of Money', in *Poverty and Prosperity: Franciscans and the Use of Money* (St Bonaventure, NY: Franciscan Institute Publications, 2009), pp. 13–37 (particularly p. 30).

18. John Fleming, *From Bonaventure to Bellini: An Essay in Franciscan Exegesis* (Princeton: Princeton University Press, 1982), p. 25.

19. Little, *Religious Poverty*, p. 34.

20. Geoffrey Ingham, for instance, at the beginning of his own very comprehensive study of the history, philosophy and sociology of money, confesses his puzzlement 'that such a commonplace as money should give rise to so much bewilderment, controversy and, it must be said, error. It is not well understood.' *The Nature of Money* (Cambridge: Polity, 2004), p. 5.

21. Little, *Religious Poverty*, p. 18.

22. Little, *Religious Poverty*, p. 17.

23. Little, *Religious Poverty*, p. 18.

24. Max Weber, 'Religious Rejections of the World and Their Directions', in H. H. Gerth and C. W. Mills (eds and trans), *From Max Weber: Essays in Sociology* (1946; New York: Oxford University Press, 1970), p. 331; quoted in Little, *Religious Poverty*, p. 33. See also Ingham, *The Nature of Money*, pp. 111–12.

25. See Valerie Allen, *On Farting: Language and Laughter in the Middle Ages* (New York: Palgrave Macmillan, 2007), pp. 76–7, 95–7.

26. For a revisionist reading, defending Chaucer's Friar as 'a multi-faceted friar-character, whose actions and interactions do not convey a strictly negative appraisal of mendicancy', see G. Geltner, *'Faux Semblants*: Antifraternalism Reconsidered in Jean de Meun and Chaucer', *Studies in Philology*, 101 (2004), 357–80 (358).

27. Bourdieu, *Practical Reason*, p. 96.

28. Bourdieu, *Practical Reason*, p. 114. Bourdieu cites Grenet, *Les Aspects économiques du bouddhisme dans la société chinoise des Ve et Xe siècles* (Saigon: École Française d'Extrême-Orient, 1956).

29. See Bernard S. Levy, 'Biblical Parody in the *Summoner's Tale*', *Tennessee Studies in Literature*, 11 (1966), 45–60; Alan Levitan, 'The Parody of the Pentecost in Chaucer's *Summoner's Tale*', *University of Toronto Quarterly*, 40 (1971), 236–46; Glending Olson, 'The End of *The Summoner's Tale* and the Uses of Pentecost', *Studies in the Age of Chaucer*, 21 (1999), 209–45.

30. Joel Kaye, *Economy and Nature in the Fourteenth Century: Money, Market Exchange, and the Emergence of Scientific Thought* (Cambridge: Cambridge University Press, 1998), pp. 2–3.

31. John Murdoch, 'From Social into Intellectual Factors: An Aspect of the Unitary Character of Late Medieval Learning', in John Murdoch and Edith Sylla (eds), *The Cultural Contexts of Medieval Learning* (Dordrecht and Boston: D. Reidel, 1975), p. 287; quoted in Kaye, *Economy and Nature*, p. 3.

32. Kaye, *Economy and Nature*, p. 190.

33. Kaye, *Economy and Nature*, pp. 166–7.

34. J. A. W. Bennett, *Chaucer at Oxford and at Cambridge* (Toronto: University of Toronto Press, 1974). On Merton College, see pp. 58–85; on Strode, see pp. 63–5; on Bradwardine, see pp. 62–3, and also Kaye, *Economy and Nature*, pp. 165–6.

35. Bennett, *Chaucer at Oxford*, p. 69.

36. Kaye, *Economy and Nature*, pp. 173–81.

37. Kaye, *Economy and Nature*, pp. 28–36.

38. Kaye, *Economy and Nature*, p. 36.

39. Chaucer's acoustical observations derive largely from Vincent of Beauvais and Robert Grosseteste. See John M. Fyler's note in the *Riverside Chaucer*, general editor Larry D. Benson (Boston: Houghton Mifflin, 1987), p. 983. See also W. O. Sypherd, *Studies in Chaucer's* House of Fame (London: L. Paul, Trench, Trübner, 1907; reprinted New York: Haskell House, 1965), pp. 95–100. Bennett remarks that Chaucer 'could hardly have made that poetical survey of the starry regions and the laws of sound but for the impetus given by the Merton School' (*Chaucer at Oxford*, p. 62).

40. Bennett, *Chaucer at Oxford*, p. 75: 'Thus one by one every astronomical trail in Chaucer leads us to Oxford, and in Oxford to Merton.' Bennett adds that Chaucer's *Treatise on the Astrolabe* 'itself became an Oxford text inasmuch as at least one copy of it (MS. Bodley 619) was made by an Oxford astronomer'.

41. Kaye, *Economy and Nature*, p. 176.

42. John Thomas Noonan, *The Scholastic Analysis of Usury* (Cambridge, MA: Harvard University Press, 1957), pp. 19–20.

43. Kaye, *Economy and Nature*, pp. 82–3. See also D. Vance Smith, *Arts of Possession: The Middle English Household Imaginary* (Minneapolis: University of Minnesota Press, 2003), pp. 131–3.

44. Little, *Religious Poverty*, p. 177.

45. Kaye, *Economy and Nature*, p. 83.

46. R. Howard Bloch, *Etymologies and Genealogies: A Literary Anthropology of the French Middle Ages* (Chicago: University of Chicago Press, 1983), p. 170.

47. Joel Kaye, *A History of Balance, 1250–1375: The Emergence of a New Model of Equilibrium and Its Impact on Thought* (Cambridge: Cambridge University Press, 2014), p. 79.

48. Kaye, *Balance*, p. 171n.

49. Alastair Minnis, 'Purchasing Pardon: Material and Spiritual Economies on the Canterbury Pilgrimage', in Lawrence L. Besserman (ed.), *Sacred and Secular in Medieval and Early Modern Cultures: New Essays* (New York: Palgrave, 2006), pp. 63–82 (82). See also Minnis, 'The Construction of Chaucer's Pardoner', in R. N. Swanson (ed.), *Promissory Notes on the Treasury of Merits: Indulgences in Late Medieval Europe* (Leiden: Brill, 2006), pp. 169–95.

50. R. N. Swanson, *Indulgences in Late Medieval England: Passports to Paradise* (Cambridge: Cambridge University Press, 2007), p. 219.

51. Bourdieu, *Practical Reason*, p. 115.

Chapter 6: 'Fy on a thousand pound!' Debt and the Possibility of Generosity in the *Franklin's Tale*

1. D. W. Robertson, *A Preface to Chaucer: Studies in Medieval Perspectives* (Princeton: Princeton University Press, 1962), p. 472.

2. See Lee Patterson, 'The Development of Chaucer Studies', in *Negotiating the Past: The Historical Understanding of Medieval Literature* (Madison: University of Wisconsin Press, 1987), pp. 3–39.

3. D. W. Robertson, Jr., *A Preface to Chaucer: Studies in Medieval Perspectives* (Princeton: Princeton University Press, 1962), p. 472. See also R. M. Lumiansky, 'The Character and the Performance of Chaucer's Franklin', *University of Toronto Quarterly*, 20 (1951), 344–56.

4. Jacques Derrida, *Given Time: I. Counterfeit Money*, translated by Peggy Kamuf (Chicago: Chicago University Press, 1992), p. 12.

5. Derrida, *Given Time*, p. 23.

6. Derrida, *Given Time*, p. 7; Derrida's emphasis.

7. Britton J. Harwood, 'Chaucer and the Gift (If There Is Any)', *Studies in Philology*, 103 (2006), 27.

8. Harwood, 'Chaucer and the Gift', 28–9.

9. Harwood, 'Chaucer and the Gift', 31.

10. Harwood, 'Chaucer and the Gift', 45.

11. Kyle Mahowald, '"It may nat be": Chaucer, Derrida, and the Impossibility of the Gift', *Studies in the Age of Chaucer*, 32 (2010), 131–2.

12. Mahowald, 'It may not be', 143.

13. Harwood, 'Chaucer and the Gift', 42.

14. Mahowald, 'It may nat be', 145.

15. See, for instance, Robert Bernasconi, 'What Goes Around Comes Around: Derrida and Levinas on the Economy of the Gift and the Gift of Genealogy', in Alan D. Schrift (ed.), *The Logic of the Gift: Toward an Ethic of Generosity* (New York: Routledge, 1997), pp. 256–73.

16. Pierre Bourdieu, 'Marginalia – Some Additional Notes on the Gift', in Schrift (ed.), *The Logic of the Gift*, p. 240.

17. Marcel Mauss, *The Gift: The Form and Reason for Exchange in Archaic Societies*, translated by W. D. Halls (New York: Norton, 1990), p. 3.

18. Derrida, *Given Time*, pp. 12, 13; Derrida's emphasis.

19. Derrida, *Given Time*, p. 7; Derrida's emphasis.

20. See *Given Time*, p. 42, where Derrida says that one of Mauss's goals in reintroducing the category of the gift is 'to succeed in maintaining an originary specificity of the process of the gift in relation to cold economic rationality, to capitalism, and mercantilism – and in that way to recognize in the gift that which sets the circle of economic exchange going.' Note that even as Derrida acknowledges that Mauss's essay is motivated by the political goal of distinguishing gifts and gift exchange from commodities and markets, he still insists (erroneously, I firmly believe) that the gift, as the elemental form of exchange, is the direct ancestor of and the first step toward the inevitable conclusion of markets and capitalism.

21. Camil Ungureanu, 'Bourdieu and Derrida on Gift: Beyond "Double Truth" and Paradox', *Human Studies*, 36 (2013), 407.

22. Chris Hann and Keith Hart, *Economic Anthropology: History, Ethnography, Critique* (Cambridge: Polity Press, 2011), p. 87.

23. David Graeber, *Toward an Anthropological Theory of Value: The False Coin of Our Own Dreams* (New York: Palgrave, 2001), pp. 220–1; Graeber's emphasis.

24. Jacques T. Godbout, in collaboration with Alain Caillé, *The World of the Gift*, translated by Donald Winkler (Montreal: McGill-Queen's University Press, 1998), p. 179.

25. Derrida, *Given Time*, p. 23.

26. Derrida, *Given Time*, p. 40; Derrida's emphasis.

27. Mauss, *The Gift*, pp. 35–6.

28. In subsequent works, notably *The Gift of Death*, translated by David Wills (Chicago: University of Chicago Press, 1995), Derrida treated the gift in relation to notions of sacrifice. See Dennis King Keenan, *The Question of Sacrifice* (Bloomington: Indiana University Press, 2005), pp. 134–59.

29. Godbout and Caillé, *The World of the Gift*, p. 197.

30. Mahowald, 'It may nat be', 145; Mahowald's emphasis.

31. Graeber, *Theory of Value*, p. 161; Graeber's emphasis. The degree to which Derrida's conception of the gift is rooted in universal moral principles is even more apparent in *The Gift of Death*. Derrida argues that the only true gift is one's own life because it is the only thing one truly owns: 'The crypto- or mysto-genealogy of responsibility is woven with the double and inextricably intertwined thread of the gift and of death: in short of the *gift of death*. The gift made to me by God as he holds me in his gaze and in his hand while remaining inaccessible to me, the terribly dissymmetrical gift of the *mysterium tremendum* only allows me to respond and only rouses me to the responsibility it gives me by making a gift of death [*en me donnant la mort*], giving the secret of death, a new experience of death' (p. 33).

32. Robert R. Edwards, 'Source, Context, and Cultural Translation in the Franklin's Tale', *Modern Philology*, 94 (1996), 161. See also Alan T. Gaylord, 'The Promises in *The Franklin's Tale*', *ELH*, 31 (1964), 331–65; Judith L. Kellogg, '"Large and Fre": The Influence of Middle English Romance on Chaucer's Chivalric Language', *Allegorica*, 9 (1987), 221–48; Susan Crane, 'The Franklin as Dorigen', *Chaucer Review*, 24 (1990), 236–52.

33. See Graeber, *Theory of Value*, p. 10, and *Debt: The First 5,000 Years* (Brooklyn, NY: Melville House, 2011), pp. 23–8. In addition to being elaborated by Adam Smith in *The Wealth of Nations*, the theory is, as Graeber notes, presented as fact at the start of just about every introductory economics textbook. Adam Smith, *The Wealth of Nations* (New York: Alfred A. Knopf, 1991), pp. 19–25.

34. See Graeber, *Debt*, pp. 55–9. A particularly insightful and valuable investigation of the questions of money and debt, and an important elaboration of primordial debt theory, are provided by Geoffrey Ingham, *The Nature of Money* (Cambridge: Polity Press, 2004). See also Georg Friedrich Knapp, *The State Theory of Money*, translated by H. M. Lucas and J. Bonar (London: Macmillan, 1924).

35. Graeber, *Debt*, p. 59.

36. See Graeber, *Debt*, especially chapter 5, 'A Brief Treatise on the Moral Grounds of Economic Relations', pp. 89–126.

37. Graeber, *Debt*, p. 446, n. 53.

38. Delloyd J. Guth, 'The Age of Debt, the Reformation, and English Law', in *Tudor Rule and Revolution: Essays for G. R. Elton from His American Friends* (Cambridge: Cambridge University Press, 1982), pp. 69–86.

39. Hann and Hart, *Economic Anthropology*, pp. 50–1. Most of Mauss's modern readers acknowledge the political origins of *The Gift*. Mauss's aim was to address the limitations of early twentieth-century market ideology. As Graeber says, 'Mauss was not trying to describe how the logic of the marketplace, with its strict distinctions between persons and things, interest and altruism, freedom and obligation, had become the common sense of modern societies. Above all, he was trying to explain the degree to which

it had *failed* to do so; to explain why so many people – and particularly, so many of the less powerful and privileged members of society – found its logic morally repugnant' (*Theory of Value*, p. 162). It has been suggested that the revival of interest in Mauss's essay in the early twenty-first century arises from similar impulses. Alan D. Schrift posits that 'the appeal of the gift as a topic for consideration and research may reflect a renewed concern for the establishment of more politically acceptable relations between citizens in response to the recent neoconservative attacks on many of the fundamental principles underlying a notion of social welfare and the accompanying neoconservative championing of a return to a fundamentally contractarian notion of human relations. This attack has allowed a narrowly self-interested notion of reciprocal return to emerge and dominate the current political discourse on giving.' 'Introduction: Why Gift?', in Schrift (ed.), *The Logic of the Gift*, p. 19.

40. Graeber, *Debt*, pp. 119, 120.
41. Graeber, *Debt*, p. 121.
42. Graeber, *Debt*, p. 332.
43. Graeber, *Debt*, p. 391.
44. Graeber, *Theory of Value*, p. xi. See also Thomas Hylland Eriksen, 'Globalization', in Keith Hart, Jean-Louis Laville and Antonio David Cattani (eds), *The Human Economy: A Citizen's Guide* (Cambridge: Polity Press, 2010), p. 24: 'The concepts of language and time exist in traditional societies, but not writing and clocks. Similarly, money-like instruments exist in many kinds of societies, but our kind of money, "all-purpose money", is recent and culture-bound. It does roughly the same thing for payment, value measurement and exchange as clocks and writing do for time and language, respectively. All make transactions more abstract and impose a standard, ultimately taking in the whole world. They place individual, mundane transactions under one invisible umbrella.'
45. Joanne Rice notes in the *Riverside Chaucer*, general editor Larry D. Benson (Boston: Houghton Mifflin, 1987), p. 901, that the phrase Aurelius uses to release Dorigen from the agreement – 'I yow relesse, madame, into youre hond / Quyt every serement and every bond / That ye han maad to me as heerbiforn' (V.1533–5) – derives from the formula for a legal release or quit-claim.
46. Graeber, *Debt*, p. 64.
47. Graeber, *Debt*, p. 87.
48. Godbout and Caillé, *The World of the Gift*, p. 210.
49. Ruth Barrie Strauss, '"Truth" and "Woman" in Chaucer's Franklin's Tale', *Exemplaria*, 4 (1992), 136–7.
50. Graeber, *Debt*, p. 65. A 'debt-peon' is a bond-slave – one who owes labour in repayment of a debt.
51. Graeber, *Debt*, p. 82.
52. Graeber, *Debt*, p. 391.

Conclusion

1. R. A. Shoaf, *Dante, Chaucer, and the Currency of the Word: Money, Images, and Reference in Late Medieval Poetry* (Norman, OK: Pilgrim Books, 1983), p. 68; Patricia J. Eberle, Commercial Language and the Commercial Outlook in the *General Prologue*', *Chaucer Review*, 18 (1983), 163.
2. Joel Kaye, 'Monetary and Market Consciousness in Thirteenth and Fourteenth Century Europe', in S. Todd Lowry and Barry Gordon (eds), *Ancient and Medieval Economic Ideas and Concepts of Social Justice* (Leiden: Brill, 1998), pp. 371–403.

BIBLIOGRAPHY

Adams, Jenny, 'Exchequers and Balances: Anxieties of Exchange in *The Tale of Beryn*', *Studies in the Age of Chaucer*, 26 (2004), 267–97.

Adams, Robert, 'The Concept of Debt in *The Shipman's Tale*', *Studies in the Age of Chaucer*, 6 (1984), 85–102.

Aers, David, *Chaucer* (Atlantic Highlands, NJ: Humanities Press International, 1986).

Algazi, Gadi, Valentin Groebner and Bernhard Jussen (eds), *Negotiating the Gift: Pre-modern Figurations of Exchange* (Göttingen: Vandenhoeck & Ruprecht, 2003).

Allen, Elizabeth, 'Chaucer Answers Gower: Constance and the Trouble with Reading', *ELH*, 64 (1997), 627–55.

Allen, Valerie, *On Farting: Language and Laughter in the Middle Ages* (New York: Palgrave Macmillan, 2007).

Anspach, Mark Rogin, *À charge de revanche: figures élémentaires de la réciprocité* (Paris: Seuil, 2002).

——, 'Violence Deceived: Changing Reciprocities from Vengeance to Gift Exchange', in Caroline Gerschlager (ed.), *Expanding the Economic Concept of Exchange: Deception, Self-Deception and Illusions* (Dordrecht: Kluwer Academic Publishers, 2001), pp. 213–24.

Archibald, Elizabeth, '"Worse Than Bogery": Incest Stories in Middle English', in Elizabeth Barnes (ed.), *Incest and the Literary Imagination* (Gainesville: University Press of Florida, 2002), pp. 17–38.

Armstrong, Regis J., J. A. Wayne Hellmann and William J. Short (eds), *Francis of Assisi: Early Documents* (New York: New City Press, 1999).

Baird, Joseph L., 'Law and the *Reeve's Tale*', *Neuphilologische Mitteilungen*, 70 (1969), 679–83.

Barney, Stephen A., 'The Plowshare of the Tongue: The Progress of a Symbol from the Bible to *Piers Plowman*', *Mediaeval Studies*, 35 (1973), 261–93.

Bataille, Georges, *The Accursed Share: An Essay on General Economy*, translated by Robert Hurley (New York: Zone Books, 1988).

Bédier, Joseph, *Les Fabliaux: Études de littétature populaire et d'histoire littéraire du moyen âge* (Paris: É. Bouillon, 1893).

Beidelman, T. O., 'Agonistic Exchange: Homeric Reciprocity and the Heritage of Simmel and Mauss', *Cultural Anthropology*, 4 (1989), 227–59.

Beidler, Peter G. (ed.), *The Wife of Bath* (Boston: Bedford, 1996).

——, 'The Price of Sex in Chaucer's *Shipman's Tale*', *Chaucer Review*, 31 (1996), 5–17.

Bennett, J. A. W., *Chaucer at Oxford and at Cambridge* (Toronto: University of Toronto Press, 1974).

Bennett, Judith, 'The Curse of the Plowman', *Yearbook of Langland Studies*, 20 (2006), 215–26.

Benson, C. David, 'Incest and Moral Poetry in Gower's *Confessio Amantis*', *Chaucer Review*, 19 (1984), 100–9.

Benson, Larry D., and Theodore M. Andersson (eds), *The Literary Context of Chaucer's Fabliaux* (Indianapolis: Bobbs-Merrill, 1971).

Bernasconi, Robert, 'What Goes Around Comes Around: Derrida and Levinas on the Economy of the Gift and the Gift of Genealogy', in Alan D. Schrift (ed.), *The Logic of the Gift: Toward an Ethic of Generosity* (New York: Routledge, 1997), pp. 256–73.

Bertolet, Craig E., *Chaucer, Gower, Hoccleve and the Commercial Practices of Late Fourteenth-Century London* (Burlington, VT: Ashgate, 2013).

——, '"Wel bet is roten appul out of hoord": Chaucer's Cook, Commerce, and Civil Order', *Studies in Philology*, 99 (2002), 229–46.

Bestor, Jane Fair, 'Marriage Transactions in Renaissance Italy and Mauss's Essay on the Gift', *Past & Present*, 164 (1999), 6–46.

Bishop, Kathleen A., 'Queer Punishments: Tragic and Comic Sodomy in the Death of Edward II and in Chaucer's *Miller's Tale*', in Kathleen A. Bishop (ed.), *The Canterbury Tales Revisited – 21st Century Interpretations* (Newcastle: Cambridge Scholars Press, 2008), pp. 16–24.

Bijsterveld, Arnoud-Jan A., 'The Medieval Gift as Agent of Social Bonding and Political Power: A Comparative Approach', in Esther Cohen and Maykè B. de Jong (eds), *Medieval Transformations: Texts, Power, and Gifts in Context* (Brill: Leiden, 2001), pp. 123–56.

Blamires, Alcuin, 'Chaucer the Reactionary: Ideology and the General Prologue to the *Canterbury Tales*', *Review of English Studies*, new series, 51, 204 (2000), 523–39.

Bloch, R. Howard, *The Scandal of the Fabliaux* (Chicago: University of Chicago Press, 1986).

——, *Etymologies and Genealogies: A Literary Anthropology of the French Middle Ages* (Chicago: University of Chicago Press, 1983).

——, 'Chaucer's Maiden's Head: The Physician's Tale and the Poetics of Virginity', *Qui Parle*, 2 (1988), 22–45.

Bolton, J. L., *Money in the Medieval English Economy: 973–1489* (Manchester: Manchester University Press, 2012).

Bourdieu, Pierre, *Practical Reason: On the Theory of Action* (Stanford: Stanford University Press, 1998).

——, *The Logic of Practice*, translated by Richard Nice (Stanford: Stanford University Press, 1980).

——, *Outline of a Theory of Practice*, translated by Richard Nice (Cambridge: Cambridge University Press, 1977).

——, 'Marginalia – Some Additional Notes on the Gift', in Alan D. Schrift (ed.), *The Logic of the Gift: Toward an Ethic of Generosity* (New York: Routledge, 1997), pp. 231–41.

Bracken, Christopher, *The Potlatch Papers: A Colonial Case History* (Chicago: University of Chicago Press, 1997).

Braswell, Mary, *Chaucer's 'Legal Fiction': Reading the Records* (Madison, NJ: Fairleigh University Press, 2001).

Breuer, Heidi, 'Being Intolerant: Rape is Not Seduction (in "The Reeve's Tale" or Anywhere Else)', in Kathleen A. Bishop (ed.), *The Canterbury Tales Revisited – 21st Century Interpretations* (Newcastle: Cambridge Scholars Press, 2008), pp. 1–15.

Brewer, Derek, 'Class Distinction in Chaucer', *Speculum*, 43 (1968), 290–305.

Britnell, R. H., *The Commercialisation of English Society, 1000–1500* (Manchester: Manchester University Press, 1996).

Bryan, W. F., and Germaine Dempster (eds), *Sources and Analogues of Chaucer's Canterbury Tales* (New York: Humanities Press, 1958).

Bullón-Fernández, Maria, *Fathers and Daughters in Gower's* Confessio Amantis: *Authority, Family, State, and Writing* (Cambridge: D. S. Brewer, 2000).

Cady, Diane, 'Damaged Goods: Merchandise, Stories, and Gender in Chaucer's *Man of Law's Tale*', *New Medieval Literatures*, 17 (2017).

Cahn, Kenneth S., 'Chaucer's Merchants and the Foreign Exchange: An Introduction to Medieval Finance', *Studies in the Age of Chaucer*, 2 (1980), 81–119.

Caillé, Alain, *Don, intérêt et désintéressement: Bourdieu, Mauss, Platon et quelques autres* (Paris: La Découverte/M.A.U.S.S., 2005).

——, *Critique de la raison utilitaire: Manifeste du MAUSS* (Paris: La Découverte, 1989).

——, 'Gift', in Keith Hart, Jean-Louis Laville and Antonio David Cattani (eds), *The Human Economy: A Citizen's Guide* (Cambridge: Polity Press, 2010), pp. 180–6.

Calhoun, Craig, Edward LiPuma and Moishe Postone (eds), *Bourdieu: Critical Perspectives* (Chicago: University of Chicago Press, 1993).

Carlson, Cindy L., and Angela Jane Weisl (eds), *Construction of Widowhood and Virginity in the Middle Ages* (New York: St. Martin's, 1999).

Carrier, James, 'Gifts, Commodities, and Social Relations: A Maussian View of Exchange', *Sociological Forum*, 6 (1991), 119–36.

Carroll, Virginia Schaefer, 'Women and Money in *The Miller's Tale* and *The Reeve's Tale*', *Medieval Perspectives*, 3 (1988), 76–88.

Chaucer, Geoffrey, *The Riverside Chaucer*, general editor Larry D. Benson (Boston: Houghton Mifflin, 1987).

Cheal, David, *The Gift Economy* (London: Routledge, 1988).

Codere, Helen, *Fighting with Property: A Study of Kwakiutl Potlatching and Warfare, 1792–1930* (Seattle: University of Washington Press, 1950).

Cooke, Thomas D., *The Old French and Chaucerian Fabliaux: A Study of Their Comic Climax* (Columbia: University of Missouri Press, 1978).

Correale, Robert M., and Mary Hamel (eds), *Sources and Analogues of the Canterbury Tales* (Cambridge: D. S. Brewer, 2005).

Crane, Susan, 'The Franklin as Dorigen', *Chaucer Review*, 24 (1990), 236–52.

——, 'Alison's Incapacity and Poetic Instability in the Wife of Bath's Tale', *PMLA*, 102 (1987), 20–8.

Crocker, Holly, 'Wifely Eye for the Manly Guy: Trading the Masculine Image in the *Shipman's Tale*', in T. L. Burton and John F. Plummer (eds), *'Seyd in Forme and Reverence': Essays on Chaucer and Chaucerians in Memory of Emerson Brown, Jr.* (Provo, UT: Chaucer Studio Press, 2005), pp. 59–73.

Cusato, Michael F., O.F.M., 'The Early Franciscans and the Use of Money', in *Poverty and Prosperity: Franciscans and the Use of Money* (St Bonaventure, NY: Franciscan Institute Publications, 2009), pp. 13–37.

De Roover, Raymond, *Business, Banking, and Economic Thought in Late Medieval and Early Modern Europe* (Chicago: University of Chicago Press, 1974).

——, *Money, Banking and Credit in Mediaeval Bruges: Italian Merchant Bankers, Lombards, and Money-changers* (Cambridge, MA: Mediaeval Academy of America, 1948).

Dempsey, Bernard W., *Interest and Usury* (Washington, DC: American Council on Public Affairs, 1943).

Derrida, Jacques, *The Gift of Death*, translated by David Wills (Chicago: University of Chicago Press, 1995).

——, *Given Time: I. Counterfeit Money*, translated by Peggy Kamuf (Chicago: University of Chicago Press, 1992).

Donaldson, E. Talbot, *Chaucer's Poetry: An Anthology for the Modern Reader* (New York: Ronald Press Company, 1958).

Donavin, Georgiana, *Incest narratives and the Structure of Gower's* Confessio amantis (Victoria, BC: English Literary Studies, 1993).

Donham, Donald L., 'Beyond the Domestic Mode of Production', *Man*, new series 16 (1981), 515–41.

Dryden, John, *The Poems and Fables of John Dryden*, edited by James Kinsley (London: Oxford University Press, 1962).

Dyer, Christopher, 'Piers Plowman and Plowmen: A Historical Perspective', *Yearbook of Langland Studies*, 8 (1995), 155–76.

Eberle, Patricia J., 'Commercial Language and the Commercial Outlook in the *General Prologue*', *Chaucer Review*, 18 (1983), 161–74.

Edwards, Elizabeth, 'The Economics of Justice in Chaucer's Miller's and Reeve's Tales', *The Dalhousie Review*, 82 (2002), 91–112.

Edwards, Robert R., *Chaucer and Boccaccio: Antiquity and Modernity* (New York: Palgrave, 2002).

——, 'Source, Context, and Cultural Translation in the Franklin's Tale', *Modern Philology*, 94 (1996), 141–62.

Epstein, Robert, 'The Lack of Interest in the *Shipman's Tale*: Chaucer and the Social Theory of the Gift', *Modern Philology*, 113 (2015), 27–48.

——, 'Sacred Commerce: Chaucer, Friars, and the Spirit of Money', in Robert Epstein and William Robins (eds), *Sacred and Profane in Chaucer and Late Medieval Literature: Essays in Honour of John V. Fleming* (Toronto: University of Toronto Press, 2010).

——, '"With many a floryn he the hewes boghte": Ekphrasis and Symbolic Violence in the *Knight's Tale*', *Philological Quarterly*, 85 (2006), 49–68.

Eriksen, Thomas Hylland, 'Globalization', in Keith Hart, Jean-Louis Laville and Antonio David Cattani (eds), *The Human Economy: A Citizen's Guide* (Cambridge: Polity, 2010), pp. 21–31.

Farber, Lianna, *An Anatomy of Trade in Medieval Writing: Value, Consent, and Community* (Ithaca: Cornell University Press, 2006).

Fleming, John V., *From Bonaventure to Bellini: An Essay in Franciscan Exegesis* (Princeton: Princeton University Press, 1982).

——, *An Introduction to the Franciscan Literature of the Middle Ages* (Chicago: Franciscan Herald Press, 1977).

——, 'Anticlerical Satire as Theological Essay: Chaucer's *Summoner's Tale*', *Thalia*, 6 (1983), 5–22.

——, 'The Summoner's Prologue: An Iconographic Adjustment', *Chaucer Review*, 2 (1967), 95–107.

——, 'The Antifraternalism of the *Summoner's Tale*', *Journal of English and Germanic Philology*, 65 (1966), 688–700.

Fowler, Elizabeth, 'Misogyny and Economic Person in Skelton, Langland, and Chaucer', *Spenser Studies*, 10 (1992), 245–73.

Frank, Robert Worth, Jr., 'The Reeve's Tale and the Comedy of Limitation', in Stanley Weintraub and Philip Young (eds), *Directions in Literary Criticism* (University Park: Penn State University Press, 1973), pp. 53–67.

Fulton, Helen, 'Mercantile Ideology in Chaucer's 'Shipman's Tale', *Chaucer Review*, 36 (2002), 311–28.

Ganim, John M., 'Double Entry in Chaucer's *Shipman's Tale*: Chaucer and Bookkeeping Before Pacioli', *Chaucer Review*, 30 (1996), 295–305.

Gaunt, Simon, *Gender and Genre in Medieval French Literature* (Cambridge: Cambridge University Press, 1995).

Gastle, Brian, 'Chaucer's "Shaply" Guildsmen and Mercantile Pretensions', *Neuphilologische Mitteilungen*, 99 (1998), 211–16.

Gaylord, Alan T., 'The Promises in *The Franklin's Tale*', *ELH*, 31 (1964), 331–65.

Geltner, G., '*Faux Semblants*: Antifraternalism Reconsidered in Jean de Meun and Chaucer', *Studies in Philology*, 101 (2004), 357–80.

Georgianna, Linda, 'Love So Dearly Bought: The Terms of Redemption in *The Canterbury Tales*', *Studies in the Age of Chaucer*, 12 (1990), 85–116.

Gerhard, Joseph, 'Chaucer's Coinage: Foreign Exchange and the Puns of the *Shipman's Tale*', *Chaucer Review*, 17 (1983), 341–57.

Godbout, Jacques T., in collaboration with Alain Caillé, *The World of the Gift*, translated by Donald Winkler (Montreal: McGill-Queen's University Press, 1998).

Goodall, Peter, 'Chaucer's "Burgesses" and the Aldermen of London', *Medium Aevum*, 50 (1981), 284–91.

Gower, John, *Confessio Amantis*, edited by Russell A. Peck, 3 vols (Kalamazoo: Medieval Institute Publications, 2000–4).

Graeber, David, *Debt: The First 5,000 Years* (Brooklyn, NY: Melville House, 2011).

——, *Toward an Anthropological Theory of Value: The False Coin of Our Own Dreams* (New York: Palgrave, 2001).

——, 'Debt, Violence, and Impersonal Markets: Polanyian Meditations', in Chris Hann and Keith Hart (eds), *Market and Society: The Great Transformation Today* (Cambridge: Cambridge University Press, 2009), pp. 106–32.

Gregory, Christopher, *Savage Money: The Anthropology and Politics of Commodity Exchange* (Amsterdam: Harwood Academic Publishers, 1997).

——, *Gifts and Commodities* (London: Academic Press, 1982).

Guth, Delloyd J., 'The Age of Debt, the Reformation, and English Law', in *Tudor Rule and Revolution: Essays for G. R. Elton from His American Friends* (Cambridge: Cambridge University Press, 1982), pp. 69–86.

Hahn, Thomas, 'Money, Sexuality, Wordplay, and Context in the *Shipman's Tale*', in Julian N. Wasserman and Robert J. Blanch (eds), *Chaucer in the Eighties* (Syracuse: Syracuse University Press, 1986), pp. 235–49.

Hann, Chris, and Keith Hart, *Economic Anthropology: History, Ethnography, Critique* (Cambridge: Polity Press, 2011).

Harper, Elizabeth, '*Pearl* in the Context of Fourteenth-Century Gift Economies', *Chaucer Review*, 44 (2010), 421–39.

Hart, Keith, 'Marcel Mauss's Economic Vision, 1920–25: Anthropology, Politics, Journalism', *Journal of Classical Sociology*, 14 (2014), 34–44.

Harwood, Britton J., 'Chaucer and the Gift (If There Is Any)', *Studies in Philology*, 103 (2006), 26–46.

——, 'The "Fraternitee" of Chaucer's Guildsmen', *Review of English Studies*, 39 (1988), 413–17.

Herzman, Ronald B., 'The *Reeve's Tale*, Symkyn and Simon the Magician', *American Benedictine Review*, 33 (1982), 325–33.

Higgs, Elton D., 'Temporal and Spiritual Indebtedness in the *Canterbury Tales*', in Susan Powell and Jeremy J. Smith (eds), *New Perspectives on Middle English Texts: A Festschrift for R. A. Waldron* (Woodbridge: Brewer, 2000), pp. 151–67.

Hirschman, Albert O., *The Passions and the Interests: Political Arguments for Capitalism before Its Triumph* (Princeton: Princeton University Press, 1977).

Holsinger, Bruce, *The Premodern Condition: Medievalism and the Making of Theory* (Chicago: University of Chicago Press, 2005).

Horrell, Joe, 'Chaucer's Symbolic Plowman', *Speculum*, 14 (1939), 82–92.

Howell, Martha C., *Commerce before Capitalism in Europe, 1300–1600* (Cambridge: Cambridge University Press, 2010).

Hsy, Jonathan H., *Trading Tongues: Merchants, Multilingualism, and Medieval Literature* (Columbus: Ohio State University Press, 2013).

Huizinga, Johan, *The Autumn of the Middle Ages*, translated by Rodney J. Payton and Ulrich Mammitzch (Chicago: University of Chicago Press, 1996).

Hume, Cathy, 'Domestic Opportunities: The Social Comedy of the *Shipman's Tale*', *Chaucer Review*, 41 (2006), 138–62.

Hunt, Edwin S., and James M. Murray, *A History of Business in Medieval Europe, 1200–1550* (Cambridge: Cambridge University Press, 1999).

Ingham, Geoffrey K., *The Nature of Money* (Cambridge: Polity Press, 2004).

Irigaray, Luce, *This Sex Which Is Not One*, translated by Catherine Porter (Ithaca: Cornell University Press, 1985).

Kay, Sarah, *The Chansons de geste in the Age of Romance: Political Fictions* (Oxford: Clarendon, 1995).

Kaye, Joel, *A History of Balance, 1250–1375: The Emergence of a New Model of Equilibrium and Its Impact on Thought* (Cambridge: Cambridge University Press, 2014).

——, *Economy and Nature in the Fourteenth Century: Money, Market Exchange, and the Emergence of Scientific Thought* (Cambridge: Cambridge University Press, 1998).

——, 'Monetary and Market Consciousness in Thirteenth and Fourteenth Century Europe', in S. Todd Lowry and Barry Gordon (eds), *Ancient and Medieval Ideas and Concepts of Social Justice* (Leiden: Brill, 1998), pp. 371–403.

Keenan, Dennis King, *The Question of Sacrifice* (Bloomington: Indiana University Press, 2005).

Keenan, Hugh T., 'The General Prologue to the *Canterbury Tales*, Lines 345–346: The Franklin's Feast and the Eucharistic Shadows', *Neuphilologische Mitteilungen*, 79 (1978), 36–40.

Kellogg, Judith L., '"Large and Fre": The Influence of Middle English Romance on Chaucer's Chivalric Language', *Allegorica*, 9 (1987), 221–48.

Kisor, Yvette, 'Moments of Silence, Acts of Speech: Uncovering the Incest Motif in the *Man of Law's Tale*', *Chaucer Review*, 40 (2005), 141–62.

Knapp, Georg Friedrich, *The State Theory of Money*, translated by H. M. Lucas and J. Bonar (London: Macmillan, 1924).

Knight, Stephen, *Geoffrey Chaucer* (Oxford: Blackwell, 1986).

Komter, Aafke E. (ed.), *The Gift: An Interdisciplinary Perspective* (Amsterdam: Amsterdam University Press, 1996).

Krueger, Roberta, 'Love, Honor, and the Exchange of Women in *Yvain*: Some Remarks on the Female Reader', *Romance Notes*, 25 (1985), 302–17.

Ladd, Roger A., *Antimercantilism in Late Medieval English Literature* (New York: Palgrave Macmillan, 2010).

——, 'Gower's Gifts', in Ana Sáez-Hidalgo and R. F. Yeager (eds), *John Gower in England and Iberia: Manuscripts, Influences, Reception* (Woodbridge: Brewer, 2014), pp. 229–39.

Langholm, Odd, *Economics in the Medieval Schools: Wealth, Exchange, Value, Money and Usury according to the Paris Theological Tradition, 1200–1350* (Leiden: Brill, 1992).

——, *The Aristotelian Analysis of Usury* (Bergen: Universitetsforlaget, 1984).

——, 'The Medieval Schoolmen (1200–1400)', in S. Todd Lowry and Barry Gordon (eds), *Ancient and Medieval Economic Ideas and Concepts of Social Justice* (Leiden: Brill, 1998), pp. 439–501.

Le Goff, Jacques, *Money and the Middle Ages*, translated by Jean Birrell (Cambridge: Polity, 2012).

——, *Your Money or Your Life: Economy and Religion in the Middle Ages* (New York: Zone Books, 1988).

Lefort, Claude, 'L'échange ou la lutte des hommes', *Les Temps modernes* (1951), 1404–17.

Lévi-Strauss, Claude, *The Elementary Structures of Kinship*, edited and translated by James Harle Bell, John Richard von Sturmer and Rodney Needham (Boston: Beacon Press, 1969).

Levitan, Alan, 'The Parody of the Pentecost in Chaucer's *Summoner's Tale*', *University of Toronto Quarterly*, 40 (1971), 236–46.

Levy, Bernard S., 'Biblical Parody in the *Summoner's Tale*', *Tennessee Studies in Literature*, 11 (1966), 45–60.

Little, Lester K., *Religious Poverty and the Profit Economy in Medieval Europe* (Ithaca: Cornell University Press, 1978).

Lumiansky, R. M., 'The Character and the Performance of Chaucer's Franklin', *University of Toronto Quarterly*, 20 (1951), 344–56.

Mahowald, Kyle, '"It may nat be": Chaucer, Derrida, and the Impossibility of the Gift', *Studies in the Age of Chaucer*, 32 (2010), 129–50.

Maifreda, Germano, *From* Oikonomia *to Political Economy: Constructing Economic Knowledge from the Renaissance to the Scientific Revolution* (Burlington, VT: Ashgate, 2012).

Mann, Jill, *Chaucer and Medieval Estates Satire: The Literature of Social Classes and the General Prologue to the* Canterbury Tales (Cambridge: Cambridge University Press, 1973).

——, 'Satisfaction and Payment in Middle English Literature', *Studies in the Age of Chaucer*, 5 (1983), 17–48.

Martindale, Wight, Jr., 'Chaucer's Merchants: A Trade-Based Speculation on Their Activities', *Chaucer Review*, 26 (1992), 309–16.

Mauss, Marcel, *Essai sur le don: Forme et raison de l'échange dans les sociétés archaïques* (Paris: Presses Universitaires de France, 2007).

——, *The Gift: The Form and Reason for Exchange in Archaic Societies*, translated by W. D. Halls (New York: Norton, 1990).

McDonald, Nicola F., '"Lusti Tresor": Avarice and the Economics of the Erotic in Gower's *Confessio Amantis*', in Elizabeth M. Tyler (ed.), *Treasure in the Medieval West* (York: York Medieval Press, 2000), pp. 135–56.

Mennell, Stephen, *All Manners of Food: Eating and Taste in England and France from the Middle Ages to the Present* (Oxford: Basil Blackwell, 1985).

Miller, Robert P., 'It Snewed in His Hous', *English Language Notes*, 22 (1985), 14–16.

Minnis, Alastair, 'The Construction of Chaucer's Pardoner', in R. N. Swanson (ed.), *Promissory Notes on the Treasury of Merits: Indulgences in Late Medieval Europe* (Leiden: Brill, 2006), pp. 169–95.

——, 'Purchasing Pardon: Material and Spiritual Economies on the Canterbury Pilgrimage', in Lawrence L. Besserman (ed.), *Sacred and Secular in Medieval and Early Modern Cultures: New Essays* (New York: Palgrave, 2006), pp. 63–82.

Miskimin, Harry A., *Money, Prices, and Foreign Exchange in Fourteenth-Century France* (New Haven: Yale University Press, 1963).

Montgomery, Franz, 'The Reeve's reference to repelling force with force is a well-known maxim of the law of England', *Philological Quarterly*, 10 (1934), 404–5.

Murdoch, John, 'From Social into Intellectual Factors: An Aspect of the Unitary Character of Late Medieval Learning', in John Murdoch and Edith Sylla (eds), *The Cultural Contexts of Medieval Learning* (Dordrecht and Boston: D. Reidel, 1975).

Muscatine, Charles, *Chaucer and the French Tradition* (Berkeley: University of California Press, 1957).

——, 'The Social Background of the Old French Fabliaux', *Genre*, 9 (1976), 1–19.

Myers, Louis McCorry, 'A Line in the Reeve's Prologue', *Modern Language Notes*, 49 (1934), 222–6.

Newman, Karen, 'Directing Traffic: Subjects, Objects, and the Politics of Exchange', *Differences*, 2 (1990), 243–70.

Noonan, John Thomas, *The Scholastic Analysis of Usury* (Cambridge, MA: Harvard University Press, 1957).

Olson, Glending, 'The End of *The Summoner's Tale* and the Uses of Pentecost', *Studies in the Age of Chaucer*, 21 (1999), 209–45.

Olson, Paul A., 'The *Reeve's Tale*: Chaucer's *Measure for Measure*', *Studies in Philology*, 59 (1962), 1–17.

Patterson, Lee, *Chaucer and the Subject of History* (Madison: University of Wisconsin Press, 1991).

——, *Negotiating the Past: The Historical Understanding of Medieval Literature* (Madison: University of Wisconsin Press, 1987).

Pearsall, Derek, *The Canterbury Tales* (London: George Allen & Unwin, 1985).

Polanyi, Karl, *The Great Transformation: The Political and Economic Origins of Our Time* (1944; Boston: Beacon Press, 1957).

——, Conrad Arensberg and Harry W. Pearson (eds), *Trade and Market in the Early Empires* (New York: The Free Press, 1957).

Purdon, Liam O., and Julian N. Wasserman, 'The Franklin, Food, and the Freemen of York', *Chaucer Review*, 33 (1998), 112–15.

Putter, Ad, 'Gifts and Commodities in *Sir Amadace*', *Review of English Studies*, 51 (2000), 371–94.

Quilligan, Maureen, *Incest and Agency in Elizabeth's England* (Philadelphia: University of Pennsylvania Press, 2005).

Rigby, Stephen H., and Alastair J. Minnis (eds), *Historians on Chaucer: The 'General Prologue' to the Canterbury Tales* (Oxford: Oxford University Press, 2014).

Robertson, D. W., Jr., *A Preface to Chaucer: Studies in Medieval Perspectives* (Princeton: Princeton University Press, 1962).

Rogers, William E., and Paul Dower, 'Thinking about Money in Chaucer's Shipman's Tale', in Robert G. Benson and Susan J. Ridyard (eds), *New Readings of Chaucer's Poetry* (Cambridge: D. S. Brewer, 2003), pp. 119–38.

Ronquist, E. C., 'The Franklin, Epicurus, and the Play of Values', in Robert Myles and David Williams (eds), *Chaucer and Language: Essays in Honor of Douglas Wurtele* (Montreal: McGill-Queen's University Press, 2001), pp. 44–60.

Root, Robert Kilburn, *The Poetry of Chaucer: A Guide to Its Study and Appreciation* (Boston: Houghton Mifflin, 1906).

Rubin, Gayle, 'The Traffic in Women: Notes on the "Political Economy" of Sex', in Raya R. Reiter (ed.), *Toward an Anthropology of Women* (New York: Monthly Review Press, 1975), pp. 157–210.

Sacrum commercium sancti Francisci cum domina Paupertate, edited by Stefano Brufani (Assisi: Edizioni Porziuncola, 1990).

Sahlins, Marshall, *Stone Age Economics* (Chicago: Aldine-Atherton, 1972).

Salih, Sarah, *Versions of Virginity in Late Medieval England* (Woodbridge: Brewer, 2001).

Saul, Nigel, 'The Social Status of Chaucer's Franklin: A Reconsideration', *Medium Aevum*, 52 (1963), 10–26.

Savage, Anne, 'Clothing Paternal Incest in *The Clerk's Tale*, *Émaré* and the *Life of St. Dympna*', in Jocelyn Wogan-Browne et al. (eds), *Medieval Women: Texts and Contexts in Late Medieval Britain: Essays for Felicity Riddy* (Turnhout, Belgium: Brepols, 2000), pp. 345–62.

Scaglione, Aldo D., 'Boccaccio, Chaucer, and the Mercantile Ethic', in David Daiches and Anthony Thorlby (eds), *Literature and Western Civilization, II: The Mediaeval World* (London: Aldus, 1973), pp. 579–600.

Scala, Elizabeth, 'Canacee and the Chaucer Canon: Incest and Other Unnarratables', *Chaucer Review*, 30 (1995), 15–39.

Scanlon, Larry, 'The Riddle of Incest: John Gower and the Problem of Medieval Sexuality', in Robert F. Yeager (ed.), *Re-Visioning Gower* (Asheville: Pegasus Press, 1998), pp. 93–128.

Schneider, Paul Stephen, '"Taillynge Ynough": The Function of Money in the *Shipman's Tale*', *Chaucer Review*, 11 (1977), 201–9.

Schrift, Alan D. (ed.), *The Logic of the Gift: Toward an Ethic of Generosity* (New York: Routledge, 1997).

Schulte-Tenckhoff, Isabelle, 'Misrepresenting the Potlatch', in Caroline Gerschlager (ed.), *Expanding the Economic Concept of Exchange: Deception, Self-Deception and Illusions* (Dordrecht: Kluwer Academic Publishers, 2001), pp. 167–88.

Shell, Marc, *Money, Language, and Thought* (Baltimore: Johns Hopkins University Press, 1982).

——, *The Economy of Literature* (Baltimore: Johns Hopkins University Press, 1978).

Sheridan, Christian, 'Conflicting Economies in the Fabliaux', in Holly A. Crocker (ed.), *Comic Provocations: Exposing the Corpus of Old French Fabliaux* (New York: Palgrave Macmillan, 2006), pp. 97–111.

Shoaf, R. A., *Dante, Chaucer, and the Currency of the Word: Money, Images, and Reference in Late Medieval Poetry* (Norman, OK: Pilgrim Books, 1983).

——, '"Unwemmed Custance": Circulation, Property, and Incest in the Man of Law's Tale', *Exemplaria*, 2 (1990), 287–302.

Sidhu, Nicole Nolan, '"To Late for to Crie": Female Desire, Fabliau Politics, and Classical Legend in Chaucer's *Reeve's Tale*', *Exemplaria*, 21 (2009), 3–23.

Silverman, Albert H., 'Sex and Money in Chaucer's *Shipman's Tale*', *Philological Quarterly*, 32 (1953), 329–36.

Simmel, Georg, *The Philosophy of Money* (London: Routledge & Kegan Paul, 1978).

Smith, Adam, *The Wealth of Nations* (New York: Alfred A. Knopf, 1991).

Smith, D. Vance, *Arts of Possession: The Middle English Household Imaginary* (Minneapolis: University of Minnesota Press, 2003).

Specht, Henrik, *Chaucer's Franklin in the Canterbury Tales* (Copenhagen: Akademisk Forlag, 1981).

Spufford, Peter, *Money and Its Use in Medieval Europe* (Cambridge: Cambridge University Press, 1988).

Stavsky, Jonathan (ed.), *Le Bone Florence of Rome: A Critical Edition and Facing Translation of a Middle English Romance Analogous to Chaucer's* Man of Law's Tale (Cardiff: University of Wales Press, 2017).

Stevens, Martin, and A. C. Cawley (eds), *The Towneley Plays*, Early English Text Society (Oxford: Oxford University Press, 1994).

Stilwell, G., 'Chaucer's Plowman and the Contemporary English Peasant', *ELH*, 6 (1939), 285–90.

Strathern, Marilyn, *The Gender of the Gift: Problems with Women and Problems with Society in Melanesia* (Berkeley: University of California Press, 1988).

Strauss, Ruth Barrie, '"Truth" and "Woman" in Chaucer's Franklin's Tale', *Exemplaria*, 4 (1992), 135–68.

Strohm, Paul, *Social Chaucer* (Cambridge, MA: Harvard University Press, 1989).

Swanson, R. N., *Indulgences in Late Medieval England: Passports to Paradise* (Cambridge: Cambridge University Press, 2007).

Sypherd, W. O., *Studies in Chaucer's* House of Fame (London: L. Paul, Trench, Trübner, 1907; reprinted New York: Haskell House, 1965).

Szittya, Penn R., *The Antifraternal Tradition in Medieval Literature* (Princeton: Princeton University Press, 1986).

Todeschini, Giacomo, *Franciscan Wealth: From Voluntary Poverty to Market Society*, translated by Donatella Melucci (St Bonaventure, NY: Franciscan Institute, 2009).

Ungureanu, Camil, 'Bourdieu and Derrida on Gift: Beyond "Double Truth" and Paradox', *Human Studies*, 36 (2013), 393–409.

Wardlow, Holly, *Wayward Women: Sexuality and Agency in a New Guinea Society* (Berkeley: University of California Press, 2006).

Watt, Diane, *Amoral Gower: Language, Sex, and Politics* (Minneapolis: University of Minnesota Press, 2003).

Weber, Max, *From Max Weber: Essays in Sociology*, edited and translated by H. H. Gerth and C. Wright Mills (1946; New York: Oxford University Press, 1970).

Weiner, Annette B., *Inalienable Possessions: The Paradox of Keeping-While-Giving* (Berkeley: University of California Press, 1992).

Weisl, Angela Jane, *Conquering the Reign of Femeny: Gender and Genre in Chaucer's Romance* (Cambridge: D. S. Brewer, 1995).

Williams, Arnold, 'Two Notes on Chaucer's Friars', *Modern Philology*, 54 (1956), 117–20.

——, 'Chaucer and the Friars', *Speculum*, 28 (1953), 499–513.

Wogan-Browne, Jocelyn, *Saints' Lives and Women's Literary Culture, c. 1150–1300: Virginity and Its Authorizations* (Oxford: Oxford University Press, 2001).

——, 'The Virgin's Tale', in Ruth Evans and Lesley Johnson (eds), *Feminist Readings in Middle English Literature: The Wife of Bath and All Her Sect* (London: Routledge, 1994), pp. 165–94.

Wood, Chauncey, 'Chaucer's Wife of Bath's Prologue, D 576 and 583', *Explicator*, 23 (1965), 9.

Wood, Diana, *Medieval Economic Thought* (Cambridge: Cambridge University Press, 2002).

Woods, William F., 'A Professional Thyng: The Wife as Merchant's Apprentice in the *Shipman's Tale*', *Chaucer Review*, 24 (1989), 139–49.

.

INDEX